CHAIN HER BY ONE FOOT

The Subjugation of Native Women in Seventeenth-Century New France

Karen Anderson

Routledge

New York   London

First Published in 1991
Paperback published in 1993 by
Routledge, Inc.
29 West 35th Street
New York, N.Y. 10001

Paperback published in Great Britain by
Routledge
11 New Fetter Lane
London EC4P 4EE

British Library Cataloguing in Publication Data
Anderson, Karen
Chain her by one foot: the subjugation of women in seventeenth-century
New France.
1. Canada. Society. Role, history of women
I. Title
305.420971

Library of Congress Cataloging in Publication Data
Anderson, Karen L.
Chain her by one foot: the subjugation of Native women in
seventeenth-century New France / Karen Anderson.
p.   cm.
Includes bibliographical references (p. 236)
1. Huron Indians – Women – History – 17th century.
2. Montagnais Indians – Women – History – 17th century. 3. Marriage –
New France – History – 17th century. 4. Sex role – New France – History
– 17th century. 5. Converts, Catholic – New France – History – 17th
century. I. Title.

ISBN 0–415–04758–7
ISBN 0–415–90827–2

CONTENTS

ACKNOWLEDGEMENTS

I wish to thank a number of people who read and commented on this book in manuscript form. Bonnie J. Fox, Kieran Keohane, Sedef Arat Koç, Katherine Kopinak, Meg Luxton, Julia O'Connor and Ester Reiter all gave me valuable suggestions, encouragement and help. My special thanks go to my husband, Gary Woodill, whose generous support, editorial skills and critical acumen helped me to shape this book.

1

'PROUD, DISOBEDIENT AND ILL-TEMPERED'

In 1643 the Jesuit missionary Barthelemy Vimont described a marriage which took place at Sillery, just above Quebec City, between Charles and Marie Meiaskawat, two native converts.

The zeal of Charles Meiaskawat is agreeable as it is fervent. Before being baptized, he had taken a wife who was of a very arrogant and violent temper, and who had no inclination toward the Faith. Nevertheless, he made himself worthy of Baptism and received it, while she always stubbornly persisted in her unbelief. He tried to soothe her, and to incline her gradually to the Faith, with admirable patience. He succeeded; she urgently asked for Baptism and obtained it. It was proposed that they be married according to the Church, so as to give their marriage the character and the grace of that Sacrament. They both agreed to this, and proceeded to the Church to receive the Blessing of the Priest, who first asked Charles if he took such a one for his wife. 'Wait a little,' answered Charles; and, turning to his wife, he said: 'But thou, wilt thou continue to be proud, disobedient and ill-tempered, as in the past? Answer me; for, if thou wilt not behave better, I will not take thee for my wife, – I shall easily find another.' She was quite abashed, and replied that she would conduct herself better in the future. 'Speak louder,' said Charles; 'we do not hear thee. When thou art angry, thou screamest like a mad woman; and now thou wilt not open thy mouth.' The poor woman had to shout aloud, and protest publicly that she would be obedient to her husband, and live with him in gentleness and in the utmost humility. 'That is right,' said Charles, 'provided thou doest as thou sayest; otherwise thou wilt cause me to be angry; and, if I get angry, I shall go to Hell, and so wilt thou.' Then speaking to the Father, 'Go on,' he said, 'I am satisfied. I will always love her as my only and my lawful wife.'

Vimont went on to comment:

God has visibly blessed this marriage, and we have never seen a greater change than in this woman, who has now become truly a lamb, and has very deep and affectionate feelings of devotion.
(Thwaites 1896–1901, 25:175–7)

The description of that marriage made up a small part of the annual report of 1642 that Lalemant, as head of the Jesuit missions in New France, was required to send to his Superior in Rome. Each report, or *Relation*, was subsequently published in France for sale to the general public.

Several things interested me about this particular passage. First, and most simply, was the way in which Charles and Marie are recorded as having spoken to each other, what they said and what they did during the ceremony, the way in which they expressed their sentiments, feelings, emotions. Marie's response to her husband's direct criticism, as well as Charles' pointed identification of Marie as a potential source of danger (if she made him angry he would go to Hell, but so would she) particularly caught my attention.

Second was the very fact that such an account of the marriage between two converts existed at all, and that it was not just a mere accounting, but something which passed for being a recording of words exchanged during the course of a wedding ceremony. If that were not enough, the commentary of the same priest who performed the ceremony was included. Why should the Jesuits, from the moment of their arrival among the Huron and the Montagnais in 1632, have made a practice of recording the details of their progress in converting them to Christianity? Why should the vows exchanged by two obscure people in the backwoods of a remote land be so painstakingly recorded? Why would those documents be sent, not only to Jesuit Superiors in France and Rome, but also to the printers?[1]

The third thing of interest was the difference between what Charles and Marie said during their marriage ceremony, and other conversations between men and women, previously recorded by the Jesuits. At first, and almost invariably, women appeared in the pages of the *Relations* in a negative light, described as 'firebrands of Hell', haughty, proud; women did as they pleased, they acted with 'wanton lewdness', they were 'Megeras',[2] they acquiesced to no one. They censured and ostracized their Christian spouses. They cursed the Jesuits and called for their deaths.

Charles's and Marie's wedding day was not the first time the couple had appeared in the pages of the *Relations*. But in earlier representations this couple had been cast in the role of example of the problems faced by a 'good Christian man' who had a 'haughty tempered' and 'spiteful' wife. Yet their relationship had changed dramatically in the one year between 1641 (the date they first appeared in the pages of the *Relations*) and their Christian marriage in 1642.

Charles and Marie were first mentioned by the Jesuit Vimont, in the course of his discussion of three Montagnais families recently settled at Sillery, a Christian village the Jesuits were in the process of establishing just above Quebec City with money donated from a wealthy and pious French patron. Marie was singled out for special attention at that time because she was the only one out of the three families who had not yet converted to the Christian faith. Her instruction was proceeding slowly, and Vimont described her as 'a rough, wild creature who gives a great deal of trouble to the poor man [i.e. to Charles]' (ibid. 20:195).

Her behaviour was apparently the cause of a great deal of distress for her husband who feared (in keeping with his Christian instruction) that his wife's anger attracted 'Demons' to his cabin. 'I fear that the Demons she keeps in my cabin', he is reputed to have said, 'are perverting the good that I received in holy Baptism' (ibid. 20:195). Charles added that 'I earnestly believe in God and I wish to obey him; and, since I have learned that sin drove God from our hearts, when another does evil in my presence, I fear that may bring loss to my soul' (ibid. 20:195). At one point Marie had apparently tried to stab Charles in the thigh with a knife but he had evaded the blow and only his blanket was slashed. It was with obvious pride that Charles displayed this evidence of his wife's misbehaviour to his fellow Christians at Sillery saying: 'See... the anger of her who considers me her servant; she thought she would be able to irritate me, but I have more power over myself than to fall into a passion at the anger of a woman' (ibid. 20:197).

At one point Charles resorted to begging Marie to believe in God, offering in return, Vimont tells us, to love her above all things, to wait on her in all her needs, to even 'perform the little duties that women do', such as fetching water and wood. Charles went so far as to threaten to leave Marie if she would not believe in God because, he claimed, he could not 'love those who do not love God'. But Marie was not immediately intimidated by either arguments or threats. She was convinced that since the Jesuits had come to their country and told them to pray to God they were all dying. 'Where are thy relatives and where are mine?', she asked Charles. 'The most of them are dead; it is no longer a time to believe' (ibid. 20:197). Concerned that she and her husband would be made beggars without food or clothing, Marie upbraided Charles for being lazy when he did not go hunting on Christian feast days. She further blamed their daughter's recent death on the fact that Charles had had her baptized.

But by the date of Marie's Christian marriage to Charles in 1643 there was a definite shift in her comportment. Nor was Marie's case unique. Like Marie, the other women who people the pages of the Jesuits' *Relations* also appear to have undergone extensive changes in behaviour. By the mid-1640s, not more than three decades after the French first arrived among them, many women had already been subdued, rendered docile and obedient. Women made fewer displays of shrewish bad temper, they no longer cursed the Jesuits as sorcerers, they were no longer portrayed as doing just as they pleased, having sex with any man that attracted them. There were fewer incidents reported of how this or that woman forced a male relative to leave her longhouse, or to give up Christianity and return to traditional practices. Now, instead, we read about how women were chained, beaten and even starved if they ran away; about how they were publicly chastised if they didn't obey their husbands. Now women were publicly cautioned to be wary of provoking any anger in their husbands, because if they did, not only would they go to Hell but they would be the cause of their husbands going there too.

My aim in this book is to answer the question: how did this happen? How were power relations within Huron and Montagnais societies so thoroughly altered that, within a period of some thirty years after the arrival of the French, men and women no longer held the same relations to each other. I do not intend, however, to write a history of the relations between men and women in Huron or Montagnais societies. Nor do I intend to write a history of the effects of seventeenth-century French colonial practices and Jesuit missionary activity, in particular, on native societies in the New World. My objective is at once more specific and more general.

It is more specific because it is concerned with the analysis of a specific instance of change in the status of women. In spite of this apparent specificity there is also a general and more theoretical side to the analysis offered in this book. In answering the historically particular questions about the conditions under which Huron and Montagnais women became subjugated to men, I also address the issue of the elements involved in women's oppression in western European culture, at least since the beginning of the seventeenth century. This book, then, is part of a larger and on-going project in feminism which has taken as its object the description, explanation and analysis of how women came to be dominated by men.

So far, attempts to construct universally applicable explanations, which try to include all of human societies, all of human history and even prehistory, in their purview, fall far short of being satisfactory. It is clear that many more case studies need to be undertaken which raise questions about institutionalized means by which relations between men and women are established and put into practice.[3] We also need to know about the specific conditions under which those relations are altered, in what direction and with what consequences. Finally, we need to know about the emotional processes involved in subjugation and domination. How do women come to accept the role of subordinate, men the role of dominator?

To ask how, why and by what means the native people of New France were able to maintain egalitarian relations between the two sexes, how the confrontation between the Jesuits and the Huron and Montagnais came to happen and why women were subsequently defeated, is to immediately raise the issue of the relations of power and, thus, of subjugation and domination. In raising this issue the first thing that we must note is that in seventeenth-century Huron and Montagnais societies, as well as in seventeenth-century French society, the social world was clearly divided into women and men. The life experiences of one sex were not the life experiences of the other sex in either Indian or in French societies. Moreover, in seventeenth-century Huron, Montagnais and French societies (and indeed, in all societies in human history to this point) the differences between men and women were seen as both significant *and* complementary. That is to say men and women together made, not only babies, but also society. Society did not, indeed could not, exist without the contributions of *both* sexes.[4]

Two outstanding differences between the Indian and French societies were the ways in which men and women were valued and the ways in which the two sexes were able to exercise power. Although both the value and the power of women and men in Huron and Montagnais societies were not perfectly symmetrical, they were, at least, relatively equally balanced.

Such was not the case between French women and men in the seventeenth century. Not only did Christian doctrine determine women to be of a lesser worth than men, more susceptible to influences of evil, weaker in every way and in need of men's guidance, but the social and institutional practices of the day assured women a position of greatly reduced powers and rewards, compared to those granted to men.[5] The Jesuits' project in the New World was to replace the relative symmetry that they found in male/female relations among the Huron and Montagnais with the asymmetry characteristic of the relations between the sexes in France. Institutional structures, ideology and ways of being in the world (including subjectivity) which called for the subjugation of women to men had to be transferred on to societies previously characterized by relatively unsubjugated relations. To analyse how this came about requires that many different paths be followed.

The explanation must be at once cognizant of the relationship between large-scale social organization, institutional structures and individual consciousness, emotionality and subjectivity. It must permit us to understand, in this particular case, how it was that Huron and Montagnais men and women came to tolerate, and indeed to pursue, lives of relative unfreedom, compared to what they had formerly enjoyed. The explanation must provide an answer to the question: how was it possible, how it could happen, that one half of society, women, came to be seen by both men and by themselves as being of lesser value, as being potential corruptors, as needing to follow guidance and direction? Finally, the explanation must help us to understand the role of aggression, anger and violence in this transformation. How was it that women became the targets of men's violence and anger? How was it that women's own anger came to be redirected, almost exclusively, either against their children or against themselves?

The work of Michel Foucault has contributed a great deal to the task of reconceptualizing power relations and their analysis. Power, for Foucault, is not a quality that is possessed by some and not by others. Power is recognized in other terms, not as a thing but as a quality of social relations; not as possessed but as constantly in play; not as exclusive, as something negative which says no, but as an acting out of potential relations according to strategies which are constantly undergoing change.

The use of this approach to frame a study of the relations between men and women prior to the arrival of the Jesuits, and the impact of the Jesuits on the decline in the status of women has certain implications. Power should not be seen as something that women or men had or possessed. Power can most usefully be conceptualized in terms of the working out of social forces, through specific social institutions, and especially through the complex of socially recognized relations that Huron and Montagnais culture called into existence between men and women. We need to know, then, what were the institutionalized arrangements that structured, underlay, defined and maintained male/female relations in such a way that women and men, for the most part, occupied different roles, but retained equal capacity to exercise power. How did this complex structure intersect with what the Jesuits sought to put in place? Through what mechanisms, and by what means did those who were being changed come to accept, believe in and practice behaviours that conformed to Christian ideals as presented by the Jesuits?

To answer these questions means to 'distinguish the events, differentiate the networks and levels to which they belong, and ...reconstitute the threads which connect them and make them give rise to one another' (Foucault 1979:33). The events in question are easily identified and took place over a period of thirty years. They centre around the arrival of French traders and missionaries in New France, the integration of the Huron and the Montagnais into the fur trade, the sudden onslaught of devastating epidemics, famines and genocidal wars with the Iroquois, the defeat of the Montagnais and the Huron by the Iroquois and the subsequent Christianization of survivors. Identifying the 'networks' and 'levels' to which these events belong is a more complex matter. Huron and Montagnais societies, with their own internal institutional organizations, characterized by specific forms of distribution, must be considered. The Jesuit missionaries who came to New France and their social, economic, political and religious interconnections with the state, the church and mercantile interests are also of central importance.

Once the 'networks' or 'levels' to which the events belong have been identified a further task remains – the historically particular and detailed task of tracing out how and by what means and at what precise points (i.e. through what institutionalized structures) different powers met, acted on each other, created reactions, acquiescence,

7

resistance or compromise. Foucault has argued that it is necessary to be concerned with the point where 'power surmounts the rules of right which organize and delimit it and extends itself beyond them, invests itself in institutions, becomes embodied in techniques and equips itself with instruments and eventually even violent means of material intervention' (ibid.: 232).

Therefore,

1. To speak about men and women is also to speak about power *relations*. Subjugation is only one possible outcome of the action of two or more sets of social forces on each other.
2. Power is constantly put into play between social actors. It never is at rest, possessed by one individual or group of individuals and not by another.
3. Power is brought into play over the entire 'social body' through localized institutional forms.
4. Power can only be said to exist when distinctions between two or more groups are made, and where those groups bear a social relationship to each other based on that distinction.

In the analysis which follows the institutionalized bases of power relations between men and women in native society, as well as the bases of the relations between the French and the native peoples of New France will be examined. The appearance of the French in New France and the interrelations between the Jesuits and native peoples were above all else struggles, a series of confrontations that were carried out along a variety of different lines, on a number of different levels, and through several different institutional structures.[6]

One set of institutional structures to be examined are the points at which power was brought into play and distributed throughout Huron and Montagnais societies during the early years of the Jesuits' missions. The sharp division which sorted men and women into the categories of good or evil, active or passive, so prevalent in western European thought of the seventeenth century, had not originally been part of the Huron or Montagnais experience. Nor were the lines of power between men and women drawn in a similar manner to those in the society the Jesuits had just left, and whose rationale they wished to impose on the people of the New World. One task will be to discern the basis on which differences between men and women were established in native society and which brought relations of power between women and men into play. This discussion will focus on the points of concern already identified by marxist and by feminist theory – production, reproduction, kinship and the formation of the psyche and emotional life.

A second set of institutionalized structures to be examined is that which existed between the Jesuits and the Hurons and Montagnais. The Jesuits arrived among the native peoples of New France with very little means of physically forcing the native people to comply with their demands. The French state, although supportive of the Jesuits' presence in New France, provided them with no means of coercion, no arms, no armies, no material wealth, no show of force. In spite of Champlain's advice to Louis XIII that force was one of the 'four buttresses' of all states, few French colonists, let alone soldiers, arrived to back up the Jesuits' claim that they were the bearers of a new and more powerful truth about existence and the way to live one's life. It was not with these external, visible and violent means of subjugation that the Jesuits brought about the Christianization of the native people of New France. Nor was it through the extensive use of physical coercion that they succeeded in seeing native women subordinated to men.

To understand how it was that the Huron and the Montagnais came to be Christianized and women subjugated to men entails an examination of those points at which the native peoples in New France became constituted as Catholics and as the subjects of the king of France. Those points included, most importantly, the instances in which and through which individual self-knowledge and behaviour, was transformed. How was it that the Huron and Montagnais came to accept 'Christian' practices, to alter their behaviour and to accept as 'true' a new social and emotional daily reality?

A final extremity of power, another point at which tactics, strategies and campaigns were set, interests put into play and positions gained and lost, is to be found in the complex set of relations between the Jesuits and the French crown, the state, the church and commercial interests and the native peoples of New France.

To begin, the subjugation of both Huron and Montagnais women took place within the context of intensive interactions with French missionaries, colonial administrators and traders. Thus, an analysis of the domination of women has to take into account not only the dynamics generated within native societies, but also those generated between native and French societies. Moreover, the interaction between French and native societies was neither one-dimensional, one-directional, consistent nor predictable. It took place on at least three different discernible levels – societal, institutional and emotional. In the first instance, the specific social, economic and political organizations of both native and French societies played an essential role in setting the boundaries of all potential interaction.

Here the marxist concepts of social formations and modes of production, particularly as they have been elaborated by late twentieth-century theorists such as Althusser, Balibar, Godelier, Hindess and Hirst and others, continue to offer a useful framework for one aspect of this study. These theories draw our attention to questions dealing with the logic of the reproduction of entire social formations. They also provide a framework for considering the nature of the interactions between members of a given social formation whose productive relations are regulated through rules of kin relations and obligations. In Chapters 6 and 7 these issues will be examined especially with reference to the extent to which kin-based modes of production can be viewed as the basis for establishing egalitarian relations between men and women.

However intriguing and useful an analysis of the logic of the reproduction of kin-based modes of production, and the relation between kin corporate social formations and women's status may be, this provides only a partial approach to answering questions concerning the subjugation of women. Although marxist analysis offers us the assurance of knowing that 'in the last analysis' it is the economic relations which are the determining ones, post-structuralist theory has successfully challenged this assumption (Weedon 1987). One of the most enduring contributions of the work of Michel Foucault has been to free up the ways in which social analysts can think about the causes of human social behaviour, making economic power relations only one set among many.

In any society, social action is always undertaken by individuals who are organized in specific ways, and who have both the knowledge and the will to follow specific rules of conduct. The institutional structures which act as focal points for individuals, and which appear as the points through which specific codes of conduct, beliefs and bodies of knowledge are communicated and imposed are also an integral part of social life. Very different institutional structures and bodies of knowledge informed native life than those which informed the lives of the Jesuits.

Thus while Huron, Montagnais and Jesuit individuals existed first within their own social world, informed and regulated by specific institutional structures and rules, each group also found itself confronting a new social world. That confrontation required the construction of new practices and knowledge by members of both sides. It required the construction of new institutional structures to facilitate the interaction. The subjugation of Huron and Montagnais women to men took place within the context of this confrontation and involved the creation of new institutional structures, rules and bodies of knowledge and ways of understanding emotional life.

There remains the question of subjectivity, conceived of as 'the conscious and unconscious thoughts and emotions of the individual, her sense of herself and her ways of understanding her relation to the world' (ibid.: 32). This is both the beginning and the end point of any social transformation, and it constitutes the third and ultimately most central focus of this study. In the end, what changed for the Huron and the Montagnais, and not for the Jesuits, was the understanding and practice of the self – more particularly of the gendered and sexed self in relation to the opposite sex. This transformation required a new construction of subjectivity for both men and women: not only were the salient characteristics of each sex redefined, but so were their ways of self-understanding and expression.

Women and men acquired new knowledge about who they were. They also learned how to put that new knowledge into action in relation to the opposite sex. Most often that knowledge was directed towards disciplining the body in order to force the soul to comply. New disciplinary practices were established to create conformity, obedience and docility through subjecting the body to the rigours of specific kinds of directed disciplinary practices. Penitents whipped each other and themselves; everyone was on alert, watching not just for misdeeds, but also for mis-thoughts. Confession and acts of contrition, both public and private, became a daily occurrence. Non-compliers were severely punished; deprived not only of liberty, but also of food, shelter and warmth. In all this women in particular were singled out for special treatment. Above all else, docility in women, and their obedience to husbands and fathers became a lynchpin, so necessary for avoiding the snares and pitfalls set by the Christian Devil.

The analysis of changes in subjectivity, of rules and regulations supporting the definition of individuals, and of the ways in which the two sexes defined themselves and learned to experience themselves as either male or female, of necessity encompasses an examination of emotional life. Individuals' lives were made over and what passed for the truth about men and women one day became reviled as the 'work

11

of the Devil' the next. To explain such a rapid transition, from one way of being in the world to another, from one set of beliefs and values in which the truth about men and women was based on their equal values to one in which the truth about men and women revealed women's inferior status, calls for a look at the basis of subjective understanding and experience.

In the end the Jesuits succeeded. In a period of just over thirty years, what had previously been true about men and women in both Huron and Montagnais societies, the qualities that had characterized their interactions, the ways in which they were defined as individuals as well as in relation to each other, had been profoundly altered. There was a 'new regime' which produced and regulated relations between them; a radical modification in the way in which 'truth' or 'knowledge' about men and women was produced, and acted upon.

The 'truth' about the subjugation of Huron and Montagnais women to men, the 'real story' behind the Jesuits' ultimate success in bringing Christianity to the 'savages' of New France is located somewhere in that complex interplay of social structure, culture and psyches.

2

'THE BLOOD OF MARTYRS IS THE SEED OF CHRISTIANS'

The stated objective of the Jesuit missionaries who were sent to Quebec in 1625 was to bring about the conversion to Christianity of the 'pagans' of that country at whatever the cost to themselves or to the would-be converts. A number of them also expressed a desire to be martyred in the course of their stay. Between 1648 and 1649 five Jesuits, Jean de Bréboeuf, Antoine Daniel, Gabriel Lalemant, Charles Garnier and Nöel Chabanel achieved their desire for martyrdom when they were tortured, killed and then eaten by the Iroquois.

The Jesuits were convinced that no conversion could be won without suffering, torment and bloodshed; that 'as a rule men yield to God only through calamities'. Plagues, wars and famines were necessary to distinguish the 'reprobate' from the 'elect', causing the former to die 'like beasts' and the latter to become 'children of God' and to 'ascend to Heaven'. Writing in the *Relation* of 1639/40 the mission Superior Paul Le Jeune revealed that:

> We have sometimes wondered whether we could hope for the conversion of this country without the shedding of blood; the principle received, it seems, in the Church of God, that the blood of martyrs is the seed of Christians, made me at one time conclude that this was not to be expected, – yea, that it was not even to be desired; considering the glory that redounds to God from the constancy of the Martyrs, with whose blood all the rest of the earth has been so lately drenched, it would be a sort of curse if this quarter of the world should not participate in the happiness of having contributed to the splendour of this glory.
> (Thwaites 1896–1901, 17:13)

But why risk so much for the conversion of so few? Jesuit fanaticism in the New World, had, as elsewhere, its clearly practical, rational side. The conversion of from 'ten to twenty thousand souls', as Le Jeune put it to his readership, may seem like folly, but in fact it was well worth the exposure to so many 'hazards and dangers'.

> [W]e are only at the entrance of a land [he wrote] which on the side of the West, as far as China, is full of Nations more populous than the Huron; toward the South we see other People beyond number, to whom we can have access only by means of this door at which we now stand.
>
> (ibid. 28:67)

The Jesuits believed, following the ideas current at the time, that the St Lawrence River was the beginning of a great waterway system that would allow them passage, ultimately, to China. For the Jesuits, then, the Montagnais, Huron and other native groups located along the beginnings of this waterway were only the first people to be encountered in their long-term project of the conversion of all the pagans of North America *and* the Far East. The strategic location of the Montagnais, but especially of the Huron, made their conversion, in spite of their relatively small numbers, of immense importance in the Jesuits' general plan for the Christianization of the world's population.

Not only were the Jesuits willing to die if it meant that in so doing they could convert even a few souls, they were equally willing to see the temporal lives of the native peoples ended if it meant that even a few of them could be baptized. They were convinced, moreover, that God himself wished the native people to die as a means of chastising, humbling and causing them to be more willing to accept Christianization. Writing in the *Relation* of 1646, for example, Jérôme Lalemant described the fate of the people living around Tadoussac in this way:

> There were reckoned, formerly, on the shores of this port, three hundred warriors or effective hunters, who made with their families about twelve or fifteen hundred souls. This little people was very proud; but God, wishing to incline it to receive his Son, has humbled it by diseases which have almost entirely exterminated it. These blows, nevertheless, are beneficent; while his justice was slaying bodies at the great deluge of the world, his mercy continued to gather up the penitent souls. We might say relatively the same, that his wrath putting to death a part of the Savages by wars and epidemics, his kindness gave to

14

others a life which must be sought amid a thousand deaths.

That is what we have seen with our own eyes; for these poor people, assailed by many diseases, and worn out with the fatigues of war, have finally thrown themselves into the haven of life and peace. They have given themselves up to Jesus Christ, who seems to wish to repeople this tribe with a goodly number of savages who land here from various places, in order to see with their own eyes that which they learn with their ears, that there are men formed like them, who preach and who publish the greatness of God, and who teach the way to Heaven.

(ibid. 29:123)

Following the virtual destruction of the Huron at the hands of the Iroquois, the then Jesuit Superior, Paul Ragueneau, claimed that the Iroquois had in fact done more good than harm because they had 'delivered many souls from the fires of Hell, while burning their bodies in an elemental fire' (ibid. 38:45). Formerly the Hurons and others had 'mocked at the Gospel, and tried to murder those who proclaimed it in their country'. They had accused the Jesuits of being sorcerers who murdered by stealth, caused crops to fail, brought droughts and other bad weather. They also accused the Jesuits of being traitors who sold out the Hurons to their enemies.

That changed when the Iroquois all but annihilated the Hurons. Then the survivors came to the Jesuits to beg for help and protection. Then they came asking for baptism, or as Ragueneau put it, 'urging that the life of the soul might be granted them, since they were losing that of the body; and desiring entrance into Heaven, since they were being driven out from their own lands' (Thwaites 1896–1901, 38:47). It seemed to Ragueneau that the Huron and other 'Nations' would have been

lost if they had not been ruined; that the greater part of those who came in quest of baptism in affliction, would never have found it in prosperity; and that those who have found Paradise in the Hell of their torments, would have found the true Hell in their earthly Paradise.

(ibid. 38:47)

Given this logic it is no surprise that we find Ragueneau claiming that the Iroquois were directly responsible for the conversion and sanctification of many souls, even though they appear now in our eyes like monsters ready to devour us ... Let people lose their property, let them lose their lives, let them be killed, massacred, burnt, roasted, broiled, and eaten alive, patience! that matters not, so long as the Gospel takes its course, and God is known, and souls saved. The gain is greater than the loss in this traffic.

(ibid. 38:49)

The most pressing problem that Ragueneau envisaged resulting from the incursions of the Iroquois against the Huron and other allies of the French was that the French might give up their attempts to press onward into the interior of the country. If this were to happen, the 'Gospel laborers and the Pastors of this fold should be banished and driven away from their flocks'. It was a potential misfortune which could easily be averted if the 'high mightinesses' who ruled France could find a way to continue to be steadfast in their support of the Jesuit missions in New France.

PAIN, SUFFERING AND SALVATION

For the seventeenth-century Jesuits, who followed the Christian beliefs of the day, bodily pain was far less to be feared than sin and eternal damnation. 'Our ingratitude would be great, and our chastisement horrible', wrote Father Baird, Jesuit Superior in Acadia in 1616, 'if we do not enhance the value of the grace we have ... by communicating it to our fellow men in proportion to our means and opportunities.' Indeed, the Jesuits felt that it was incumbent upon them to suffer as much as possible in the course of doing what they considered to be God's will. The more each of them personally suffered, the more attractive God found them. Certain among them wrote out rules for their own behaviour in these matters which were discovered and published in the *Relations* after their deaths.

Father Enemond Massé, for example, wrote that what he called the 'delights' Canada had to offer could be attained only 'through a frame of mind conformed to the Cross'. Massé enumerated eight practices to be 'observed inviolably' if one wanted to fully experience these 'delights', including to: sleep only on the bare ground, wear no linen except around the neck, say mass only in a hair shirt, take the discipline (i.e. whip yourself) daily, fast three times a week, and if you should happen to offend anyone, however little, 'thou shalt gather up secretly with thy tongue the spittle and phlegm proceeding from the mouths of others' (ibid. 29:33–5).

In the Jesuits' view, because Satan was particularly powerful in the New World, it was their task to struggle on behalf of God and Jesus against him and his legions. This struggle was justified because not only did the Huron offer the means of access to many other more numerous nations, but because the people of New France were considered to be human. Although 'barbarians', 'savages' or 'pagans', they were also, in one Jesuit's words, 'images of our God as we are, and as capable of enjoying him . . . . [C]ompanions of our own species and almost of the same quality as we' (ibid. 4:117).

By 1639 the Jesuit Paul Le Jeune had come to the conclusion that 'if animals are capable of discipline, the young Savage children are much more so' and that 'education alone is wanting to these poor children, whose minds are as good as those of our Europeans' (Thwaites 1896–1901, 16:179). Indeed, the Jesuits' opinion of the Montagnais and Huron, while often disparaging, was also at times admiring. Paul Le Jeune, for example, wrote that the Huron had 'fine bodies' and found 'nothing effeminate in their appearance . . . . Those little Fops seen elsewhere', he wrote, 'are only caricatures of men, compared with our Savages.' Their minds, he contended were 'of good quality'. They lacked education and instruction only, being 'more intelligent than our ordinary peasants' and without ambition and avarice (ibid. 6:229–31).

Jesuit belief in the correctness and necessity of their mission is reflected in the particular brand of fanaticism that they brought to their work among the native people. To take any other course of action than the one they had chosen would have meant accepting responsibility for the native peoples of New France continuing to be 'precipitated every day into eternal torments, and profound depths of everlasting punishment, without hope of deliverance' (ibid. 4:117). It truly did not matter if all the native people in New France died in the attempt to Christianize them, as long as one soul was assured of eternal salvation.

But the Jesuits' project in New France did not merely rest on the conversion and baptism of people who were dying. They were not content with a verbal avowal of faith. They wanted much more than to hear former 'pagans' say they believed in the Christian God, that they recognized His power, authority, and that of His Son Jesus Christ. The Jesuits wanted the Huron and the Montagnais to recognize, accept and be grateful for French authority over them. 'The Savages', wrote Vimont in the *Relation* of 1642/3, 'are scantily grateful in their natural state, especially toward the Europeans;

Christianity trains them, little by little, in this virtue' (ibid. 24:233). They wanted the converts to follow rules of behaviour, to adopt beliefs about morals and to acknowledge and submit themselves to a set of social relations they believed to be dictated by God. They wanted, especially, for the Huron and Montagnais to be afraid of offending God, and of incurring His anger (ibid. 26:135; 27:233). They wanted, too, to be recognized by the native people for their selfless devotion to their salvation. Conversations, in which native converts express sentiments in keeping with these objectives, were proudly repeated in the pages of *Relations*. One of the 'principal Christians of Sillery', for example, was recorded as having said to a visiting non-Christian about a passing Jesuit:

> There... are those who teach us, and show us the way to Heaven. They spare no pains for this purpose, they make themselves poor for us, they become sick for us; if thou spend a Winter here, thou wilt know by experience the truth of what I tell thee. What they teach us is of importance; they forbid us everything that is bad, – the feasts where all the food is eaten, the invocations of evil spirits, the belief in dreams, the multiplicity of wives in marriage, and, in a word, all our wicked customs which betray us and cast us into a fire after death. That is a fire... which will never go out, of which the one that warms us here on earth is only a faint outline. It is terrible in its eternal duration; those who go into it burn, without hope of getting out of it.
>
> (ibid. 24:23–5).

It was the native women who were the most difficult to convert. They were the Jesuits' most vociferous and relentless opponents. Wild, ill-mannered, rude and dangerously lewd they challenged Jesuit beliefs, and teachings. As women, they refused to conform to the behaviour that the Jesuits knew God had ordained for their sex. They would not submit themselves to the authority of their husbands and fathers. They would not behave in a modest and gentle fashion. They made no attempt to hide their sexuality, did not value virginity, chastity, or sexual continence and refused to remain married to an unsuitable spouse. If the Devil's plans for the New World were to be thwarted, if the forces of good that the Jesuits believed they represented were to be triumphant and souls to be saved, native women would have to submit. In order for that to happen there had to be

18

profound changes in the relationships between women and men and a drastic reduction in women's independence and powers.

CHRIST AND THE ANTICHRIST

One overriding theme runs through all of the *Jesuit Relations* written during the early years of the missions. The central theme is that a great struggle was being waged in New France between the forces of good and those of evil. The theme of the struggle between good and evil, of course, was not particular to the Jesuits, but was consistent with the way in which fear had been rationalized and dealt with for several centuries throughout western Europe.

The Jesuits, along with many other Europeans of the seventeenth century, feared the appearance on earth of the Antichrist,[1] a monster of chaos who would herald the coming of war, plagues, famine and devastation. At times represented as the Devil himself, at other times as an aspect of the Devil, as his son or as some human possessed by him, the Antichrist was Christ's exact opposite. Born of a whore, while Christ was born of a virgin, a destroyer, while Christ was a Saviour, a worker of sham illusions, while Christ performed true miracles, the Antichrist was pure evil, to Christ's pure goodness (Cavendish 1975:17).

The fear of the rule of chaos was given institutionalized expression by both Catholic and Protestant churches. The Antichrist, or his servants, were variously identified as heretics (for Catholics), the papacy and the Roman Catholic clergy (for Protestants), Turks, Jews, women and all the pagan people of the world.[2] The Antichrist and Christ were seen as locked in a struggle for control of the fate of the world. The immense fear was that the Antichrist might gain dominion, and that untold catastrophes would accompany this reign; thus the Jesuits devoted their lives to being soldiers for Christ in this struggle. Established by their founder, Inigo Lopez de Loyola, to be Christ's standard bearers, they were convinced that, with their help, the Antichrist could be defeated, Christ's majesty would restore order and eternal peace in the kingdom of God would be assured for all believers.

The discovery in America of previously unknown people in the fifteenth century had already been interpreted in Europe either as a sign that the end of the world was near (following Matthew XXIV, 14) or that the reign of the Saints was to follow. In any case the possibility of extending the struggle of the forces of order against those of chaos into newly discovered territory where, up to that moment, the Demon had held full sway, inspired many Spanish, Portuguese and, later, French missionaries. It was a noble mission indeed to be able to present millions of new converts to Jesus, on his Second Coming (Delumeau 1978:205).

The conquest and pillage of the peoples of America was thereby justifiable because idolatry had to be suppressed at all costs. The pagan peoples of America were to be forced to make a complete break with their past practices. In the combat of Christ and the Antichrist a choice had to be made. For the European missionaries who worked among the native peoples of the New World, only one choice was acceptable: the Demon, the Antichrist, had to be vanquished everywhere.

It is no accident that there was a chronological coincidence between the merciless conversion, suppression and annihilation of the native peoples of the New World, and the suppression of women, in theological teachings and practices, in laws excluding women from economic activities,[3] and especially through witch-hunting, in the Old World. Pagans and women, among others, were identified as real or potential allies of the common enemy, the Antichrist. The Devil was at work in the world against God's divine plan for the universe and his initiates were spread throughout the New World. The Devil's allies could also be found at home, where they practised the Satanic mass as a secret nocturnal cult. The major work of the Church during the sixteenth and seventeenth centuries was to combat the forces of evil and to destroy them, for the 'greater glory of God' (Muchembled 1987:13).

This theme, which appears frequently in the Jesuit writings from New France, is illustrated by Father Bressani when he wrote in his *Relation* of 1653 about the early difficulties that the Jesuits had in even gaining passage to the country of the Huron:

> The Demon, who feared this enemy, [i.e. the Jesuit missionary's arrival in their territory] tried to hinder the journey, and indeed, in the year 1633, prevented it . . . . It lacked but little that he hindered it also in the following year, 1634. [T]he Huron . . . would gladly have embarked a certain young Frenchman, with arms for the chase and the war: but they did not wish to load themselves with people who wore cassocks, – esteeming them useless, and even prejudicial, to their interests; but the time appointed by the divine providence having arrived, the consistency of ours overcame all the opposition of Hell. Here follows

Father de Brébeuf's letter on this matter to the Superior of the Mission: 'I have never seen any departure so much thwarted by the skill, as I believe, of the Demon... but the great Saint Joseph, to whom I made a vow, caused us successfully to overcome all the difficulties.'

(Thwaites 1896–1901, 39:51)

Jesuit missionaries observed that, in general, the native people of New France knew neither fear of nor submission to some higher authority. Women, in particular, did not submit to the authority of men. Here lay a great threat to Christianization and a constant danger to the potential salvation of so many 'souls'. Men and women would have to be made to fear God, to fear the Devil and to fear themselves as potential 'sinners', as potentially corruptible by the Devil, and as his dupes. Due to their weak natures, women were particularly susceptible to the influences of the Devil, and special care needed to be taken to bring them under the control of men. Thus the Jesuits were convinced that it was necessary to transform the existing behaviour of the native peoples to conform with European standards, with all that entailed in terms of domination and obedience between men and women.

THE PREOCCUPATION WITH SAVING 'SOULS'

In order to save the world from the forces of evil the Jesuits believed it absolutely necessary that Christianization of all pagans should proceed as quickly as possible. Christianization, of course, implied that everyone be brought under the same rules of conduct, and that they learn to fear and obey God's rules and authority, which the Jesuits believed they represented. Thus, the most frequent complaint voiced by writers of the *Relations*, especially in the early years of their mission, was the extent to which women and men, but especially women, exercised what appeared to be free will. As long as the people of New France recognized no one's authority or control over them they would continue to live in constant danger of being the dupes or allies of Satan. This, of course, could only serve to prolong and intensify the danger of their eternal damnation. It also intensified the danger of God's wrath being visited on the entire world, because many people in it continued to refuse to acknowledge His power.

In 1636, just a few years after his arrival in New France, the Jesuit Superior Paul Le Jeune wrote, describing the Montagnais and the Huron:

There is nothing so difficult as to control the tribes of America. All these Barbarians share the law of wild asses, they are born, live and die in a liberty without restraint; they do not know what is meant by bridle or bit. With them, to conquer one's passions is considered a great joke, while to give free reign to the senses a lofty Philosophy.

(ibid. 12:61

Le Jeune compared the freedom of the 'Barbarians' to life lived under the 'Law of our Lord'. The latter, he contended, was 'far removed from this dissoluteness; it gives us boundaries and prescribes limits, outside of which we cannot step without offending God and reason' (ibid. 12:61).

The Jesuits abhorred what they felt was libertinage and lawlessness, so prevalent among the people of New France, for without laws and punishment God's will would not be obeyed. This was an exceedingly dangerous situation, not only because the Devil might actually find himself welcome, but because the entire society put itself in danger of incurring God's wrath and punishment. It was the Jesuits' undeniable duty to instil the fear of God and the desire to follow His rules in all those people who did not yet worship Him. Should these rules be broken, punishment given out by those who were pious enough to uphold God's laws seemed to be the only way to avoid a situation in which God took matters into His own hands and extended His wrath to everyone – sinners for their sins, others for their failing to see that God's laws were followed and that the non-complying were punished.

The kind of personality structure common to those Jesuits, whose feelings are expressed throughout the *Relations*, indicates a complex mixture of fearfulness, submissiveness, vengefulness and courage. Most possessed an immense determination to follow through with a course of action regardless of its consequence. Self-abnegation, denial and a strong death wish, which often presented itself as a desire for martyrdom, were also prevalent. The writings of Paul Le Jeune, Superior of the mission at Quebec, indicate such a personality; a man who clearly delighted in what he saw as the punishment of others who had not followed a rigidly set code of behaviour that included fearful submission to the authority of God. Two examples from his *Relation* of 1636 illustrate this.

Early in their mission to New France the Jesuits had succeeded in converting a young Montagnais whom they had expected to help them with the conversion of other Montagnais. The young man, however, soon renounced his conversion, earning himself the name 'The Apostate' in Le Jeune's subsequent *Relations*. In 1636 Le Jeune wrote: 'That wretch [the 'Apostate'] died this year of hunger abandoned in the woods like a dog' (ibid. 9:71). About this young man's death Le Jeune had written:

> It was very reasonable that his impious mouth, which so often blasphemed God, should lack food; and that God should condemn this kind of death to him who had seen poor, sick persons die before his eyes, without ever consenting to aid in giving them a piece of the bread of the word of God.
>
> (ibid. 9:71)

Le Jeune went to some lengths to explain to his readers that, even though this young 'Apostate' had done him great wrong, he (Le Jeune) would have done anything in his power to 'free [the Apostate] from the iron chains in which he now is' and to 'procure for him, in exchange for all the wrongs he has done me, the greatest blessing that can be obtained for a reasonable creature, eternal salvation' (ibid. 9:71). Thus Le Jeune covered himself on both fronts. On the one hand, he was quite satisfied that the 'Apostate' got what was coming to him. It was only fitting that he experienced God's wrath in a way that Le Jeune must have found particularly appropriate. Moreover, the fact that the young Montagnais did suffer a horrible death is taken by Le Jeune as evidence confirming his belief that God righteously punishes those who sin. On the other hand, Le Jeune took the opportunity to state that, although he personally had suffered a number of wrongs at the hands of this young Montagnais, he would not only be willing to forgive him, but to put his own life on the line in order to bring the young man back to Christianity.

At one and the same time, then, Le Jeune sees his fears of God's punishment justified and gets an opportunity to demonstrate that he is *not* like the 'Apostate'; that he will, even under the most trying of circumstances, give his life to convert someone, no matter how lowly, to Christianity, and that therefore he himself is beyond reproach and punishment. Le Jeune's position, then, is completely justified; his life and the beliefs that guide it vindicated. He can continue to live in fear, and to deny himself his own desires by keeping the rigid rules that he believes God demands of him. At the same time he can justifiably be glad that someone else got what he deserved, confirming his beliefs and justifying the voluntary suffering he has undertaken in this life in order to win divine recognition in the next.

A second example of this need to see rules followed and punishment meted out, as well as an immense sense of satisfaction when it occurs, is also found in Le Jeune's writings of 1636. In that *Relation* Le Jeune comments that 'libertine spirits' who are discontent with law are suffering from a 'disease of the mind'. The laws of God are not severe, he contends, because they are not characterized by bitterness (ibid. 9:15). To illustrate his point Le Jeune refers to the establishment of laws at Quebec in December 1635 against blasphemy, drunkenness and failing to attend mass or divine service on Holy days.

On 26 December 1635 a notice to this effect was placed on a pillar outside the church, and an iron collar was fastened to the same pillar, while a chevalet was placed nearby.[4] A few days later, according to Le Jeune, a 'drunkard and blasphemer was placed on the chevalet, to receive his justly deserved punishment'. The best laws in the world, he commented, are of no value if they are not observed. It was therefore fitting and necessary to have the means of enforcement at hand, however severe they might be. The severe and public punishment of a few often was all that was needed to prevent the same lawless and impious behaviour in many. Elsewhere Le Jeune wrote, 'God takes as it pleases him, and it is upon him we must wait in patience and in meekness' (ibid. 8:243). There are no accounts available of Le Jeune's childhood, but if it followed what was typical of the period it is not difficult to see how easy it would be for a young child to form such ideas of the capricious and vicious nature of adult authority. Wilfulness, exuberance and defiance were considered characteristics that no child should be allowed to possess. Obedience was taught at the earliest possible moment. The child's will was to be broken and replaced by that of another in such a way that the child could no longer distinguish between their own will and the other's will.[5]

But whatever produced in Le Jeune such an immense fearfulness, combined with a determination to avoid punishment, and the ability to experience satisfaction in seeing others punished, it was almost certainly shared by many other Jesuits. Examples of this kind of reaction to 'richly deserved' punishment on the part of other Jesuits are readily available throughout the *Relations*. Le Jeune's discussion of a Huron woman who fell ill and received baptism, and who later renounced her newly acquired Christianity when she regained her health is illustrative. This particular Huron woman ridiculed the sacraments and laughed at confession once she recovered from the serious illness that had caused her to be baptized in the first place. But shortly after her initial recovery she was stricken with 'a catarrh which almost closed the respiratory passage and deprived her of speech' (ibid. 16:143).

Seizing the opportunity to frighten her, the Jesuit who was visiting her informed her that the Devil wanted to prevent her from confession, and that was why she couldn't speak. She'd refused the sacrament when she was healthy and had a chance. Now it looked like the Devil had made sure that she would never be able to confess and would go to Hell as a result. This apparently had its desired effect, because the woman managed to confess by a series of signs. Her health recovered for a second time she 'now behaves like a person who believes in God and has the will to obey him' (ibid. 16:145). In this case the woman got a second chance to become a true believer. But had she died, according to Le Jeune, she would have richly deserved her fate for having reneged on the promise she made at her baptism.

In his *Relation* of 1647, Jérôme Lalemant wrote:

This place has both its joys and its desolation, its sweetness and its bitterness; it has had strokes of the divine Justice, and effects of its mercies. Let us begin with the severity which God has displayed in the punishment of some refractory ones. Three men of influence among the Savages were placing some obstacles against the expansion of the Faith, by their polygamy, openly retaining two wives. A thunderbolt hurled from Heaven, I mean to say, an extraordinary punishment, has killed their bodies, and, perhaps, wretchedly destroyed their souls.

(ibid. 30:257)

One of these young men had married a Christian girl, but 'allowing himself to be beguiled by a mad love', he then took a second wife. According to Lalemant, 'God, who waits for the sinner as long as he pleases, gave this one several months to come to his senses; and then, all at once, took away his life by the hands of his own friend.' Out hunting with his friend, the polygamist was mistaken for an animal and shot. The death had a positive effect, however, for the kinsmen of the slain man spent the night on their knees, 'asking pardon of God for their sins, with firm resolutions to lead a life very different from that which they had lived up to that moment' (ibid. 31:257–59).

The second of the three died shortly after the first, from some sudden illness, and his two wives, terrified by such a 'strange and sudden' death, immediately converted. But it required the death of the third before some 'Apostates and some hardened Pagans' were sufficiently shaken to behave better. As Le Jeune wrote:

> This thunderbolt, while killing one man, raised several others to life; the good Christians gave a thousand blessings to God, the lukewarm ones became warm, the Apostates became reconciled to the Church; and the Pagans, honoring Jesus Christ, asked his holy Baptism. No one dared any longer open his lips against the Faith; it was now spoken of only with a dread and a respect that all together pleased us.
>
> (ibid. 31:267)

There are many indications throughout the *Relations* of personality characteristics that the Jesuits esteemed in others and hoped to manifest in themselves. The eulogies written after the deaths of certain Jesuits, and published in the pages of the *Relations*, provide some insight into the kinds of personality structure and behaviour patterns that were most admired.

Called *Echon* by the Huron, Brébeuf was apparently considered among the chief enemies of the country and attributed with causing much of the death and destruction that had occurred after his arrival. As Paul Ragueneau noted, 'the name of *Echon* has been, for the space of some years, held in such abhorrence that it was used for terrifying the children' (ibid. 34:79). The sick often believed that a look from *Echon* was enough to cause them to get sick and die. In Ragueneau's view the fact that the Huron despised Brébeuf and treated him badly, and that he was constantly under threat of death, made him even more attractive.

Brébeuf was special because he had been granted a number of 'notable apparitions of Our Lady, of Saint Joseph, of the Angels and of the Saints'. Brébeuf kept these favours secret, only telling them to his own confessor, and he did not use them to guide his behaviour. Instead he relied on 'the principles of Faith, through the operations of obedience and in the lights of reason' (ibid. 34:177). Another lesser person so favoured would have made these favours known and would have sought to use them in his daily life. Brébeuf, instead, was content to be lead by and to obey apparently lesser men who did not enjoy the same favours from the Saints and the mother of Jesus.

Brébeuf's willingness to obey at all times marked him as a particularly worthy person. Indeed, he distinguished himself by his obedience. According to his eulogist, Brébeuf

> saw that he was fit only to obey, and that this virtue was natural to him, because not having great intelligence and great prudence, and being incapable of guiding himself he had as much pleasure in obeying as a child, who, not having enough strength to walk, takes pleasure in allowing himself to be carried in his mother's bosom.
>
> (ibid. 34:177)

Brébeuf was reputed to be detached from passions, indicated by the fact that he always asked for the most humble posts and by his patience, courage, suffering and zeal. He bore the heaviest loads on a journey, paddled the hardest, was the first into and the last out of freezing water. He called himself an ox (alluding to his name) and claimed to be 'fit only to bear burdens' (ibid. 34:181).

To all of the hardships he embraced he also added voluntary mortifications: 'disciplines everyday, and often twice each day; very frequent fasts; haircloths and belts with iron points; vigils which advanced far into the night'.[6] Even with this, Brébeuf felt that he had not suffered enough. Brébeuf adored humiliation. According to Ragueneau:

> When any humiliation befell him, he blessed God for it, and felt from it an inward joy, saying to those from whom he could not conceal all the emotions of his heart that those were not humiliations for him, because whatever low places he might be, he always saw himself higher than he wished; and that he had as much inclination for descending continually lower as has a stone, which never has a tendency to rise.
>
> (ibid. 34:183)

Brébeuf frequently asked his fellow Jesuits to humiliate him and Ragueneau noted that 'the good thing is that when, in order to cooperate with the grace of God upon him, we did not spare him, we always found an even spirit, a contented heart, and a most serene countenance' (ibid. 34:183–5). Even under the most trying circumstances Brébeuf always wore a benign look. Of his own gifts he is reputed to have said that:

> God . . . through his goodness has given me a gentleness, benignity, and a charity with respect to everyone; an indifference to

whatsoever may happen; a patience for suffering adversities; and the same goodness has willed that, through these talents which he has given me, I shall advance to perfection, and shall lead others to eternal life.

(ibid. 34:187)

In his own writings Brébeuf expressed his desire to die as a martyr while 'enduring all the torments which the Martyrs have suffered' (ibid. 34:189). He was said to be devoid of sexual feelings, and could not be tempted by women, writing himself that he had 'no attachment for any venial sin, nor the least pleasure in the world, that his will was averse to it as to his greatest enemy; and that he would rather choose all the pains of hell than the least sin' (ibid. 34:193). Ragueneau concluded his eulogy with the observation that Brébeuf had no faults whatsoever when he achieved his desire and was martyred on 16 March 1649.

Gabriel Lalemant, who had the dubious fortune of dying at the same time, and in the same manner as Brébeuf, was equally devoted to seeking a martyr's death. Among the papers found after his death was one in which he 'consecrated himself to Our Lord for the purpose of receiving from his hand a violent death, either in exposing himself among the plague-stricken in Old France, or in seeking to save the Savages in the New'. Lalemant asked the added favour of being allowed to die 'in the flower of his age'(ibid. 34:229).

Some of the same personality traits that Ragueneau eulogized in others he also claimed for himself. Ragueneau wrote, for example, to the Father General Vincent Caraffa in Rome, telling the general that he always rejoiced in 'these evils by which God permits us to be tried' (ibid. 35:19). The Jesuit Charles Garnier, eulogized in the *Relation* of 1650 by Ragueneau, was described as an 'indefatigable worker.... His face, his eyes, even his laugh, and every movement of his body, – preached sanctity'. Ragueneau claimed to personally know of 'several who were converted to God by the mere aspect of his countenance, which was truly Angelic, and which imparted a spirit of devotion, and chaste impressions, to those approaching him' (ibid. 35:123).

The 'heroic' virtues of Garnier included a 'perfect Obedience', and a profound humility which caused him to view himself as the 'most unworthy of the mission'. He always believed himself to be punished terribly by God if someone 'thought highly of him and he always tried to persuade others to have a low opinion of himself' (ibid. 35:123–5). Like the others, Garnier was fond of self-mortification and 'sought it day and night'. He slept on the ground, and wore a belt with iron points turned into his flesh, which he regularly sharpened. He used a discipline made of wire and added sharp points to it, ate 'meagerly and miserably'. According to Ragueneau:

> During the last year of famine, acorns and bitter roots were, to him, delicacies, not that he was insensible to their bitterness, but that love gave a relish to them. And yet he had ever been the cherished child of a rich and noble house, and the object of all a Father's endearments, brought up from the cradle, on other foods than those of swine.
>
> (ibid. 35:125–7)

THE JESUITS' PROJECT

The Jesuits came to New France as conscientious and determined bearers of a new moral and social order. They came prepared to do battle with the forces of evil and to sacrifice their lives in order to see the kingdom of God established among former pagans. Once in New France they discovered just how difficult their task would be. The native people they were to convert seemed to them to be without even the most rudimentary laws. Each individual exercised an extra-ordinary degree of personal freedom; no one seemed willing to accept the rule of another. In 1636, just a few years after his arrival in New France, the Jesuit Superior Paul Le Jeune wrote describing the Montagnais and the Huron as, 'A little wild ass is not born into greater freedom than is a little Canadian' (ibid. 16:179).

Without laws, without submission to higher authority, the Jesuits were convinced that the native people of New France were truly a fertile ground for the Demon. Not only did men not submit to the authority of other men, but women had the temerity to not submit to the authority of their fathers or husbands. Here lay a great threat to the Jesuit project to save the world from the forces of evil. The Jesuits were convinced that it was necessary to transform the existing behav-iour of the native peoples to conform with God's standards, with all that entailed in terms of domination and obedience between women and men. Once in New France, and working among the Huron and the Montagnais, they discovered just how dangerously free women were. In order to instil a new social and moral order, in order to save the souls of so many potentially damned people, the Jesuits would have to shut women up: both to confine them and to stop up their voices. Yet at the same time they would have to make women speak, to cause them to use an entirely new conceptual framework to examine their most intimate feelings and actions, and to interpret them according to new rules. Silenced as social beings, women's husbands and fathers would now speak for them. As spiritual beings, however, the Jesuits' project demanded that women learn to reveal their most private thoughts and that they be told in minute detail how to understand them.

The Jesuits recorded the conversations and actions of Huron and Montagnais women and men as they spoke to each other, often in confusion, pain and desperation, in those years when the world as they once knew it ceased to exist but no new order had fully or clearly emerged to take its place. The missionaries interpreted this point of disjuncture as evidence that the old order was falling away, and that the new Christian one was taking its place. As historical documents the *Jesuit Relations* contain a record of the transition from an old to a new order, a transition in which a new structuring of human relations was put into place, new understandings of women and men rationalized, and new power relations brought into play.

In the new order, which conformed as much as possible to Jesuit ideals, every act by a woman in which she subordinated herself, her will, her emotional life to that of her husband or father, was an act of moral reform and a profession of faith. Such acts were intended to reveal the true nature of women by purging them of their previous natures formed under too much liberty, too little education and insufficient sexual restraint. A new 'site of constraint' emerged, centring on women and their emotional lives: a site of constraint in which a new morality was combined with French-style administrative forces to police even the most private thoughts and feelings of each individual.

The Christian marriage of Charles and Marie Meiaskawat, celebrated in front of the Jesuit missionary at Sillery in 1642, in which Charles asks Marie if she will continue 'to be proud, disobedient and ill-tempered, as in the past' and Marie responds by promising to 'be obedient to her husband, and live with him in gentleness and in the utmost humility' may be taken as a sort of historical marker. It indicates that significant progress had been made towards the subjugation of women, that previous relations between women and men had been transformed.

3

'THAT THEY MAY ALSO ACQUIRE A FRENCH HEART AND SPIRIT'

While the Huron and Montagnais were born into 'great freedom', knowing little personal subordination and domination within their own society, the experience of the French who came to colonize them was rather different. Wealth, power, prestige, fear, submission and loyalty – these were the watch words of the seventeenth-century French. These themes were institutionally tied to two projects which served to characterize the *ancien régime*: the centralization and concentration of political power into one institution, the absolutist state, and the concomitant creation of an obedient and loyal citizenry.

It was the Jesuits and their servants (along with a few seamen-adventurers, like Samuel de Champlain) who had direct contact with members of native societies in the New World. But it was through the activities of the king, his first ministers, other aristocrats, fur merchants and their employees that the immediate conditions which allowed the Jesuits to begin their work in New France were created. The project in the New World was an outgrowth of a much larger project in the Old World – one which lead, ultimately, to the creation of a modern state, and a national population governed by that state. An analysis of the changes in the relations between men and women in Huron and Montagnais societies begins with the related projects of state formation in France and the colonization of New France. The Jesuits' activities in both the Old and New Worlds were closely tied to, although not homologous with, these two projects.

During the sixteenth and seventeenth centuries French monarchs and their ministers took major steps towards developing the fiscal, administrative and policing apparatuses needed for the functioning of a powerful and centralized state. These included 'procedures which allowed the effects of power to circulate in a manner at once continuous, uninterrupted, adapted and individualised throughout the entire

31

social body' (Foucault 1979:36–7). In the late sixteenth and early seventeenth centuries, the institutional structures through which these changes were effected were not yet under the strict control of the state and its administrators. Institutional structures of the state proper were not yet disentangled from those which supported the network of power surrounding church, aristocratic or mercantile interests. Nor was the question of who would occupy key positions within the nexus of competing interests firmly decided.

As a consequence of this (a consequence, moreover, played out through the very person of monarchs who felt that they *were* the state and a significant part of the church), the body of knowledge, the truths and the objectives which guided state activities were often closely interwoven with those guiding church, noble and mercantile interests. Although already aware of their differences, the social actors clustered around these four foci of social organization often proceeded together as if they were pursuing a common interest. Drawn from the same backgrounds and frequently occupying positions within more than one of these organizations, the leaders of the state, church, aristocracy and bourgeoisie were ever mindful of each other's presence; suspicious and mistrustful of each other they none the less found each other mutually useful.[1]

It was only later that other techniques for the control of large populations which encompass the entire social body were developed, and the members of state-based institutions of social organization were able to claim more of the field of action for themselves. In the early years of the seventeenth century, the church, the nobility and the bourgeoisie (or rather that network of interests, strategies, beliefs, sentiments and will to action that made them up) were all competing forces, especially where the questions of wealth and military power were concerned. Members of state-based social institutions, including the king and his first ministers, had to be content with allowing many others whose foci of power lay outside the state-based institutions into the field of action in order to further their projects of expansion. In spite of the struggles for positions of dominance, in spite of the uncertainties about who would occupy what position, and what amount of power, wealth and prestige would accrue to them, there was a clear commitment on everyone's part to the necessity of enforcing relations of hierarchy, and the subordination of one part of society to another. The subjugation of the native people in New France to God and king, and within that, of women to men, was a complex part of this world-view.

THE PROJECT IN NEW FRANCE

In the autumn of 1612, Charles de Bourbon, le comte de Soissons, became the new governor of New France. By his commission, he was enjoined to keep Canada under obedience to the king and to bring the 'savages' of the country to the knowledge and service of God, through instructing them in the Roman Catholic religion. Soisson's death soon followed and the governorship of Canada passed to his nephew, the prince of Condé. At the same time a commercial society was formed composed of merchants of Rouen, Le Havre, St Malo and La Rochelle, with an eleven-year monopoly for trading in pelts. In return for that monopoly, the company was to fortify Quebec, convert the 'savages' and bring over French colonists.

In order to accomplish this, Samuel de Champlain, seaman, adventurer, cartographer, explorer and representative of the king, and his viceroys in New France made arrangements with the Recollect order to send missionaries to New France. By 1618, Champlain had completed his ninth voyage to New France. In the following year he dedicated the third volume of his *Voyages and Discoveries Made in New France, from 1615 to 1618*, to his king, Louis XIII. In his dedication, Champlain expressed the hope that the young king would continue to encourage colonization and Christianization in New France. To begin with, Champlain stated, the people of New France are 'by no means so savage but that in time and through intercourse with a civilization they may be refined'. Acknowledging that many of his majesty's subjects had interested themselves in New France only because they were 'urged on by the lust of gain', Champlain expressed his belief that 'these are the means which God employs to give more scope to the holy desires of others'.

In thanking Louis for his protection against those who were only interested in financial gain Champlain claims that the king has given him good reason

> for increasing our long-cherished desire to send out yonder communities and colonies to teach those peoples, along with the knowledge of God, the glory and triumphs of your Majesty, so that with the French speech they may also acquire a French heart and spirit, which, next to the fear of God, shall breathe nothing but the desire to serve you. And should our design succeed, the glory thereof will redound first to God, and then to your Majesty, who, in addition to a thousand blessings from Heaven as a reward for so many souls granted admission

there by this means, will gain an immortal name for carrying the glory and sceptre of the French as far westward as your predecessors extended it eastward, and over the whole habitable Earth. This will augment the quality of Most Christian which belongs to you above all the kings of the earth.

(Biggar (ed.) 1922–36, III:5–6)

God's due being rendered, Champlain was also quite willing to promote the financial side of things as well. In a letter addressed to the Chamber of Commerce of Paris the year previously, Champlain outlined the attractions of, and his hopes for the country. The letter is worth quoting from at length:

Firstly, His Majesty (Louis XIII) will establish the Christian faith among an infinite number of souls....

Secondly, the King will make himself master and lord of a country nearly 1,800 leagues in length, watered by the fairest rivers in the world and by the greatest and most numerous lakes, the richest and most abundant in all varieties of fish that exist, and full also of the greatest meadows, fields and forests....

Thirdly, the Sieur de Champlain undertakes to discover the South Sea passage to China and the East Indies by way of the River St Lawrence, which traverses the lands of the said New France, and which river issues from a lake about 300 leagues in length, from which lake flows a river that empties into the said South Sea, according to the account given to the said Sieur de Champlain by a great number of people....

That his Majesty would derive a great and notable profit from the taxes and duties he could levy on the merchandise coming from the said country, as likewise from the customs duties on the merchandise that would come from China and from the Indies, which would surpass in value at least ten times all those levied in France, inasmuch as all the merchants of Christendom would pass through the passage sought by the Sieur de Champlain ... in order to shorten the said journey by more than a year and a half and without any risk from pirates and from the perils of the sea....

Furthermore the said Sieur de Champlain proposes to build at Quebec a town ... which shall be called LUDOVICA, in the centre of which will be built ... the Church of the Redeemer, as a memorial and commemoration of the good that it shall please

God to do to these poor people, who have no knowledge of His
holy name, to incline the will of the King to bring them to the
knowledge of the holy Christian faith and to the bosom of our
holy mother Church....

And inasmuch as all existing states are supported politically
on four buttresses, which are force, justice, trade and husband-
ry, it is necessary to add force, which will consist of three
hundred good men well armed and disciplined, and who nevertheless will have to work by turns on whatever will be necessary, as it is inexpedient in founding colonies to carry thither
people, whatever their quality may be, who are incapable of
earning their living.

(Bishop 1964: 235–6).

Appended to Champlain's promotional letter was an itemized list
estimating the potential wealth that could be extracted from country.
A total of 5,400,000 livres could be earned yearly from such resources
as fisheries, whale oil, forest and agricultural products, dyes, hemp,
silver and iron mines, textiles, furs, building materials and hides (ibid.
1964:237).

Here, in his letter and his dedication, Champlain offers both a
rationale for French presence in the New World and a list of objectives for dealing with the native people. Wealth, power and prestige
for the king (and by association for other well placed members of the
society) were explicitly tied to the creation of a Gallicized, Catholi-
cized and obedient population in New France. In Champlain's tidy
turn of phrase a population was to be created in New France who, in
acquiring a 'French heart and spirit', would learn simultaneously the
fear of God and of Louis XIII. Moreover, Louis XIII would really
earn his title of 'most Christian' by bringing the 'holy name of God to
so many nations that had never heard of it' (Bishop 1964:7). Louis
XIII's interests would be furthered (and thus those of the French
state and the people of France) because New France had such rich
potential for providing new sources of revenues.

Champlain was convinced that a great deal of wealth could be
extracted from New France. Especially important were the native
populations which could be interbred with French settlers to produce a new race of people. This natural resource, like any other
resource that might provide its masters with riches, required careful
'husbanding'. The native population had to be tamed, civilized and
intermarried with French peasant stock. Once created, however, not

35

only would this new race produce riches for France, it would also defend the country against all other monarchs' claims.

The potential for success, as Champlain saw it, was all there. To realize that potential, however, required extensive co-ordination between the state, religious and mercantile interests. In the seventeenth century, the success of such a co-ordinated effort was not at all assured especially in view of centralizing attempts by the king and his first minister to concentrate political, economic and military power within one institutional structure, i.e. the state. Such centralization of control required that other institutional structures be systematically stripped of their powers. This made co-operation between those who headed the state and those whose basis of power lay elsewhere a constant struggle and jockeying for leverage.

It is not surprising, then, to find that Champlain's arguments, which were directed at inducing the king and other members of the aristocracy with money and military power to throw their resources and energies behind the New World project, were later echoed by Jesuit writers, once they had been able to establish their own presence in the New World. Paul Le Jeune, in his *Relation* of 1635, argued that it would be an 'enterprise very honorable and very profitable to Old France' to establish a colony in New France. 'Shall the French, alone of all the nations of the earth', Le Jeune asked his king, 'be deprived of the honor of expanding and spreading over this New World' (Thwaites 1896–1901, 8:9). It would be much better, he argued, if French emigrants could go to a French colony than to people the colonies of some other foreign power. To establish a French colony in New France would:

> weaken the strength of the Foreigner, ... banish famine from the houses of a multitude of poor workmen, ... [and] also strengthen France; for those who would be born in New France, will be French, and in case of need can render good service to their King, a thing which cannot be expected from those who dwell among our neighbors and outside of the dominion of their Prince.[2]
>
> (ibid.)

Lacking sufficient institutional and financial strength to accomplish much on their own, the men who headed the French state of the seventeenth century had to rely on the strength of the very institutional structures they were seeking to absorb, subsume or subjugate in order to carry out many of their policies. It is this interplay of forces, this uncertainty of outcome, of balance of powers, that gave French presence in the New World during the seventeenth century its precarious and tentative nature. There were never enough men, never sufficient resources, never adequate authority or military strength to prevent the Iroquois from raiding, to force the native people to comply with French laws and the Catholic religion, or even to enforce trading monopolies. Indeed, the fortunes of the colony were bound up in the struggles taking place in Old France. In the end, New France was treated as a resource, there to be exploited by whomever had sufficient means to enforce their claim.

The rapid decline in the status of Montagnais and Huron women during the early to mid-seventeenth century took place within the context of the often convoluted interplay of power that was simultaneously taking place in France. This struggle for control centred around state building and the consolidation of institutions intended to bring about the centralized control and management of large populations. Those who came to the New World and who had direct contact with native peoples – especially the missionaries, merchants and adventurers – all participated, in one way or another, in this great and historically significant project. Along with the nobility and the monarch they shared in the project of the creation of a subject and obedient population, in both Old and New Worlds (the major differences in their objectives focusing around the question of who was to be made obedient to whom?).

The events in France, which allowed sometimes conflicting, sometimes co-operating combinations of interests to form temporary alliances, helped give direction to the ways in which the restructuring of the lives of the native peoples of New France took place. The same institutions and forces that were in motion in France creating a subject population under the institutional aegis of the absolutist state were also unleashed in New France. Confronted with a new land and new peoples so different from themselves, the French, but especially the Jesuits, set about to the best of their ability to reshape the New World in the image of the Old.

One thing that the king, his first minister and the various members of the nobility who held the post of viceroy of Canada, as well as the various missionaries who arrived to carry out the project, were clear about and in agreement on: the natives of New France should be converted to Christianity. Champlain's commission of 1612, appointing him 'lieutenant particulier' for Canada, under Charles de Bourbon, le comte de Soissons, merely directed Champlain to do what Soissons's own commission from Louis XIII called for: to keep Canada 'under obedience to His Majesty', and 'to bring the savages to the knowledge and service of God, to the light of the faith, and of the apostolic and Roman Catholic religion' (Fouqueray 1925:293).

The events surrounding the colonization and commercial exploitation of New France illustrate the successes and failures of the attempts to centralize power within one institution (the state) and to assure that institution a sufficient source of income. During the seventeenth century efforts were made by those who directed the interests of the fledgling state to regulate the colonization of New France, to control the direction of the development of the colony, to assure that the native population became properly Gallicized and loyal to the crown and, finally, to assure an independent and growing source of revenue. The limited success and extensive failure of these attempts underlines the degree to which kings and prime ministers remained stymied in their attempts to make the state a primary focus of institutional power.

In New France, as in France, the direction of development was shaped through the interplay of many powerful institutions, including the missionizing order of the Jesuits. The success that was experienced in the creation of an obedient and subject population out of previously 'uncivilized savages' was accomplished largely through the efforts of this group of religious, whose own links with both the church in France and the curia in Rome were complex and conflicted. Yet, even here, the work of the Jesuits cannot be understood outside of the context of the interplay of their interests and activities with those of a multiplicity of others whose interests at times coincided with and at other times ran contrary to the activities and interests of the missionizing order. Missionaries, members of the state, the merchants and the nobility all had a hand in directing the development of events and in extracting a certain portion of the profit from the New World. As curious as it may sound, they proceeded from a basis of personal action which on the one hand required vast amounts of courage and dedication to accomplish, and which, on the other, sought to establish fear, obedience and submission in all they came in contact with.

THE PROMOTION OF 'NOUVELLE FRANCE'

French colonization in America began quite late. While the Portuguese and the Spanish had been exploiting the New World for almost a century, and while fishing vessels had regularly visited Newfoundland, it was only in 1524 with Verranzo's mapping of the coastline of Nova Gallia, extending between Florida and Newfoundland, that France seriously considered the New World (Trudel 1973:1). A decade later the French king, François I, commissioned a St Malo seaman, Jacques Cartier, to explore the Gulf of St Lawrence with the objective of locating a sea route through North America to the Pacific Ocean.[3] Cartier was also instructed explore 'certain isles and countries where it is said there must be great quantities of gold and other riches' (Biggar (ed.) 1930:42).

While Cartier did not find a passage to the Pacific, he did encounter a group of Iroquoian-speaking people who lived in a village called Stadacona near present-day Quebec City, and he later travelled up river to visit another village, Hochelaga. The inhabitants of Stadacona regaled Cartier with tales of the 'Kingdom of Saguenay', reputed to lie to the west of their village. It was a kingdom, they maintained, 'where there are infinite quantities of gold, rubies and other riches and where there are white men, as in France, dressed in woollen cloth'. Dreaming of immense riches, Cartier hoped to establish a French colony on the St Lawrence which could be used as a base for exploring the rich interior of New France (Trudel 1973:133).

To further that objective, he kidnapped a number of the Stadaconians he had encountered, including a leader by the name of Donnacona, and had them accompany him back to France.[4] In an interview with François I, Cartier and Donnacona were able to impress the king with the possibilities of great riches that the country held in store, ready for the taking. Determined to challenge Spanish claims to North America, François I proceeded with a plan of colonization.

That plan of colonization, however, was conceived of within, and constrained, structured and shaped by the economic, political and social conditions of the period. The king himself had insufficient resources with which to pursue money-making projects, such as the development of trade in New France. He had even less for ventures such as colonization, that promised to be a drain on finances at least in the short term. Yet colonization was in the 'interests of the state' and by promoting trade with and colonization of New France the king could hope to gain new sources of revenues. Moreover, to colonize meant to have citizens, and to have citizens meant to have a possibility of holding a territory loyal to the state (and thus to the king). In the short term colonization was an expense that detracted from immediate profits. In the long run it was a means of assuring that the area remained both open to trade and within the sphere of influence of the monarch.

It was for these reasons that in January 1541 François I directed a commission to a Protestant nobleman, Jean-François de La Rocque, Sieur de Roberval. Roberval had fought in the Italian wars attached to the duc de Bouillon, attended court regularly and figured among François I's immediate entourage. He was chosen, in François I's own words, because he was an 'excellent personage of great loyalty and integrity towards us' who would be able to give 'greater order and dispatch to the accomplishment of this enterprise' (ibid.: 36). Moreover, Roberval seems to have had the requisite financial resources. But what is equally important is that Roberval was in no position to challenge the king from any quarter. Ennobled, but not a member of one of the great families, a Protestant and not a Catholic, Roberval had to be content with whatever François I decided to allot to him.

The details of Roberval's commission are interesting, largely because they underline the complex relations between mercantile, state-making and colonizing projects. They are interesting too, because, for the first time, they provide an outline of the role that religious conversion of the natives was expected to take. It is these elements, written down by François I in 1540, that can be read again, repeated several decades later, in Champlain's missive to Louis XIII.

François I's commission to Roberval directed the latter to send out 'men-at-arms', as well as members of the general population 'of each sex and every liberal and mechanic art' into the lands of 'Canada and Ochelaga and others around and about them'. To this list was added 'all lands beyond and bordering the seas uninhabited or not possessed and dominated by a Christian prince' and even to the 'very land of Saguenay'. Colonists were to 'converse with these foreign peoples', and to live with them if necessary. Roberval, moreover, was enjoined to build 'towns, and forts and temples and churches for the communication of our Holy Catholic faith and Christian doctrine'. He was instructed to establish the institution of laws and law officers that converts might live 'with reason and order in the fear and love of God' (ibid.). To accomplish all of this he was given carte blanche vice-regal powers.

The communication of Catholicism was a fundamental part of the rationalization of European presence in, and conquest of, the New World. The discovery of new territories with non-Christian populations coincided with the growing movement in Europe towards the consolidation of absolutist states, as well as with internal turmoil brought about by wars, the Reformation and the Counter-Reformation. The refusal of monarchs of emerging absolutist states to submit to the pope's temporal authority, combined with growing centralist and mercantilist pressures towards making new conquests that would yield new sources of wealth, produced a renewed interest in debates surrounding the 'laws of nations'.

Even in the Middle Ages, European jurists had been divided on the issue of the rights of 'infidels' to sovereignty and personal property. While in the thirteenth century Pope Innocent IV, for example, defended the right of all rational creatures to hold property, at the same time Henry of Susa, Cardinal of Ostia was claiming that no secular power existed outside of the church and that 'heathens' lost their political and personal rights when Christ became king of the earth. Christ had transferred his power to Peter, and thus to the popes; 'heathens', therefore, held their property only with the approval of the pope who could appoint a ruler to see to their conversion to Catholicism (Dickason 1977:98).

In 1493 Pope Alexander VI issued his bulls which divided the New World between Spain and Portugal, and threatened to excommunicate anyone who contravened those rights. Pope Alexander VI's partitioning of the New World included not only those lands already discovered, but also those lands to be discovered, a wording that François I later tried to have changed and restricted to territories already discovered.

By the mid-sixteenth century the French had finally entered into the race for territory in the New World. Montchrestien, for example, argued that if anyone had the right to civilize the non-Christian world it was the French, who were known for their art and civilities. Others argued that the 'Barbarians' should be made over in the French image, and would in the future have to submit to the 'gentleness' of France's domination (ibid.).

Although there was important debate on whether or not the pope had civil or temporal domination in the world, and could transfer that to whomever he chose, the right and duty of Christians to preach the gospel and to convert pagans was never questioned. Nor was the idea that recalcitrant pagans could be forced to submit if they resisted, or that Christians had a right and duty to 'rescue' them from such horrifying practices as human sacrifice and cannibalism. While by 1637 Pope Urban VIII had threatened excommunication for those who deprived native peoples of their liberty and property, none of the states involved in colonizing the New World were willing to comply with this edict. The French lawyer, Marc Lescarbot, who spent 1606 to 1607 at Port Royal, wrote that 'there is here no question of applying the law and policy of Nations, by which it would not be permissible to claim the territory of another. This being so, we must possess it and preserve its natural inhabitants.'[5] Why bother conquering a new territory, Lescarbot reasoned, if not to possess it entirely.

With a similar objective in mind Roberval had accompanied Cartier and several hundred prospective colonists to establish, in 1541, a settlement near present-day Quebec, at Cap Rouge. The colony failed miserably when they did not find the promised 'kingdom of Saguenay'. Gold and diamonds turned out to be worthless iron pyrites and quartz and colonists suffered from scurvy, food shortages and native hostility. In 1543 Roberval and those colonists who had survived returned to France without the expected riches. The king and the nobility quickly lost interest in New France and for several decades commerce there was left in the hands of fishermen and fur traders.

While sixteenth-century attempts to colonize and to exploit the resources of New France led to disappointment for most of those involved, almost all of the competing, carefully interwoven interests that would later be present in more successful attempts were already in place. Represented in this first attempt in the New World is the king who grants certain prerogatives to a member of the nobility, who in turn grants certain trading rights to specific mercantile groups. As part of the conditions of the grant, colonization is specified by the king. In addition we find the explorer/adventurer, captain/organizer, in this case Cartier, balanced between king, nobility and merchants. Finally, the native population was already viewed as a natural resource to be exploited and used at will, and importantly, to be converted to Christianity. Only missionizing orders to carry out this conversion are missing from the first attempts in the sixteenth century. It was Samuel de Champlain, following the orders of his various commissions from Louis XIII, who first introduced missionaries to New France.

THE JESUITS, THE COUNTER-REFORMATION AND THE FRENCH STATE

The Society of Jesus was established by Inigo Lopez de Loyola, the thirteenth and youngest child of a Basque nobleman, Bertrand de

Loyola. Orphaned at the age of 14, Inigo was sent to the court of don Juan Velasquez, treasurer general of Castille, where he became known for his 'gallant' exploits – gaming, womanizing and fighting duels. Implicated in some criminal affair (probably murder) he was forced to flee the court, giving himself over to the ecclesiastic tribunal at Pampelune, where he spent some time in prison (Woodrow 1984:23–6).

In 1521, at the age of 30, Loyola was badly wounded while in the service of the viceroy of Navarre, defending the town of Pampelune against the French. Sent to his family's chateau to recover from near death and from three operations on his leg, Loyola experienced some sort of religious conversion. He then set out to translate his own spiritual experiences into direct action, conceiving of his life as a military mission, under the standard of Christ, whose objective was to defend and propagate Christianity.

Loyola's ideas about the role the Jesuits were to play for Christianity drew heavily on the feudal idea of an overlord who was followed, without question, by his loyal troops. With Christ as their general, at the head of the Christian army, the Society of Jesus (the order that Loyola was soon to found) was to constitute His bodyguard, in much the same way as knights protected their liege lord. Loyola envisaged Jesus calling his volunteers into a pacifist but heroic combat. Both in practice and in his writings, Loyola was to stress self-abnegation, submission to authority and obedience as the most desirable personal characteristics of his followers (Guibert 1964:90).

In 1528 Loyola travelled to Paris to study theology. He was a student there during the same period as Calvin, although the two never met (Tüchle, Bouman and Le Brun 1968:159). In 1534, at Montmartre in Paris, Loyola and six friends formed themselves into a community, promising poverty and chastity and apostolic labours in the Holy Land. At first the members of this community were pledged to convert the Turks to Christianity. When this objective proved to be too limiting, Loyola adopted the more general objective of 'defending the kingdom of Christ among all classes, in all countries and by all legitimate means' (Schwickerath 1904:76).

Loyola received a masters degree in 1535 and was ordained as a priest two years later. Finally, in 1540, the Society of Jesus was recognized by Pope Paul III with the Bull *Regimini Militantis Ecclesiae* (Broderick 1934:898; Woodrow 1984:39). Members were bound by the usual vows of poverty, chastity and obedience as well as by a fourth vow tying them to the pope. The constitution required perfect obedience of each member to the personal judgement of the superior, and directly linked them to obedience to the pope (Woodrow 1984:58). By this vow the Jesuits undertook to go wherever the pope wished to send them.

In 1558 the constitution of the Society was finally accepted. Among other things it stipulated that the Jesuits could only accept as members men who had distinguished themselves by their intelligence, their culture and their saintly lives. Great stress was placed on theology and philosophy, and members were required to undergo many years of study. The major objectives of the Society were to be preaching, teaching and 'the conversion of heathens', and the constitution made it clear that teaching was considered 'apostolic' work (Donohue 1963:8).

The structure of the Society was totally hierarchical and centralized, with a General being elected for life. By the time of Loyola's death in 1556 the Jesuits could be found in four continents, and counted over a thousand members. In 1600 they had 353 establishments, a century later that number had more than tripled (Tüchle, Bouman and Le Brun 1968:160–1).

Very quickly the major objectives of the Jesuits came to be teaching and missionizing. Both of these activities were seen as central to the task of the fight against the Protestant Reformation, and the securing, or reclamation of people to the Catholic faith. Jesuit colleges, in particular, were intended to become important strongholds, points of offence as well as defence in the struggle against the Reformation. Father Jouvancy, one of the earlier members of the Society, wrote that Jesuit missionaries were 'enflamed with a marvelous ardour for spreading the Faith and Religion among those nations lacking in morals and culture'. These brave men, he added 'labour under the most brutal conditions, with the grossest kinds of human beings often going hungry, cold, thirsty and naked' (Charmot 1951:80–1).

IMPORTANT AND WELL-PLACED FRIENDS

As with most things in the late sixteenth and early seventeenth centuries, religion, politics, state building, inter- and intra-class struggles cannot easily be separated from each other. It is a simple matter to note that the Jesuit undertakings of educating and missionizing throughout the world were directly tied to their stated objectives of promoting and securing their own and everyone else's salvation. It is another matter, however, to try to explain Jesuit actions in any one particular instance on the basis of such simple principles. Moreover, it is very difficult to speak of a single 'Jesuit policy' or plan of action. While the Society was extremely hierarchical and centralized on paper, in actual practice the generals of the late-sixteenth to mid-seventeenth centuries often had problems keeping dissident members under control.[6]

One section of the Jesuits in France, allied with the Catholic League, were bitterly opposed to Henri IV who, they felt, was too supportive of Protestants. The League had been established by the duc de Guise in 1576, ostensibly with the objective of defending Catholicism against the Calvinists. This defence, however, was not without its clearly political side and involved the overthrow of Henri III, himself a Protestant and his replacement by the duc de Guise. Henri III's successor, Henri IV, renounced his Protestantism, and embraced Catholicism, thus undercutting the League, which had already discredited itself through its alliance with France's sworn enemy, Spain. However, Henri's Catholicism was suspect and in 1594, after an attempt on his life by a student of the Jesuits, Henri IV banished the Jesuits from France, on suspicion of their complicity (Aveling 1981:209).[7]

By 1604 Henri had changed his mind and recalled the Jesuits to France. His decision was probably influenced by the role played by the Jesuit, Cardinal Tolet, in bringing about the revocation of his excommunication, a necessary step in allowing him to once again embrace Catholicism and thus to become king of France (Woodrow 1984:72). Henri IV went so far as to take a Jesuit, Father Joseph Coton, as his personal confessor. The Jesuits flourished and by 1610 the order had possibly 1,400 members in France, and possessed thirty-six colleges devoted to educating the children of the nobility and the bourgeoisie (Tüchle, Bouman and Le Brun 1968:221). Not only did the Jesuits occupy themselves with the children of members of powerful groups, but they regularly became the personal confessors of the wealthy, the high-placed and the powerful.

It was in this way that the first Jesuit missionaries came to New France. Financed by Mme de Guercheville, a wealthy aristocrat who was one of his private penitents, Father Massé and several other Jesuit missionaries were sent to Acadia in 1611. Widowed, Mme de Guercheville had purchased a part interest in the company trading to Acadia, and had given over a portion of her profits to support the missionaries. Two years later, however, a Virginian by the name of

Samuel Argall, seized the settlement, claiming that it was within English territory and the Jesuits were ousted (Grant 1984:7).

In seeking to fulfil his commission from Louis XIII, and to bring the Roman Catholic faith to the native peoples, Champlain subsequently approached Mme de Guercheville to buy the habitation of Quebec and sponsor the Jesuits to that settlement. When she declined Champlain secured the services of the Recollects, a branch of the Franciscans. This order of missionaries already had over 500 missions in Spanish America and was also active throughout France (Fouqueray 1925:294). In 1615 three priests and a lay brother arrived at Quebec City: one to cover the St Lawrence from Trois Rivières to a point below Quebec, a second to go to Tadoussac to preach to the Montagnais of the Saguenay region, and a third to travel to the Huron, who were living on the shores of Georgian Bay (Grant 1984:7). By 1624, however, the Recollects could no longer find support for their efforts, and were forced to make way for the Jesuits.

The Jesuits' arrival in New France to replace the Recollects was, as in Acadia, financed by wealthy and high-placed friends, in this case the connections of the Jesuit Father Noyrot. Among Noyrot's friends and penitents was Henri de Lévis, duc de Ventadour. Ventadour was nephew of the current viceroy to Canada, the duc de Montmorency.[8] When Montmorency decided to sell his title of viceroy, Ventadour, who by this time had developed a 'great affection for the mission of Canada', was persuaded by his Jesuit friends to purchase it (Fouqueray 1925:297–8). Thus, it was under the viceroyalty of Henri de Lévis, duc de Ventadour, friend and penitent, that the Jesuits were to come to replace the Recollects as missionaries in New France.

Ventadour, who was especially fanatical, gathered around him members of both the Capuchin and Jesuit orders, as well as individuals such as St Vincent de Paul. In France, he organized a secret society, called the Company of the Holy Sacrament, with the objective of 'promoting the Glory of God by all means'. The company supported works of assistance to the poor, the sick and prisoners. It also spied on deviants, actors and libertines and kept close watch over public opinion (Goubert and Roche 1984, II:73).

In the early summer of 1625, three Jesuit priests, Fathers Charles Lalemant, Enemond Massé and Jean de Brébeuf, accompanied by three lay brothers, and financed by Henri de Lévis, duc de Ventadour,[9] arrived in Quebec (Thwaites 1896–1901, 4:118). Lalemant, former professor of grammar, literature and mathematics, and principal of the boarders at the Jesuit college in Paris, was put in charge of the mission. They were joined, a year later, by two more Jesuits, Anne de Noüe, and Philibert Noyrot (Ventadour's personal confessor).

Although support for the Jesuits' presence in New France came directly from the viceroy himself this support was by no means sufficient to see them comfortably installed in their new missions. The merchant company trading to Quebec was especially unwelcoming of Jesuit presence. Ventadour had made it known to the merchants that not only were they to welcome the Jesuits into the colony, but that they would be expected to contribute to their upkeep. Additional moneys for the Jesuits' work in New France came in the form of a 3,000,000 livre gift from the marquis de Rohault de Gamache whose son first studied with the Jesuits, and later joined their order (Fouqueray 1925:229). The inheritance of the latter also went to support the Jesuit seminary at Quebec.

With the help of their friends, Jesuit missionaries finally made their way to Huronia in 1626. Although Noyrot and Noüe had brought along twenty workers who had been engaged to help build for them, things were not as the Jesuits would have wished in the colony. Charles Lalemant, writing to his brother, noted that 'the affairs of the colony are not yet in the order that God would want them . . . Heresy reigns here even more than ever' (ibid.: 303). Foremost on the Jesuits' list of grievances was the fact that the mercantile company, inherited from Montmorency's days as viceroy, was composed both of Calvinists and of Catholics. The Jesuits, who were committed to the eradication of any form of Protestantism, saw the presence of any Protestants in New France as a potential challenge to God's true work.

Not only did the Jesuits in New France have to contend with opposition from outside of their order, there also appears to have been internal opposition to their involvement. In a letter written to Mutio Vitelleschi, general of the Society at Rome, and dated 28 July 1625, Father Charles Lalemant noted that Father Noyrot, Ventadour's friend and confessor, was in need of Vitelleschi's assistance. As Lalemant wrote:

> With the consent of his superiors, Father Philibert Noyrot returns to France to promote as hitherto in the interests of our enterprises. He stands in need of the influence of Your Paternity in order to negotiate freely with those who have

charge of our affairs. Our own Fathers in Paris, for some reason, put difficulties in our way, and seem rather unfriendly to our missions; so that, but for the favour of Father Coton, of blessed memory, our affairs would have fallen to the ground.

(Thwaites 1896–1901, 4:181)

In Paris, Noyrot talked to Louis XIII and his councillors, describing what he believed to be the bad state of affairs in the colony, blaming the Protestants for the problems, and proposing, instead, a society of Catholics committed to the honour of the country and the Catholic faith. Noyrot was finally able to persuade Cardinal Richelieu to take an interest in the colony. Richelieu became so convinced of the potential of New France that in 1627 he purchased the post of viceroy of New France from Ventadour, and established his own trading company, the Company of New France, also called the Company of One Hundred Associates.[10] By the new company's constitution, only Catholics were allowed to participate in it. No Protestant was to set foot in New France again. Interestingly, the idea that Christianized Indians should share in all the privileges of French citizenship was also formally enshrined (Grant 1984:14; Thwaites 1896–1901, 4:257–8).

The Company of New France was personally controlled and managed by Richelieu. It drew its membership from those who held official positions around the court, as well as from merchants resident in Rouen, Paris and other cities.[11]

But as soon as Richelieu's company undertook its first trading mission in 1627 the colony of Quebec was seized by English adventurers, and was not returned to France until several years later, in 1632. Even then, the Jesuits' right to dominate the missionary field in New France was uncertain. At first Richelieu (who was deeply suspicious of Jesuit ambitions and power) offered the prize to the Capuchins. Most likely Richelieu was influenced in this matter by his adviser, the Capuchin Father Joseph. The Jesuits countered the Capuchin move through Jean de Lauson, a director of the Company of New France and intendent for Canada. It was Lauson who finally persuaded Richelieu to grant Acadia to the Capuchins and the rest of New France to the Jesuits. With Lauson's help the Jesuits were also able to prevent the Recollect from returning to their former mission and thus kept New France under their exclusive jurisdiction (Trigger 1976:467).

Paul Le Jeune's letter, written in 1634 to 'Monseigneur the

Cardinal' is a study in self-abnegation and humility, a sort of grovelling praise of Richelieu. The kind of language Le Jeune employed was usually reserved for addressing the king or for speaking to others about one's feelings about God, so it is indicative of the extent to which Le Jeune was trying to curry the favour of Richelieu, who was a potentially dangerous adversary. Le Jeune portrays Richelieu as God-like, with the power to make things happen or to prevent the Jesuits from realizing their projects in New France. He praises Richelieu for ridding France of the 'poison' (i.e. the Huguenots) that was threatening to destroy her:

> [I]t is hard to remain from day to day in a state of wonder at your great deeds and benefactions, and not allow the tongue to give some evidence of the sentiments of the heart. All Europe, yes, all the old world regards you with admiration. The Church cherishes and honors you as one of its greatest princes, full of joy at seeing the arrogance of its enemies crushed by your government. All of France owes her recovery to you, who dissipated the poison which was creeping into her heart. Alas, what misfortunes would have befallen her in these past years, if this poison had retained its strength in the midst of the State!
> (Thwaites 1896–1901, 7:239)[12]

Father Jérôme Lalemant's letter to Richelieu, written a few years later in 1640, repeats Le Jeune's sentiments, praising Richelieu for expelling the Huguenots from France. Lalemant's letter is intended to encourage Richelieu to take action against the

> English and the Flemish, who line the seacoast on our side, and who excite and strongly fortify the courage of the enemies of the tribes allied to us, among whom we live, and by whose means alone we can advance further, to the south or to the west.
> (ibid. 17:223)

Lalemant was convinced that if Richelieu did not take action against the Flemish and the English 'not for a hundred years hence, and perhaps never, shall we see ourselves rid of these other enemies of God and the State' (ibid. 17:223). As with Le Jeune's letter, Lalemant's is a fascinating study in the expression of the kind of submissive and fearful obedience that the Jesuits wished to see established in all peoples of the world. The letters portray a world the Jesuits were familiar with and wanted to see replicated. A capricious superior, just as capable of handing out pain, suffering, denial or punishment as he is of giving his blessings, must be courted, flattered and petitioned with as much show of submission as possible.

Although the relationship between the Jesuits and Richelieu was an uneasy one at best, the Jesuits could in good conscience support Richelieu's domestic policies when, in the interests of the state, he had rid France of Protestant strongholds. It was Richelieu's foreign policies which were more troubling, especially because, again for reasons of state, Richelieu had allied himself with Protestant princes against more aggressive, competitive Catholic ones. The Jesuits extended themselves to the very limit in trying to influence Richelieu's foreign policy. Given their past history in relation to the kings of France and their professed vows which bound them to carry out the orders of the popes, the Jesuits were always in a rather precarious position, especially in a nation state like France, where the will of the king and that of the pope often conflicted.

The Jesuits were able to remain in the New World and, indeed, in France, as long as they carefully balanced all of their actions so that they created an impression that the political interests of the king, and not the pope, or whichever European sovereign he was currently supporting, were placed foremost on their agenda for action. Such political considerations must have prompted Le Jeune in 1640 when he wrote in his *Relation* the following concerning the Jesuits enthusiasm for and loyalty to the king:

> [W]e do not think of ourselves as being alone in a strange country, nor are we so, since we all have only one and the same Prince and the same King, whom alone we love and honor. Last year, we made bonfires for the birth of Monseigneur, the Dauphin; we entreated God, by solemn procession to make this child like his father. Our joy and our affection were not kept within the bounds of one year; Monsieur the Chevalier de Montmagny, our Governor, wishing to prolong it, has had a Tragi-comedy represented this year, in honor of this newborn Prince.
>
> (ibid. 18:85)

The extent to which the Jesuits were deeply involved in gathering information and in recommending a course of political action in relationship to New France is made clear in a letter written in 1642 by Father Charles Lalemant to Father Etienne Charlet in Rome, concerning armed action against the Iroquois. In that letter, Lalemant makes it known that Paul Le Jeune has been in France and has raised 10,000 écus 'with which to send men over there (i.e. to New France) in order to drive away those who are sustaining the said iroquois in this war, and furnishing them with firearms' (ibid. 21:269).

Lalemant enumerated the reasons why this undertaking might be hazardous, including the lack of knowledge about the enemy's strength, the cost of such a war, the chance that 'if the attempt failed, what great outlays we would cause the King without gaining any-thing which would result in our not being listened to when we might need some lesser help' (ibid. 21:269). He also expressed doubts that they would be able to hold on to what they had gained in the face of reprisal attacks against Quebec and feared that they would furnish the Iroquois with even more arms if they failed to repel the attack. Finally, he noted, there was no assurance that they could force the Iroquois to make peace with 'our Savages' – and that assurance was absolutely necessary for peace. If they didn't act, however, the conse-quences would be dire. Lalemant reported that it was Le Jeune's opinion that:

> If these people are not driven away by making terms with them, or by force of arms, the country is always in danger of being ruined, the missions of being broken up, the nuns of returning, and the colony of being destroyed; the door of the gospel is closed to many very populous nations, and our fathers are in peril of being taken and burned.
>
> (ibid. 21:271)

Whatever else their role in New France, the Jesuits were clearly in a position to collect intelligence and to advise the king and Cardinal Richelieu on policy and to assist in raising money to undertake wars against the enemy. In this case the enemies of France were also the enemies of the Jesuits – England and Holland, two Protestant coun-tries hostile to the Jesuits and their efforts to Catholicize the people of the New World.

The Jesuits were not just involved in the politics and the religious life of New France. They were also implicated in its economy, although the extent of that involvement is not at all clear. Certainly they participated in the fur trade, at least as petty traders. But suspicions ran high that they were much more closely involved in the economic affairs of the Company of New France. Accusations against them were strong enough, and bothersome enough to pro-voke the directors and associates of the company to publish a formal denial of Jesuit involvement in December 1643. According to that denial, rumours were being circulated in order to 'disparage and destroy the reputation and value of the great labours of the Jesuits' work in New France' (Thwaites 1896–1901, 25:77). The declaration noted that 'the Jesuit Fathers are not associated in the said Company in New France, directly or indirectly, and have no part in the traffic of merchandise which is carried on by it' (ibid. 25:77).

The Jesuits, however, clearly participated in the fur trade, even if not as official members of the Company of New France. Much of the money for the support and expansion of their missions in the New World probably came from fur trade profits (Du Creux 1951–52:92). This dependence on the successful operation of the fur trade certainly helped to align the interests of the Jesuits, the trading company and the French state. But it was not enough to secure the future of the colony.

When the Jesuits returned to their work among the Montagnais and Algonkians in 1632, after their expulsion by the English, they established a new station at Trois Rivières in 1634. In that year Father Brébeuf also managed to reopen the mission to the Huron. In 1637 other Jesuits began their project at Sillery, near Quebec for the Montagnais and Algonkians. By 1639 there were twenty-seven French living among the Huron, including nineteen Jesuits. The Jesuits were able to report 300 baptisms in that year, including 100 baptisms of healthy adults. Smallpox epidemics quickly wiped out any gains the Jesuits had made and in 1646 they reported a total of only 400 professing Huron Christians (Grant 1984:28). Two years later, however, almost every Huron who had not died from epidemic disease, starvation or in Iroquois raids on their villages had converted to Christianity.

By 1650, then, the Jesuits could report that the majority of the surviving Huron and Montagnais had become obedient and submissive Christians. Women, especially, had been profoundly changed, accepting the domination of their husbands and fathers. Of course there were few people left to realize Champlain's vision of a well populated country, filled with a new race of people, the result of judicious interbreeding of French and native stock. Nor was the fur trade in good shape; most of the traders and producers having died in the previous decade from war or disease. In the end, for the most part abandoned by state-makers, and the aristocracy, without the support of the king, who could have sent troops to protect them, the French colonies in New France were teetering on the brink of annihilation at the hands of the Iroquois. Once again, Paul Le Jeune wrote to his king, begging for support for the colony:

> Behold your New France at Your Majesty's feet. She has, as this little Book will show you, been reduced to extremities by a band of Barbarians. Hear, SIRE, if you please, her languid voice and her last words. 'Save me', she cries; 'I am about to lose the Catholic Religion; the Lilies are to be snatched away from me. I shall cease to be French, being robbed of that beautiful Name with which I have been so long honored; I shall fall into the foreigners' hands, when the Iroquois shall have drained the last drop of my blood, which has almost ceased to flow. I shall soon end my life in their fires; and the Evil One is on the point of carrying away many Nations which were looking to your Piety, your Might, and your Generosity for their salvation'....
> If you consult Heaven, it will tell you that your salvation is perhaps dependent upon that of so many Peoples, who will be lost unless they are rescued by Your Majesty's efforts. If you consider the French name, you will know, SIRE, that you are a great King, who, while making Europe tremble, ought not to be held in contempt in America.... The Queen, your highly-honored Mother, whose goodness is known beyond the Seas, has hitherto prevented the total ruin of New France, but has not set her free. She has delayed her death, but has not restored her to health and strength. That is reserved for Your Majesty, who, by saving the lives and property of your French Colony and the souls of a vast number of nations, will oblige them all to entreat God to confer upon you the name of Saint, as he has conferred it upon your illustrious Ancestor, whose zeal you will imitate by undertaking a holy war.
>
> (ibid. 46:197–9)

In many ways the project in New France took on a life of its own. Louis XIV, encouraged by Le Jeune, to fulfil his duties to God, to save the souls of 'so many Peoples', and thus to become a saint, like his 'illustrious Ancestor', Saint Louis who undertook so many crusades against the Turks in the thirteenth century, in many ways seems like another pawn in this massive game. Driven by the desire for prestige, for being simultaneously feared, loved and obeyed by all, the economic, social and political objectives of the state-makers of the seventeenth century found an uneasy, yet familiar alliance with the religious ideologues who believed in and promoted a hierarchically organized society. With God at the head, demanding submissiveness, fearfulness and love, and giving in return eternal salvation and forgiveness, the Jesuits' objectives for bringing about the conversion of all the world's non-believers fit (albeit at times uneasily) with the other, worldly project of the French kings and their ministers. Obedience and submissiveness, after all, had to be learned and practised in this life, in order to assure eternal salvation in the next.

4

'THE MALE IS MORE FITTED TO RULE THAN THE FEMALE'

The Jesuits who came to New France to convert the Huron and the Montagnais had very clear ideas about relations between men and women. Among other things they were convinced that women were created to be men's 'helpmates'. Women were more feeble than men; they possessed less capacity to reason. Weak and lacking in reason, women were made to be governed by men. For the seventeenth-century Jesuits, women's subordination to men was part of God's plan for humanity, necessary for good order in society, essential for the existence of Christian marriages, indispensable for human salvation.

Writing about the Hospital and Ursuline nuns who had missions to the Indians of New France,[1] Father Vimont noted that they constantly gave love and service to the Indians. 'I know very well', he wrote,

> that virtue is loveable everywhere, but it is more agreeable under plush and satin, and in refined minds and cleanly bodies, than it is under rags and in persons who do not know what rudeness is because they have not even the elementary principles of politeness. The love constantly felt by the Hospital Nuns for the sick and the poor, and by the Ursulines for the pupils of their Seminary and for the Savage women, in whom they see but Jesus Christ alone, without any attraction that pleases the senses, is an enthusiasm in which I expect perseverance from only Jesus Christ himself.
>
> (Thwaites 1896–1901, 22:171)

'Their sex', Vimont added, 'does not possess such consistency' (ibid. 22:171). The nun's capacity to make such sacrifices comes, he concluded, from Jesus himself, who imbued these women with His own (and therefore male) Spirit. It was this male spirit that allowed them to overcome their female nature and to meet the challenges of the missions. Likewise, Christian Huron and Montagnais women, who escaped from the Iroquois and who made the arduous journey by themselves back to their own country, were able to do so because their female natures had been overcome.

This point of view was widely held, even by the nuns themselves. Correspondence written by Ursuline nuns to Father Paul Le Jeune during negotiations to establish the Ursulines in New France reveal similar convictions. Writing about their desire to begin working in New France, one member of the Ursuline order related to Le Jeune that 'although the weakness and infirmity of our sex is great, our Lord so powerfully fortifies and enhances our courage, that we are emboldened to say with Saint Paul, we can do all in him who strengthens us.' (ibid. 8:241).

The issue to be noted here, although we will return to this in greater detail below, pp. 74–100, is the shared idea that women and men have different natures, that women's nature is to be 'weak and infirm', and that when women do show strength and courage, contrary to their natures, it is due largely to a gaining of a male nature through the auspices of divine intervention.

A second point, concerning the nature of women, also emerges from a reading of the *Relations*. Women were potentially the allies of Satan, dangerous to the good ordering of society. They were particularly dangerous as sexual, pleasure-seeking beings. While the best among them were capable of turning aside from pleasure seeking, to direct their passions entirely towards the service and love of God, the rest had to be kept under constant vigilance. Christian marriages, devoted not to bodily pleasure, but to procreation, although much less preferable than the state of holy virginity,[2] were the only hope for the salvation of most members of the society.

In the previous chapter we saw some of the ways in which relations between the state, the church, the nobility and the bourgeoisie worked to limit, delimit and set the tone for the way in which New France was to be colonized. We saw how relations between various institutionalized groups and individuals who had an interest in New France were balanced and worked out on the basis of general rules, strategies and beliefs about correct social practice held alike by merchants, the king and his ministers, members of the nobility and missionaries. In this chapter we return to the theme of the Jesuits' project in New France and examine more closely the ideas and

56

especially the roots of those ideas held by the Jesuits about men, women and their interrelations.

These ideas formed an important part of the rationale behind the Jesuits' attempts to convert native peoples to Catholicism. The beliefs about the true nature of women and men and what had to be done to make the people of New France conform to God's plans were a major part of the overall plan that was set in place to make New France into a thriving and profitable, loyal and obedient French colony. The Devil was at work in the New World and women's nature made them even more susceptible to his influence than did men's.

DANGEROUS AND INFERIOR WOMEN

There are two streams of thought which provide the basis for seventeenth century Jesuit ideas about women's natural, God-given inferiority to men, and women's potential alliance with Satan. The conception of women both as the physical and moral inferiors of men that dominated the writings of the Jesuits in New France had become institutionalized in France by 1255 when the works of Aristotle were included among the subjects prescribed in the Faculty of Arts at Paris (Tredennick 1984:365). Although Aristotle's works had previously been subjected to pontifical interdiction, by the mid-fourteenth century they formed the core of the examination syllabus (Lawson–Tancred 1986:99). The overwhelming acceptance of Aristotelian ideas, and their incorporation into Christian doctrine in the thirteenth century reflected a growing tendency in western Europe towards the subjugation of women.

By the mid-fourteenth century the sex polarity[3] argument, in which women and men were seen as both different and unequal with regards to their role in generation, their wisdom and their virtue, had become part of French academic and religious thought. Women's subordination to men was justified on the grounds of their bodily differences which, it was argued, ultimately led to differences in virtues and wisdom for men and women. In this view the nature of a woman was to be passive, that of a man, active. Thus women's virtue lay in their obedience to the rule of men. Women who were not controlled by their husbands or fathers, or women who showed independence of spirit or a hint of active sexuality[4] were, therefore, unnatural.

The significance of the special relationship between Satan and women as his chosen agents, in comparison, was not a part of the Greek philosophical heritage. It grew out of a culturally based, and socially sanctioned fear and mistrust of women, combined with the association of women with responsibility for the fall from earthly paradise. Yet even this association had its historical development. Satan did not play a significant role in Christian thought until well into the Middle Ages. It was only in the eleventh and twelfth centuries that Satan appears in church art as a red-eyed, flame-haired, man eater, associated in the feudal code with a felonious vassal.

In spite of this association, early characterizations of Satan, as simultaneously a seducer and a persecutor, often made him out to be more ridiculous than terrifying. But by the fourteenth century Satan had taken on a great significance as the persecutor, tempter and seducer of humanity (Delumeau 1978:232). At the same time, beginning in the eleventh and twelfth centuries, anti-feminism began to increase in the west, and found a growing expression and virulence in Christian theology and practices. For example an abbot of the Premonstratensian Order, Conrad of Marchtal, rationalized the expulsion of women from that order at the end of the twelfth century in the following way:[5]

> We and our whole community of canons, recognizing that the wickedness of women is greater than all the other wickedness of the world, and that there is no anger like that of women, and that the poison of asps and dragons is more curable and less dangerous to men than the familiarity of women, have unanimously decreed for the safety of our souls, no less than for that of our bodies and goods, that we will on no account receive any more sisters to the increase of our perdition, but will avoid them like poisonous animals.

But it was really in the sixteenth and seventeenth centuries that the association of women with the Devil's plan to disorganize the universe, to bring about calamitous decline, were fully developed. Many members of the laity and clergy alike considered the world as a citadel under siege by the legions of Satan, and betrayed by enemies from within who had to be identified and punished. Foremost among the Devil's allies could be found women, who, according to the texts of the time, were weak and therefore more easily duped and seduced by Satan.[6]

The demonologues of the sixteenth and seventeenth centuries claimed that women were more fragile, had less intelligence, and greater bestial cupidity than men. They were therefore capable of going to any extremity to satisfy their appetites or to revenge themselves (Dulong 1984:236). The Jesuits who came to New France shared this view.

WOMEN AS MEN'S INFERIORS

Although many other philosophers before him had addressed the issue of sex identity it was Aristotle (384–322 BC) who first developed the comprehensive rationale supporting the claim that differences between men and women were philosophically significant and that by nature men were superior to women. In constructing his arguments about the nature of men and women, Aristotle devoted a certain amount of attention to attacking Plato (428–355 BC). Plato had maintained that on the level of existence in the world, there was an identity between men and women because both sexes possessed souls. For Plato, the soul was immaterial, and therefore sexless, and could reincarnate in either male or female bodies. Thus the fundamental natures of man and woman were the same although being a female was an inferior state to being a male.

In *The Republic*, where he lays out his version of an ideal society, Plato makes Socrates and Glaucon discuss the idea of similar natures in men and women, and thus the reasonableness of choosing women as well as men to be members of the Guardian Class of this ideal state. Socrates begins by laying out the logical ground rules for the acceptance or rejection of the argument to follow:

> 'if men or women as a sex appear to be qualified for different skills or occupations ... we shall assign these to each accordingly; but if the only difference apparent between them is that the female bears and the male begets, we shall not admit that this is a difference relevant for our purpose, but shall still maintain that our male and female Guardians ought to follow the same occupations.'
>
> (Plato 1987: 454d–e)

Socrates is thus suggesting that having different bodies and roles in the reproductive process is no basis on which to differentiate the natures of the two sexes. Glaucon agrees to these ground rules and Socrates proceeds to develop his argument:

'There is ... no administrative occupation which is peculiar to woman as woman or man as man; natural capacities are similarly distributed in each sex, and it is natural for women to take part in all occupations as well as men, though in all women will be the weaker partners.'

'Agreed.'

'Are we therefore to confine all occupations to men only?'

'How can we?' ...

'So men and women have the same natural capacity for Guardianship, save in so far as woman is the weaker of the two.'

'That is clear.' ...

'We come back again, then, to our former position, and agree that it is not unnatural that our Guardians' wives should share their intellectual and physical training.'

(ibid.: 455d–456b)

In *The Republic*, Plato argues that the fact that 'the female bears' and the 'male begets' has no bearing on their natures and thus their occupations in the real world. Both men and women possess souls, and those souls are sexless. Moreover, it is their souls and not their material bodies which determine their capacities (Allen 1985:61). It is on the basis of their souls, which for Plato were spiritual, non-physical substances, and not their bodies that their natures and their strengths and limitations should be considered.[7]

Female incarnations, however, were decidedly inferior to male incarnations. In the *Timaeus*, Plato tells the story of the creation of the universe. In a section entitled 'The differences between the sexes: the creation of women, birds, animals, reptiles and fish', he argues that women were created in this way:

Of those who were born as men, all that were cowardly and spent their life in wrongdoing were, according to the probable account, transformed at second birth into women; for this reason it was at that time that the gods constructed the desire of sexual intercourse, fashioning one creative instinct with life in us, another in woman.

(Plato 1959: 90e–91a)

Birds, animals, reptiles and fish came into being by a process of transformation of original men who were foolish by varying degrees. Birds, for example, were the second generation 'reincarnation of harmless but light-witted men, who studied the heavens but imagined in their simplicity that the surest evidence in these matters comes throught the eye.' (ibid.: 91e–f).

What is important, in all of this, is Plato's articulation of the separation between mind/soul and the body and his emphasis that human nature is based not on the body but on the soul. Indeed, for Plato, the body is a rather unimportant aspect of human existence when it comes to delimiting nature.[8] One receives a better or worse human body, or the physical body of an animal or bird on the basis of one's behaviour in a previous incarnation. The body is a punishment or a reward for past behaviour, but is not what determines one's nature. The nature of men and women are not different because, while possessing different kinds of bodies, they do not possess different kinds of souls.

The issue of whether or not women's bodies, their material existence, confines them, or makes them suitable for one kind of experience and not others which are only suited to men, the issue of whether or not men and women possess the same capacities and are fit to engage in the same endeavours, continues to be argued today. I will return to twentieth-century developments of these arguments in the final chapter, but for the moment it is more important to consider Aristotle, whose ideas directly opposed those of Plato. For it was Aristotle, and not Plato, whose ideas were to have a profound influence on the conceptualization of women and men in Christian thought beginning in the thirteenth century. It was at this time that three members of the Dominican Order, William of Moerbeke (in Flanders), Albert of Cologne and, most of all, St Thomas Aquinas, translated and used Aristotle's *Ethics* and *Politics* in their own work (Sinclair 1986:16).

Aristotle, who at the age of 17 became a pupil of Plato's at the latter's academy in Athens, originally accepted most of Plato's philosophical views, including that of the soul (Lawson–Tancred 1986:17, 45). He later changed his conceptualization of the mind/body relationship, rejecting reincarnation, and claiming that the soul did not exist separately from the body. The rational soul, for Aristotle, became the form of the body, and not, as it was for Plato, the prisoner of the body, 'divine stuff which really belonged elsewhere' (ibid.: 61). Thus Aristotle's arguments about men and women were developed on a metaphysical basis that was opposed to the one that Plato had used to defend an argument for the equality of the nature of men and women (i.e. reincarnation of the soul). Form, in Aristotle's view, could not exist separate from matter:

If then we must say something in general about all types of souls, it would be the first actuality of a natural body with organs. We should not then inquire whether the soul and the body are one thing, any more than whether the wax and its imprint are, or in general whether the matter of each thing is one with that of which it is the matter. For although unity and being are spoken of in a number of ways, it is of the actuality that they are most properly said.

(Aristotle 1947:412b 8, 413a 3–8)

One important consequence of Aristotle's rejection of the concept of reincarnation, and his subsequent formulation of what constituted a human being, was that it led to the conceptualizing of bodily differences between men and women as being philosophically significant (Allen 1985:99). This differentiation in itself does not necessarily lead to the conclusion that women are the inferiors of men; yet that was the conclusion which Aristotle reached. In order to do so Aristotle built another side of his argument based on the ideas of Pythagoras.

Pythagoras had founded a religious order in southern Italy around 530 BC. He left no writings[9] but taught, among other things, that the soul was immortal, and that it was reincarnated in different forms in subsequent lifetimes, according to the kind of life it had previously led. It was this idea which Plato picked up on and repeated, through Socrates, in *The Republic*. The separation between good and evil resulted in the development of 'the first dualistic system of philosophy' (Lawson–Tancred 1986:345). As a part of this philosophy, Pythagoras argued that there are ten principles, consisting of contrary pairs which he set out in a table of opposites (Tredennick 1984:346).

The pairs were arranged in the table so that those on the left-hand side were associated with order, limit and form and were given a higher valuation (Aristotle speaks of the 'column of goods' in *Ethics*). Those on the right-hand side were associated with the corresponding defects of those on the left-hand side, with matter, with what Aristotle termed the 'class of the unlimited' (Tredennick 1984:346; Allen 1985:20). Male and female make up one of the ten pairs of opposites: male was placed on the left-hand side of the table, female on the right-hand side.

On the issue of action involving human material existence Pythagoras is reputed to have argued that harmony between the sexes required that women be obedient to their husbands. Women should either not oppose their husbands at all or 'consider that they would achieve a victory if they gave in to their husbands' (Vogel 1966:130–1). It was men's virtue to rule, women's to obey. Moreover, Pythagoras considered it a superior function of reason to rule, than to obey. It was only on the plane of the soul, with regards to reincarnation, that Pythagoreans considered sex to be relatively unimportant in terms of identity (Allen 1985:22–3).

Plato, who had accepted the Pythagorean concept of the transmigration of souls, used it to maintain that on the level of existence in the world there was an identity between men and women because both sexes possessed souls. It was only on the cosmic level that the distinctions between male and female applied. For Aristotle, who came to reject the concept of reincarnation, the Pythagorean distinction between men and women, on the basis of their material bodies, took on a meaning for everyday life.

Drawing on the logic of the table of opposites, Aristotle argued that female is the opposite, and the contrary of male. In pairs of contraries, such as male and female, one is always the privation of the other, that is, one of the pair is incapable of becoming its opposite (Aristotle 1924:1055b, 25–9; and cited in Allen 1985: 91). Moreover, privation implied a negative valuation; therefore the female was associated with the lower and negative elements of passivity and matter while male was associated with the higher elements of form and activity (Allen 1985:89). Thus, for example, Aristotle argues:

> When a pair of factors, the one active and the other passive, come into contact in the way in which one is active and the other passive (by 'way' I mean the manner, the place, and the time of contact), then immediately both are brought into play, the one acting, the other being acted upon. In this case, it is the female which provides the matter, and the male which provides the principle of movement.
>
> (Aristotle 1943a:740b, 20–5; and cited in Allen 1985:93)

Aristotle further developed the implications of the assumption of the female as the privation of the male for the question of their roles in the reproductive process. The male was associated with hot, the female with the privative opposite, cold (Aristotle 1943a:729b,9–17). This has important consequences for the female. Unable to 'concoct semen' because of her cold, she is an imperfect or deformed kind of human.

> Just as it sometimes happens that deformed offspring are produced by deformed parents, and sometimes not, so the offspring produced by a female are sometimes female, sometimes not, but male. The reason is that the female is as it were a deformed male; and the menstrual discharge is semen though in an impure condition: i.e., it lacks one constituent, and one only, the principle of soul.
>
> (Aristotle 1937:737a, 26–30; and cited in Allen 1988:97)

Because he identified soul with form, a male and not female quality, it followed that it was the male who acted on the passive matter of the female to organize it into the form that would make a person. It was the soul principle in the male seed which brought the matter of the female to perfection. Not only was the deformity of the female evident in the act of conception, but it persisted throughout her life (Allen 1985:98). According to Aristotle, 'we should look upon the female state as being as it were a deformity, though one which occurs in the ordinary course of nature' (Aristotle 1937:755a, 12–16).

Arguing against Plato's vision in *The Republic*, Aristotle maintained that the husband should exercise his rule over his wife, within the household, as a statesman does over his fellow citizens, 'for the male is more fitted to rule than the female' (Aristotle 1974:1259a, 37). Aristotle extended men's right to rule, not just over women but also over children and slaves, as these constituted part of the household. Because 'every household is part of the state', the virtue of one part had to be considered in relation to the virtue of the whole. In short, how well the state was run depended on how well men ran their households (ibid.:1260a, 36–1260b, 8).

Pointing to Sparta, Aristotle argued that the lack of control over women was 'detrimental both to the attainment of the aims of the constitution and to the happiness of the state' (ibid.:1269b, 12). Because Sparta had a constitution in which women's position was 'ill-regulated' it was Aristotle's further opinion that one-half of the state was 'not properly legislated for'. He accused the Spartan women of living 'intemperately, enjoying every licence and indulging in every luxury', and concluded that their influence had been nothing but 'very harmful' for the state.

ARISTOTELIAN INFLUENCE
ON CHRISTIAN THOUGHT

It was Aristotle, and not Plato whose works were to influence the writings of St Thomas Aquinas in the thirteenth century. And it was the work of St Thomas Aquinas which in turn influenced the writings of sixteenth- and seventeenth-century moralists on men, women and their interrelations. These opinions, in turn, were frequently repeated in the *Jesuit Relations*, and constitute a sort of ideal object for reform that the Jesuit missionaries followed in their dealings with the Huron and the Montagnais.

St Thomas Aquinas used Aristotelian thought as a foundation on which to build Christian theology, particularly the idea that the female was a defective or deformed male in body and in mind (Allen 1985:389). While man was created in the image and glory of God, woman 'is the glory of man'. Woman was created for man, and not man for woman (Aquinas 1948, 1a:93, 94). Thomas took from Aristotle the idea of the importance of the identity between body and soul, materiality and rationality. Thus identity always had to be either male identity or female identity and the notion of the transmigration of souls was rejected (Aquinas 1923–9 II:44, 7). Also taken from Aristotle was the argument that women were born as a result of an accident in the order of nature (Aquinas 1952a quest. 5, art. 9:245; and cited in Allen 1985:392). Males were the 'perfect sex', females the 'imperfect' sex; with regard to 'nature in the individual [the] female is something defective' (Aquinas 1948, 1a:74, 4). However, as a whole the female is not defective but is as God intended.

For Aquinas, women contributed only matter to the process of reproduction, in a passive capacity, as compared to the active capacity in which males contributed semen, and thus the soul or form of the foetus (Aquinas 1952b quest. 3, art. 9:158). It was in the nature of the passive to yield to the active (Aquinas 1948, 1a:98, 1, 2; and cited in Allen 1985:395). Moreover, the passivity of women meant that they had no role to play beyond their contribution to regeneration. In particular, women had no role to play in public life; it was their virtue to remain silent:

> For what is appropriate for the ornament of a woman or her integrity, that she is silent, proceeds from the modesty which is owed to women; but this does not relate to the ornament of a man, instead, it is fitting that he speaks. Therefore, the Apostle (Paul) warns (I Cor. 14:34,35) *Let women keep silent in the*

churches and if they wish to learn anything, let them ask their husbands at home.
(Aquinas 1940, 1: 41; and cited in Allen 1985:400)
(my emphasis)

The female, Aquinas argued, needs the male, not only for reproduction, but also for government (Aquinas 1923–9, III, II:123, 3; and cited in Allen 1985:403). Male and female are joined together to 'establish a home life', where 'the man is the head of the woman'. Aquinas concluded from this that 'the woman was rightly formed from the man, as her origin and chief' (Aquinas 1948 1a:92, 2; and cited in Allen 1985:403). She was doubly under the power of the man as a result of sin (ibid. 1a:92, 1; and cited in Allen 1985: 403). A feeble being, marked by the stupidity that is her nature, she gave in to the temptations of Satan. As a result she must live always under the tutelage of men.

With regard to running the household, Aquinas argued that 'one ruler is better than two, and the ruler of a household is called a father' (Allen 1985:405). He is the 'active and more excellent principle', while the mother is the passive principle. Hence, he concluded, the father should be better loved than the mother (Allen 1985:405). Moreover, in marriage, attraction between spouses is unequal. The man, as protector, is endowed with the power to make decisions. The wife, as his auxiliary, must submit to him. The woman is merely the matrix for her husband's semen, and her virtue remains tied to her domesticity.

The husband, on the other hand, is a political creature whose attention is turned towards society. Completely subsumed by her husband, the woman is only capable of looking after the home and the children; her tenderness towards her husband and her children is semi-instinctual. Because reason is so much less developed in her, she can offer her husband neither friendship nor services equal to those he gives to her. She exists as a wife in order that her husband may have heirs. By her very nature a woman never becomes an adult. She remains weak all her life and must continually rely on the support of men, first her father and later her husband. In spite of these glaring inequalities between men and women, Aquinas maintained that marriage was important; by assuring the reproduction of the species it also assured the future of society (Métral 1977:88–9).

It was these themes – the rightness of and the need for women's submissiveness and obedience to their husbands' and fathers' authority; women's physical, moral and mental weakness; their relative immaturity and semi-instinctual devotion to husband and children and their attraction to and for the Devil – that were elaborated on during the Middle Ages and into the sixteenth century. It is these ideas, too, that the Jesuits brought with them to New France to be translated into reality in Huron and Montagnais societies. If the Devil was to be driven from New France, if the souls of the 'savages' of that country were to be saved, if Catholicism and the true 'faith' were to be victorious, then women would have to be made to submit to men. Christian society could not be called into being on any other basis.

WOMEN, MEN AND MARRIAGE IN THE *JESUIT RELATIONS*

These same themes can also be found in abundance in the theological writings from the thirteenth century onwards. In 1330, at the request of Pope Jean XXII, the Franciscan Alvaro Pelayo wrote his *De planctu ecclesiae*. The book was intended as a guide for directors of conscience, and the second part contained a list of 102 vices and evil acts which could be committed by women. It is a virulent antifeminine text in which a call to all clergy is made to conduct a holy war against the alliance of women with the Devil. Women are 'deceivers', they are 'full of malice', they 'kill their children', some among them are 'incorrigible'. Eve began all this and thus was the 'mother of sin'. Since Eve, women have been the 'arm of the Devil'. They will do anything to seduce men, to engage them in sexual acts outside of marriage. Women cast spells, use enchantments, impede procreation, provoke sterility. They are the 'ministers of idolatry', and they use illicit sex in the worship of the Devil. Because of this the husband must always watch over his wife, to keep her in good behaviour (cited in Métral 1977:318–22).

A bull, *Summis desiderantes affectisus*, issued by Pope Innocent VIII in December 1484, delegated Heinrich Kramer and James Sprenger as inquisitors into the subject 'the power and prevalence of witch organization'. The result was the *Malleus Maleficarum*, written most likely in 1486. In this treatise, Kramer and Sprenger ask why it is that 'a greater number of witches is found in the fragile feminine sex than among men' (Summers 1971:41). Among the answers are that women are more credulous, light-minded and impressionable than men and therefore more susceptible to the Devil, and that they are intellectually like children, unable to understand philosophy. But even more important is the 'natural reason' that women are more carnal than men. Moreover, there was a 'defect in the formation of the first woman, since she was formed from a bent rib, that is a rib of the breast, which is bent as it were in a contrary direction to a man' (ibid.:44). Women, therefore are contrary, they have weak memories, are liars by nature and are vain. All witchcraft, Kramer and Sprenger conclude, 'comes from carnal lust, which is in women insatiable' (ibid.:47). For the sake of fulfilling their lust, women will even consort with devils.

The authors of the *Malleus Maleficarum* used the anti-feminine sentiments rampant in church writings and doctrine to justify witch-hunts. Caton d'Utique concluded the document by noting that 'if there had not been the evil of women to say nothing of that of witches, the world would be free of innumerable perils' (cited in Delumeau 1978:323). Fifteenth- and sixteenth-century confessors, such as Ménot, Maillard and Glapion, found that women used fashion as a means to seduce men and to cause them to fall into mortal sin. Maillard, for example, wrote that wearing rich collars, chains of gold and the like was a sign that the Devil had taken a woman under his control. Glapion, confessor of Charles Quint, refused to believe the testimony of Mary Magdalene about Jesus's resurrection because, he argued, women are fickle and not to be believed (Métral 1977:316).

A manual for confessors, written by the Italian, Jean Benedicti, and first published in France in 1584 as *Sommes des Pechez*, drew on the Aristotelian conceptions of women's and men's nature to develop statements on men's sins towards their wives, and women's sins towards their husbands. The difference between the two is striking. A husband commits a transgression against the commandments when he refuses to feed his wife and family and to provide them with the necessities of life, according to his ability (Benedicti 1600:29). He also sins if he fails to make his wife obey him. Women, on the other hand, commit a transgression if they refuse to obey their husbands.

Men were responsible for the good conduct of their wives, and any man who allowed his wife to do evil, to paint herself up to please men or to do anything else that was beyond the bounds of decency, also sinned. According to the scriptures, wrote Benedicti, the husband was in charge of his wife. If a wife sinned because her husband had not kept her under control, he was equally responsible for her sins (ibid.:30). What a husband decided, a wife was obliged to do.

A man's power over his wife, however, had some limitations, and an over-stepping of those limits was also defined by Benedicti in terms of sin. Thus a husband also sinned if he 'seriously and atrociously' beat his wife, even if it were for some fault. He sinned, too, if he called his wife injurious names, such as prostitute, when in fact she was an honourable woman, or if he left her because he was jealous and wrongly suspected her of adultery. Nor could a man prevent his wife attending mass, or serving God (Benedicti 1600:32–5).

The sins of a woman against her husband were much more numerous, and of a quite different order. According to Benedicti, a wife sinned who refused to obey her husband concerning the government of the family, the home or in any matter concerning good morals and virtues. To refuse to submit to the will of her husband was to refuse to submit to both divine and human law (ibid.:37). A wife was obliged to live where her husband decided, unless he wished to do something against God's laws, the salvation of her soul, or unless he tried to tyrannize her and cause her death. It is God's judgement, Benedicti further stated, that a wife be subjected to her husband 'who is more noble and more excellent than the wife, seeing that he is the image of God and woman is merely the image of Man' (ibid.:41).[10]

Any woman who provoked her husband was 'quarrelsome, unruly and impatient'. Even if she was partly in the right, she should 'keep silent and champ the bit instead of making him blaspheme and swear knowing well his temperament and knowing full well that he is prone to this vice' (cited in Flandrin 1979:127). Writing on the subject of wife beating, Benedicti suggested that while 'he who severely and atrociously beats or chastises his wife, even if it be for some fault, sins.... He may, nevertheless, chastise her for her misconduct as long as he does not overstep the bounds of modesty and reason' (ibid.: 129). Misconduct involved not obeying a husband or not 'suffering his shortcomings with patience and with charity'. It also involved giving the husband reason to be angry by displaying 'arrogance and obstinacy' (ibid.: 127).

Women sinned who were proud of the refined development of their spirituality, their beauty, their goods and their parentage and who, in despising their husbands, refused to obey them especially in matters concerning service to God, the government of the home and the kind of company they kept. These women sinned because they resisted God's will, who commanded that women at all times be submissive to their husbands. Women, in Benedicti's view, were shrews to be tamed by their husbands. A man might legitimately rage at his wife if she thwarted or opposed his will, but a wife had to show patience, and a willingness to oblige her husband regardless of what he did to her. More important, however, was the link that Benedicti made between all women and the corruption of men:

> The ancient sages taught us that whenever men speak for a long time with women they are ruined; their thoughts are turned from the contemplation of heavenly things and they finally descend to hell. Such are the dangers that come from taking too much pleasure in talking, laughing and gossiping with women, whether she be good or bad.
>
> (cited in Delumeau 1978:323–4; my translation)

Other theologians reinforced the theme that women were meant to be dominated by men. Cornelius a Lapide wrote:

> woman is an excellent ornament of man since she is granted to man not only to help him to procreate children, and administer the family, but also in possession and, as it were, in domination, over which man may exercise his jurisdiction and authority. For the authority of man extends not only to inanimate things and brute beasts, but also to reasonable creatures, that is, women and wives.
>
> (cited in Maclean 1980:11)

Equally revealing is a letter of instruction to confessors sent by the Jesuit St Francis Xavier to Father Gaspard Barzé, in charge of the mission of Ormuz. This letter was published as an addition to the famous *Instructions to Confessors*, written by St Charles Borromée, re-edited over several centuries by the post-Trident church and sent to all Catholic dioceses. According to St Francis:

> The flightiness of a woman's spirit and disposition ordinarily causes many problems for confessors. One of the best precautions to be taken is to tend to the souls of the Christian husbands before those of the wives. Nature has given more strength and firmness of spirit to men, so there is more to be gained in instructing them; even the good running of the family and the piety of the wife depends on the virtue of the husband....
>
> Never find fault with the husband in the presence of his wife, even if he is obviously guilty. Rather, dissimulate while she is present, then take him aside and give him a thorough

70

confession. It is there that you can instruct him, once again, as to what his obligations are to mutual peace and agreement. Do not show yourself to be partisan to his wife. If you berate the husband in front of his wife (seeing as women are naturally given to imitation and are not at all discrete) she will not cease to peck away at him and to reproach him for the fault that you have found in him ... such that the husband will become despised and his wife insolent. In such cases as this my advice is to demonstrate to the wife the respect that she owes her husband. She should be apprised of the great pain that God has prepared for the immodesty and arrogance of those who forget so holy and legitimate a task. The wife should be instructed that it is she who is responsible for all quarrels which result from her own indiscretion and disobedience. She must patiently suffer her husband's behaviour and not complain which only indicates a lack of submissiveness on her part.

(cited in Delumeau 1978:325; my translation)

It was the opinion of the theologians and moralists that even conversation with women could prove to be dangerous for men. Another seventeenth-century Jesuit, Father J. J. Surin, wrote instructing young students in the Jesuit colleges that in order not to be debauched they should avoid reading impure books, keeping the company of those who had already fallen into vice and visits to or conversation with women.[11]

According to this Jesuit moralist, there were certain characteristics of girls which made them very dangerous to young boys. Girls are very weak minded and incapable of moderation; when not thinking about God their spirit is occupied only with insignificant things. But most importantly, it is the girls who are guilty of causing all those who succumb by looking at them to fall into sin.[12] Using the image of sheep and wolves, Surin advised that each sex must have the same horror for the other as sheep have for wolves. The same advice came from another contemporary of Surin's who argued that 'without doubt there is danger in the conversation with women'. Women are the 'Devil's snares'. They are the 'nets' that he uses to catch 'those who are not well enough on their guard'.

Sixteenth- and seventeenth-century theologians and moralists were concerned with establishing and enforcing definitions which made women subordinate to their husbands and obliged men to watch over their wives' morals and to chastise them whenever they strayed. The effect was to establish a line of power and obedience in which women and children submitted to men, and where men, in turn, carried out the orders of the church (and the state).

Where women could not be controlled by their husbands and fathers at least two institutionalized structures were established to deal with them: the first was witch-hunts, trials and burnings, and the second was the incarceration of prostitutes. Tens of thousands of women were executed in France as witches during the sixteenth and seventeenth centuries (Muchembled 1987). During the same period repressive measures were introduced against prostitutes. In the thirteenth to fifteenth centuries prostitution had been tolerated, and even institutionalized and legitimated. Actions against prostitutes were rare and prostitution was considered a legitimate occupation (Capul 1984:II 201; Otis 1987:15–39). But by the mid-sixteenth century attempts to control prostitutes were made in many urban communities and were supported by the ever-growing centralist, mercantilist monarchy, and by emotions engendered in the Reformation and Counter-Reformation. The 101st article of the ordinance of Orléan of 1561 proclaimed the prohibition of all brothels, ringing the 'official death knell of the late-medieval policy of authorized prostitution' (Otis 1987:40). Throughout the sixteenth and into the seventeenth centuries women's position in French law steadily declined (Dulong 1984:12; Otis 1987:42). Women were prohibited from making contracts and from acting in justice. In criminal law women were considered irresponsible because of their inferiority (Otis 1987:42). By the seventeenth century French women had been reduced to the status of minors and completely placed under the control of their fathers and husbands.

Prostitution figured strongly in Benedicti's list of sins. Prostitutes, he argued, 'sin grievously and are daily in a state of damnation' (Benedicti 1600:172). Such women 'corrupt the youth on whom the maintenance of the Republic depends'. They incite young men to try to debauch girls and women of good standing; 'those who learn to make love with prostitutes become inflamed and try to do the same thing with wise and honest women' (ibid.:173).

As the position of women became more and more precarious, as they were identified as being dangerous to public morals, and especially to those of men, efforts were increased to moralize them and to put individuals to 'honest work'. Members of the Company of the Holy Sacrament (whom we encountered in the previous chapter, p. 46) were significant here in establishing institutionalized systems of surveillance and control of those individuals, especially prostitutes, who in refusing to conform to the requirement of sex only in marriages, and then only for the purposes of reproduction, were to blame for enticing men to sin. Believing that prostitutes represented a great threat to individual control and thus to moral life, members of the Company of the Holy Sacrament, as well as others, helped to organize institutionalized means whereby prostitutes could be subjected to increasingly repressive measures, including being put on public display, locked up and whipped (Capul 1984 II:203).

This, then, was the intellectual, social and moral climate that the Jesuits who came to proselytize the native people of New France were familiar with. It was a morality that they believed represented the will of God, a morality that was called into being by the necessity of evading the dangers posed by the Devil. These dangers were most evident in relation to women's sexuality and could be best averted through women's rightful subjugation to men's authority.

5

'THIS LITTLE FURY OF HELL'

The Jesuits began their work in New France with the clear under-standing that Christian behaviour, morals and beliefs could be adopted by the people of New France because they were, in fact, humans. The Jesuits were part of a humanist movement that saw all 'races', all 'nations', as human and as capable of instruction. It was a matter of education and not of humanity that separated the 'Savages' of New France from the civilized people of Old France. 'There is no nature so wild', wrote Father Vimont from New France, 'that gentle-ness, grace, and education cannot polish . . . . There is no doubt that if the means were at hand to lodge a number of them, they would be made as dexterous and as well-mannered as our Europeans' (Thwaites 1896–1901, 22:183–5). As humans capable of instruction, of education and of being made to have written 'upon their hearts the love and fear' of God, the people of New France were fit to be moulded into good Christians.

But if the native peoples of New France were human, they con-formed neither to God's laws, nor to the laws of nature which dictated the proper relations between men and women. The Jesuits found many aspects of the relationship between native women and men intolerable, contrary both to God's laws and to the laws of human nature. They were willing to risk their lives to see it all changed. Because the Jesuits were concerned with the process of conversion which included not just abstract beliefs, but concrete social practices, and because they recorded their efforts as yearly reports sent to superiors in France and Rome, the *Relations* are a rich source of information on what relations between men and women were like both before and after Christianization. They contain detailed descriptions both of the resistance offered to the Jesuit attempts at enforcing new codes of behaviour and of the native

74

peoples' capitulation to European morality, beliefs and social practices.

The *Relations* are especially good sources for information on the issue of the subordination of women to men, within both Huron and Montagnais societies, as it occurred under the influence of European traders, colonial administrators and missionaries. For while important economic changes had been taking place in these two societies, at least since the fourteenth century,[1] the adoption of Christianity, and the incorporation of Christian philosophy and moral categories into daily life only occurred after the arrival of the French missionaries. And it was clearly within the context of the adoption of Christianity that the subjugation of women to men was rationalized and found its justification as well as its forms of observance.

Whether as Christians or as pagans, the actions, behaviours and beliefs of the Huron and the Montagnais all passed through the interpretative screen of Jesuit morality. Good behaviour or bad behaviour, praiseworthy actions or actions that would lead to sure damnation, everything that the Jesuits wrote about native women and men fit the prescribed formula.

NEW WORLD APPLICATIONS OF OLD WORLD MORALITY

Jesuit definitions of men and women derived from Christian doctrine current in the seventeenth century. Marriage played a central role in the formulation of these ideas, especially because women's subordination could be directly justified through reference to Eve's original sin (Maclean 1980:26). Sixteenth- and seventeenth-century theologians considered women to be inherently inferior to men for other reasons too: women, they believed, were less robust than men; they were passive while men were active, men had greater dignity and thus pre-eminence must be given to them over women as members of the same species. Because woman was made after man, and from man, she was naturally inferior to him. Moreover, women were often identified with unbridled sensuality and, thus, with lewdness. For this reason theological tracts often counselled men to avoid women's company at all times.

The Jesuits were especially concerned with practices around marriage, divorce and sexuality in Huron and Montagnais societies. The freedom that individual Huron and Montagnais exercised in these areas constituted the greatest impediments to their conversion, and the surest invitation to the Devil to continue his reign among them. Both men and women exercised a great deal of autonomy in entering into marriage, and were equally free in seeking divorce. The Jesuits found the 'sexual license' of young girls and women particularly disturbing. Girls, they claimed, boasted of seeking young men while married women refused to convert to Christianity, claiming 'they could not bind themselves to marital fidelity' or that they could not promise to live with one man for the rest of their lives. 'Conjugal continence, and the indissolubility of marriage', wrote Le Jeune in 1633, numbered among 'the most serious obstacles in the progress of the Gospel.' (ibid. 10:63).

The 'license in marriage', one Jesuit contended, gave both the Huron and the Montagnais the freedom to leave one another on the slightest 'pretext'. 'The Church', he continued, 'cannot hold the women to the marriages' (ibid. 24:187). Women and men, Vimont complained, look upon marriage as nothing more than 'a conditional promise to live together so long as each shall continue to render the service that they mutually expected from each other'(ibid. 28:51). The Jesuits were convinced that this 'lewdness and licentiousness hinders them from finding God'. As Paul Le Jeune wrote in his *Relation* of 1637, 'The bond, so strong which holds man and wife under the same yoke, will be very hard to fasten upon the savages' (ibid. 28:51). This theme was a popular one with the Jesuits and it continued to be reiterated throughout most of the *Relations*, regardless of author. The native practice of leaving an unsuitable spouse ran contrary to Christian teachings of the inviolability of marriage, and, in the Jesuit view, provided a constant opportunity for sin, and thus for the Devil to be served.

Illustrations of their obsession with this issue abound, but the Jesuits were most articulate when they were able to record their concerns as coming from the mouths of native converts. The following conversation, recorded as having taken place between two Huron seminarians[2] at Quebec City, is an example. Discussing the likelihood of marriage, one of the seminarians is reported to have said:

> If we take a wife, at the first whim that seizes her, she will at once leave us, and then we are reduced to a wretched life, seeing that it is the women in our country who sow, plant and cultivate the land and prepare the food for their husbands.
>
> (ibid. 14:235)

The seminarians were apparently commiserating with each other over how difficult it would be for them to marry, as they were now Christians, and they would be prohibited from taking another wife if their first one left them. A few years later, in 1643, Jérôme Lalemant complained that:

> License in Marriages is so great, and the freedom of leaving one another on the slightest pretext is so generally admitted as a fundamental Law of these Peoples, that every Christian who marries is exposed, on the morrow of his Nuptials, to the danger of being compelled to observe continence for the remainder of his life. What therefore can a Christian young Man do if, on his very Wedding day, his wife should abandon the Faith, and thereby at the same time break that sacred tie. She will at once take a new husband; and, were he to burn with passion a thousand times over, he must grow old in chastity without having ever made a vow to do so. The Church in this case has no sword. A woman who would act thus could not be at all blamed for it by the Infidels.
>
> (ibid. 23:187)

Although marriage, divorce and remarriage among the Huron and the Montagnais did not follow the same rigid rules as the Jesuits were hoping to instil, they were not as uncomplicated, or as free as the Jesuits made them out to be. Divorce and remarriage between man and women was relatively simple if they had no children. Remarriage became more difficult for widows and widowers. The relatives of a deceased man or women did not look favourably on the remarriage of their kin's surviving spouse until three years after their kin's death. A man who remarried before, without the permission of his former spouse's kin, was held in contempt, while a woman who thus married could expect to see her new husband 'plundered' (ibid. 16:203–5).

Among the Montagnais, girls who became engaged had the practice of cutting bangs 'in the fashion in which girls in France wear it, hanging over the forehead'. The Jesuit commentator writing about this found the fashion 'very ungraceful' both in Old and in New France, 'Saint Paul prohibiting women from making a show of their hair' (ibid. 16:205). All women wore their hair 'fastened on the back of their heads in bunches, which they ornament with Porcelain when they have it'. If an engaged girl accepted presents from her suitor and later left him, or if a married woman left her husband without cause, the rejected man might cut off this hair. According to Le Jeune, 'this makes them very despicable and prevents them from finding another husband' (ibid. 16:205).

Sex, it would seem, was something that the Huron and Montagnais thought should be enjoyed. Gabriel Sagard, a Recollect lay brother who was part of an earlier mission to the Huron, wrote that young girls vied with each other over who could have the greatest number of lovers (Tooker 1964:125). Each village, he added, had its 'procurers' whose occupation was to bring young men and women together for intercourse (Wrong (ed.) 1939:133–4). The explorer/adventurer Samuel de Champlain, even more fanciful than Brother Sagard, claimed that a woman could have twelve or fifteen husbands, 'not including other men'. He recorded in his diary how he had firmly refused an offer of sex when, leaving his cabin one evening to 'escape the fleas', he was followed and propositioned by a woman who had understood that his intention was otherwise (Biggar (ed.) 1922–36 III:47)

Thirty years later the Jesuit Superior Jérôme Lalemant commented on the same 'problem' of meetings in the woods between men and women initiated equally by either sex. He expressed disgust at the 'libertinage to which the girls and women here abandon themselves' noting, in common with Sagard, that 'the girls boast of seeking the young men' (Thwaites 1896–1901, 15:107; 38:253). He was equally appalled by the use of sexual intercourse in curing ceremonies. Any ill person could call for a number of young people to come and have sexual relations in his or her cabin as part of a their treatment. Lalemant commented that there were 'certain remedies where indecency is, as it were, in its kingdom the girls deeming it an honour, on these occasions to prostitute their honour itself' (ibid. 34:197). But by this point he was also able to add, encouraged, that 'the good Christians always refuse this horrid deed.'

Christian marriages were important, too, because they provided children who could in turn be Christianized and made obedient. The Jesuits' pleas for money for their missions often focused on this issue. As Le Jeune wrote in 1639:

> The freedom of the children in these countries is so great, they prove so incapable of government and discipline, that, far from being able to hope for the conversion of the country through the instruction of the children, we must even despair of their instruction without the conversion of their parents. And consequently, as well considered, the first matter to which we should attend is the stability of the marriages of our Christians, who

give us children that may in good time be reared in the fear of
God and their parents.

(ibid. 16:251)

In short, Christian marriages were necessary if the Jesuits were
ever going to be able to get access to the children. Indeed, the key to
the control of the entire society seemed to them to be the institution
of Christian marriages. It was here that the good management of the
society would begin. Thus, the transformation of women and men
and their means of inter-relating was essential to the whole project.
As long as parents believed themselves to be free and independent
they would allow their children to do the same.

Without fear of God and of their parents children grew up to be
disobedient adults. It was thus imperative to begin with the family
and more importantly with mothers and fathers themselves. Women
had to be brought to obedience. All this would take, in one Jesuit's
estimation, was about thirty people giving 12 ecus apiece. This would
be enough to establish fifty stable marriages which would 'after
sometime form a world, or rather a Paradise entirely new' (ibid.
17:251).

Relations between husbands and wives, particularly with regard to
men's rights to chastise and beat their spouses, was also a favourite
theme. In the manner of Benedicti, or of St Francis Xavier, for
example, Jesuit missionaries in New France conveyed the understanding that Huron and Montagnais women must submit to the
wishes of their Christianized husbands and fathers. Women were to
serve and obey. If women failed to do so and their husbands became
angry with them, they would have to bear full responsibility. Following this theme, for example, they reported on a young Christian
Montagnais, who, getting into a passion, 'beat his wife who had
insolently provoked him'. Both the man and his wife were repri-
manded for this incident, but especially the wife 'who was more
guilty than her husband' (ibid. 18:155).

Another man beat his disobedient wife to such an extent that 'he
gave her a bloody nose'. Although he went to confession the following day and offered to be publicly whipped or beaten by the French
he was allowed a much lesser punishment and 'became reconciled
with his wife in a Christian manner' (ibid. 26:99). Yet another Montagnais, on marrying his wife, is reported to have warned her: 'Be
careful of what you are about to say. I do not conceal my bad temper
from you. I am a hasty and irritable man; I make all serve me; I wish

my wife to obey me.' 'Apart from this', the Jesuit writer adds, 'the man is of a very good disposition' (ibid. 27:151).

Women were clearly meant to be under the tutelage of their husbands, as a child to a parent. Commenting on a recently converted Huron couple, Paul Le Jeune says of the wife that 'she is only too fortunate in having encountered so good a father in so faithful a husband' (ibid. 18:107). This woman was particularly worthy in her own right because she had 'never lived in the libertinage to which the girls and women here abandon themselves' (ibid. 18:107). The Jesuits reserved their praises for 'good and simple' women who allowed themselves to be 'easily lead to the right' (ibid. 16:145). In yet another example, reported on at length in the *Relations*, a Christian man confessed to beating his wife out of anger. She irritated him because she did not obey his request to follow him to mass. 'I wish no person with me ... who does not pray to God', he is reported to have said (ibid. 20:147–9). In the interview with the Jesuit missionary following this incident the beaten wife was 'full of mildness and regret'. The conclusion of the incident was that the next day the couple appeared at confession together. The Jesuit was delighted to be able to report that the 'good woman' never excused herself, whatever her husband said to her, or however he reproached her.

> Notwithstanding she had an excellent reason for excuse; for she told us afterwards that when her husband called her to go to mass, she did not hear him; nevertheless for fear of offending him, she had preferred to appear guilty, rather than excuse herself.
>
> (ibid. 20:149)

A thwarted woman who expressed her anger only gave way to resentment and vexation. The Jesuits labelled women who refused to obey their husbands and fathers 'haughty and spiteful' or 'rough and wild' (ibid. 24:57). These were women who gave a great deal of trouble to their 'poor husbands' and Jesuit sympathies went out to men saddled with such wives. Calling these women 'unlovable', 'arrogant', 'overbearing', 'jeering' or 'scornful' the Jesuits did what they could to help Christianized men bring them into line.

In 1642, for example, a Jesuit wrote about one of their poor neophytes, who was 'united to a wife who was as averse to the Faith as her husband honored it' (ibid. 22:75). This man, using the 'privilege that saint Paul gives him', left her. Some of the other Christians, however, reproached him, accusing him of only paying lip service to the commandment that a true Christian never leaves his wife. The man was in a quandary 'for he could not love a woman who did not love God, and who, moreover, was of a very arrogant and over-bearing disposition'. The man had a dream in which a band of French, along with two Jesuits commanded him: 'Leave that woman; who will not be reasonable.' In spite of such a dream the man went to his director to ask his opinion, saying 'If you order me to sit down once more beside her who has so often scoffed at God, and who has so long treated me as her lackey, I will give up my ideas to follow yours'. The man's confessor was apparently much astonished 'at seeing such courage and such firmness in the soul of a man whose gentleness is not in keeping with the ill humor of a jeering and scornful woman' (ibid. 22:77). The man's wife, under pressure from the community, agreed to receive Christian instruction, 'admitting that, in reality, she had scoffed at the prayers because she had a horror of them; but that her mind has changed, and that she has adopted other sentiments' (ibid.).

Not only were the Jesuits concerned with establishing Christian marriage as the legitimate mode of expression of relations between women and men, they were also concerned with confining sexual expression within its boundaries. Sexuality, as Michel Foucault has pointed out, is an

> especially dense transfer point for relations of power... Sexu-ality is not the most intractable element in power relations, but rather one of those endowed with the greatest instrumentality; useful for the greatest number of maneuvers and capable of serving as a point of support, as a linchpin for the most varied strategies.
>
> (Foucault 1980:103)

To be able to define the legitimate modes of expression of sexuality is to occupy a strategic place in a schemata of power relations. Church doctrine of the seventeenth century placed the locus of sexuality exclusively within the conjugal couple. While it gave men the power to enforce the moral behaviour of their wives, it placed women in a position of either submitting to or rebelling against that authority. Because men's right to rule over women was derived from their natures (active for men, passive for women) any woman who actively expressed her sexuality was 'unnatural' and thus dangerous and in need of controlling. Moreover, Christian doctrine held a complex and contradictory attitude towards marriage, love, passion and sexuality. On the one hand, for Christian theology, virginity was taken as the model of the perfection of Christianity. Before their expulsion from Eden, Adam and Eve were believed to have lived as virgins. Christ, born of a virgin, carried his own virginity with him to the cross. Virginity became a central theme of the Christian church, and the church fathers used the texts of the disciples as the basis on which to found a doctrine of continence (Brown 1988:428–47; Métral 1977:23–4).

But sexual coupling was necessary for the reproduction of the society. Sexual intercourse was a gift from God and thus necessary. It has been a consistent part of Christianity to be suspicious of pleasure and of sexual intercourse without daring to forbid it, because, in the logic of creation, 'pleasure and sexuality are gifts of God, and therefore good' (Métral 1977:184). But pleasure in and of itself is bad. It is only when it has as its end the satisfaction of some need that it can have any value. Thus, in Christian theology, sexual pleasure is a sin if it is dissociated from the reproduction of the species.

In order not to sin, sexual pleasure must be limited to coition which is undertaken for reproductive purposes only, i.e. coition within marriage (ibid.:184). Benedicti cautioned husbands and wives against 'committing excesses in their marriages that might displease God' (Benedicti 1600:201). Anyone who tried to prevent conception by any manner whatsoever, also sinned, as did those who had sexual intercourse on communion or feast days. Men were forbidden to 'to know' their wives during the 'indisposition and purging of the month' or when they were 'very close to birth'. Even a woman who sat in a window to be seen, or who went to church to be seen, and who did not dress honestly and piously, but dressed rather in order to be 'loved carnally', was committing a sin (ibid.: 202–5).

The Jesuits' own position on the question of the relative merits of marriage and chastity are made clear in this exchange between a Huron convert and an Ursuline. The conversation was recorded in a letter sent to François Le Mercier, the then Jesuit Superior at Quebec and quoted by him in his *Relation* of 1653/4. According to the unnamed Ursuline who sent the letter:

> The holy Fathers, in speaking of chastity, affirm it to be a virtue descended from Heaven, a beauty unknown to nature, and one of the fairest daughters, or one of the finest fruits, of heavenly grace. This fruit is beginning to appear in the orchards of these new Churches. I learned that a young Huron, who is about

thirty years old, and has been for the past four years strongly urged to marry, has always resisted. At length, when his relatives, by weighty arguments, pressed him with unusual persistence to take this step, he went in quest of one of the Fathers who have charge of that Church, and thus briefly addressed him: 'My Father, I am told every day to marry; what is thy opinion? Decide for me.' The Father answered him that it was not forbidden to marry, and that he could do so. 'Yes,' returned the young man; 'but which of the two is more pleasing to God, to marry or not to marry?' The Father replied that those who renounced the pleasures of earth, for sake of serving Jesus Christ better, were more acceptable to him. 'That is enough,' rejoined this good Neophyte; 'there must be no more talk of marriage to me. Good-bye, Father; that is all I had to say to thee.'

(Thwaites 1896–1901, 40:227)

A young widow also expressed the same feelings when she was confronted by a Jesuit who noticed she was walking barefoot because of her poverty. Asked why she did not find a good husband to help her, the widow replied she was determined not to marry again. 'If I had been permitted to do as I wished, I would, long ago, have lived with my husband as a sister. Regard for my salvation estranges me from the thought of marriage' (ibid. 40:229). As the Jesuit added:

As good trees bring forth good fruit, this noble Christian woman has a daughter who inherits the holy inclinations of her good mother. This child lives with the hospital Nuns, acting as Interpreter for the poor Huron patients.... She is of so excellent a disposition that she never excuses herself when her little faults are corrected; and if anyone of her companions is accused of error, she is wont to say that it was she who committed the offense, and that she has no sense. Not long ago she made her first Communion; and, in proof that she knew him who had just visited her, she voluntarily offered herself to him, imploring him to retain her in his house and graciously permit her to become a Nun.

(ibid. 40:231)

It is interesting here to compare the Jesuits' notions concerning the role of mothers and fathers in conception with those proposed by Aristotle. In recording one of his arguments made to convince the

Huron about the 'truth of one God, Creator, Governor and Preserver of all things', Paul Le Jeune touched on the issue of responsibility for conception and the growth of the infant in the womb. In contrast to Aristotle who attributed the active process to male sperm, Le Jeune attributes the action to the will of God.

'Who... but God', asks Le Jeune, 'forms the body of the child. Who out of one and the same material forms the heart, the liver, the lungs, in short, an infinite variety of members all necessary, all well-proportioned, and all joined one to another?' Not the father, Le Jeune answers, who is absent, and 'may even be dead'. Nor is it the mother, 'who does not know what is taking place in her womb'. Neither of the parents could be in charge, otherwise they would beget a 'son or a daughter at will', and produce tall, handsome, strong, active children with great minds, and other worthy qualities (ibid. 10:17).

Within the framework of legitimate sex only for reproductive purposes, and within Christian marriage, the recurrent image of wanton lewdness in non-Christianized native women that permeates Jesuit writings becomes more easily understandable. That lewdness (read the pursuit of sexual relations for the purpose of pleasure) left native women vulnerable to divine punishment. In commenting on a young Montagnais woman who had died, and whose parents had died before her from some contagious disease, the Jesuit Le Mercier wrote:

> it was, in my opinion, through a righteous chastisement of God that she was deprived of the grace of Baptism. Two things contributed materially to her misfortune. The first was that she was excessively lewd, and although the Savages show little restraint in the matter of chastity, yet she made herself conspicuous in this regard, and had prostituted herself at every opportunity.
>
> (ibid. 13:135–7)

The other cause was the inordinate desire that she and her parents felt for her health. Her mother could do nothing but talk about her sickness and the means of securing her recovery, much to the consternation of the Jesuits who wanted to discuss what had to be done to secure her eternal salvation.

The Jesuits believed that children were born with no knowledge of sex and only later were corrupted by others. They attributed the 'lewdness' of Montagnais and Huron women, and thus their consistent propensity to sin, to their lack of proper education. 'It makes our hearts ache to see these innocent young girls so soon defile their purity of body and beauty of soul', Le Jeune lamented, 'for lack of a good example and good instruction' (ibid. 10:33).

The discussion of the behaviour of young native girls who had been educated in the Ursuline convent at Quebec illustrates clearly what the Jesuits considered expressions of 'purity of body and beauty of the soul'. The Ursulines' students were instructed to avoid all contact with men, and the pupils of that convent did not fail to delight the Jesuits by having such a high regard for purity that 'when they go out walking, they avoid meeting men; and they are so careful to cover themselves with decency, that their deportment is very different from the customs of the Savages' (ibid. 22:185).

The uncontained sexuality of women was perceived as a direct threat to male converts and even to the Jesuits themselves. Reporting on a Christian convert who had previously been 'greatly addicted to women, gaming and the superstitions of the Country', Le Jeune describes how that particular convert barely avoided being seduced by a 'firebrand of hell' (ibid. 37:171–3). Another convert, while on a journey, met an 'infidel woman' who 'solicited him to do what he could not yield to her without prejudice to his conscience'. He rebuffed the woman, calling her a 'bitch', and telling her that he rejected her out of fear of 'the great master of our lives' who had his 'eyes fixed' on them (ibid. 22:63). Yet another Christian convert left a village in the middle of the night which he had been invited to as a guest at a warriors' feast. He left in a hurry when a woman of that village offered him a chance to spend the night with her and he became frightened that the Devil might make him give in to her request (ibid. 22:63).

Even the Jesuits themselves were not immune to attacks on their chastity by 'lewd women'. In his eulogy on the martyred Brébeuf, Lalemant remarks:

> His chastity was proof of his virtue; and in that matter his eyes were so faithful to his heart, that they had no sight for the objects which might have soiled purity. His body was not rebellious to the spirit; and in the midst of impurity itself, – which reigns, it seems, in this country, – he lived an innocence as great as if he had sojourned in the midst of a desert inaccessible to that sin. A woman presented herself one day to him, in a place somewhat isolated, uttering to him unseemly

language, and breathing a fire which could come only from hell. The Father, seeing himself thus attacked, made upon himself the sign of the cross, without answering any word; and this spectre, disguised beneath a woman's dress, disappeared at the same moment.

(ibid. 34:191–3)

Men's steadfast refusal to be seduced by women marked, for the Jesuits, the actions of true Christians and gave them hope that others could be converted. To emphasize the necessity of funding for their missions, Le Jeune wrote in 1639 that

if we had the means to give considerable assistance to the Savages and to induce them to become sedentary we would see a great blessing overspread these people who are much more docile in matters of the Faith than we had dared to expect.

(ibid. 16:61)

The events that gave Le Jeune such cause for hope were the stories that he had heard 'on good authority' about some 'shameless women' who had approached some Christian men at night hoping to 'solicit them to do evil in secret'. These women were rebuffed, Le Jeune reports, with these words: 'I believe in God, I pray to him everyday; he forbids such actions, I can not commit them' (ibid. 16:61).

Seductress, emissary from hell, temptress; these were some of the images the sexually active native women of New France conjured up for the Jesuits. If new definitions of men and women were to be established, the actions and self-expression of the Huron and Montagnais had to be scrutinized and directed; and their sexuality had to be redefined and controlled. Open expression of sexuality, typical in traditional Huron and Montagnais society, were sins within Christian theology. Moreover, expression of sexuality, uninformed and unregulated by the concept of 'sin' posed a threat to the very power relations the Jesuits hoped to instil. Freedom of sexual expression denoted a lack of control, a certain wildness that appeared to threaten civilization itself. Freedom of sexual expression meant that pleasure for its own sake could be experienced. This in turn meant that relations between men and women, marriage and even the very idea of a hierarchical ordering of societal relations were also open to challenge. In the Jesuits' view, God's laws could not brook such a challenge.

NATIVES, NOBLES AND SALVATION

In order to control the sexuality of young girls and women and to ensure Christian marriages the Jesuits appealed to aristocratic and monied women of France to help materially in their education. The preoccupation with saving the souls of the 'Savages of New France' was not confined to a few Jesuits and Ursuline. It had become fashionable, within the court of Louis XIII, to display a concern for the spiritual lives of the little 'heathens'. Members of the court vied with one another in shows of piety, by adopting or sponsoring native people who were brought to court to be shown the wonders of French civilization.

Aristocrats often seized upon whatever opportunity presented itself to demonstrate their 'high mindedness' and impeccable morality by making public displays of helping the lowly native people of New France find their way to Heaven. Charlotte, princess of Condé, for example, wrote to the Jesuits asking to sponsor in France one of the little native girls left in the care of the Jesuits. In response to her request, Le Jeune made it known in his *Relation* of 1637, that:

> If someone would give her a dowry [the native girl in their charge], when she is of marriageable age, and then send her back to these countries, I believe that much would be accomplished for the glory of our Lord. For a little Savage girl comfortably settled here, and married to some Frenchman or Christian Savage, would be a powerful check upon some of her wandering countrymen.
>
> (ibid. 11:53)

In 1636 the Jesuits had sent a young Iroquois woman, along with a little boy and three Montagnais girls to live with Madame de Combalet in Paris. Madame de Combalet apparently took some time out of her busy schedule to instruct the Iroquois woman herself in 'the faith of Jesus Christ and in the fear of God'. The hope was that living in 'virtue should so take possession of her heart' that she would be made fit to return to New France with an number of French nuns to help them with their work with other native girls. In order to be made fit for such work, however, it was decided that the young woman should be removed from Madame de Combalet's home and placed somewhere where she could do gardening. 'Otherwise, having too long tasted the sweetness and repose and abundance of a great house, she would afterwards shun labour' (ibid. 11:95).

One of the three young Montagnais girls sent to France went to live with nuns at Dieppe where her 'sweetness, compliance, obedience, devoutness and modesty' inspired the nuns themselves (ibid. 11:95). The other two Montagnais girls were placed under the care of Madame de Combalet who had them baptized. The popularity of sponsoring these children at court is demonstrated by their 'illustrious' godparents. The princess of Condé and Monsieur the Chancellor served as godparents for one, and Monsieur des Noiers, secretary of state, as godfather for the other.

Only one of the three young girls survived the year. Addressing the survivor in the pages of the *Relations*, Le Jeune exclaimed; 'alas my daughter, who has drawn you from your lowly estate to place you in the affection of nobles? What have you rendered to God for your deliverance from slavery, and for your enrollment among the members of his children?' (ibid. 11:99–101). It also became fashionable for persons of 'rank' to request that Christianized natives be asked to mention them in their prayers when they received communion. The queen herself made a request to the Jesuits that native Christians be asked to pray for the dauphin and gave some alms to support her request (ibid. 19:89). This, according to Le Jeune made the Christian Indians admire the 'goodness and lofty character of Christianity, which abases great things and exalts the most humble' (ibid. 19:85).

Even Louis XIII seems to have taken an interest in meeting with and talking to 'Canadian Savages' who visited his court. The *Relations* report how the king took special care to meet one of his native guests while he was at prayer, and to enquire whether or not he had been baptized (ibid. 15:235). Louis XIII and his queen were apparently so 'full of ardour for the salvation of these needy people' that they paid the Canadian the great compliment of showing him their new-born dauphin. Added to this royal favour was the gift of six suits of truly royal clothing', which the Jesuits later distributed among the various groups of natives in order to avoid jealousy (ibid. 15:223).

Le Jeune's *Relation* of 1639 is particularly skilfully laid out as a device for soliciting donations from 'persons of wealth for the project in New France'. After describing the trip of the 'Canadian Savage' to the court of Louis XIII, and the king's attention, concerns, and gifts, Le Jeune turns to a description of a meeting with a group of Christianized Montagnais that took place in Quebec following the celebrations of the birth of the dauphin, in which the king's gift of clothing had been worn. 'Some had nothing savage about them but their tanned color', he wrote, 'their demeanour and gait were full of dignity and real grace' (ibid. 15:229).

Madame the duchess d'Aiguillon and Madame de la Peltrie donated funds to establish nuns in Quebec. The duchess, who was a niece of Cardinal Richelieu, got the best of the praise the Jesuits had to offer. The duchess was labelled an 'Amazon' for her efforts, while Madame de la Peltrie, who had a significantly lower social standing, and fewer funds to make available, earned their praise as 'a modest and virtuous lady' (ibid. 16:9). But whatever funds were available were never enough. Le Jeune wrote in the *Relation* of 1638 that, through a lack of temporal assistance, 'Satan ever keeps these poor souls under his dominion'. Madame de la Peltrie, in her turn, is quoted as having exclaimed:

> Alas! how many souls could be saved in this country with what is spent for a single repast in Paris, or for a single ballet that lasts but two or three hours! I have brought only a few labourers with me but I will do what I can to help these good people.
>
> (ibid. 15:233)

Speaking of a French nobleman who had contributed funds for building French-style houses at Saint Joseph, the name given by the Jesuits to one of the Huron villages, Le Jeune writes, 'would to God that several persons of abundant wealth would imitate the devoutness of that great man! There is no loss in exchanging earth for Heaven' (ibid. 15:233).

CHRISTIAN, FEARFUL AND SUBMISSIVE

We find, then, throughout the *Relations*, a clear contrast being drawn between female non-converts, who are lewd, unnatural seductresses, and the chaste, innocent women and girls who had embraced Christianity and who were now compliant and fearful. Once the Montagnais were settled at Sillery the *Jesuit Relations* contains several references to the actions and sentiments of these women and girls. In one case a young girl, described as 'very innocent', spent the night crying with her parents after a Jesuit told her (in jest) that he had heard tales about her honour. In another case a 'good woman who was very ill' requested not to be stripped when she died, but to be left dressed to preserve her chastity.

Women and girls who avoided the approach of men showed an

'instinct of a superior Spirit'. The 'most worthy' of them either ran away at the approach of men or were willing to kill the 'impudent fellow who was importuning her with violence' (Thwaites 1896–1901, 40:215). Widows and young girls who were solicited to give themselves to men who helped to support them replied that 'they were baptised and never committed such offences' (ibid. 16:61). Prior to their Christianization it had been the custom for young men and women to sleep together at night. Following the Jesuits advice, though, Christianized girls either ignored their suitors or sent them to the Jesuits (ibid. 16:63). Young girls applied to the Jesuits to lock them up at night, 'fearing that they are not safe from the young men', even in 'parents' cabins' (ibid. 38:73). Some even went so far as to claim that they preferred death to having sexual relations with men, as this story, told by Lalemant attests.

> A young Pagan, who had frequently been refused by a Christian girl, sought for an opportunity of meeting her alone, when she went for wood in the adjacent forest. 'No one sees thee', he said to her, 'why shouldst thou be ashamed to sin with me?' 'Kill me in the midst of these woods,' replied the Christian maiden, 'No one sees thee now. Why shouldst thou have a horror of thy crime? For my part, I would more willingly suffer death than commit the sin to which thou solicitest me.' The scoundrel did not repeat his request. 'Cursed race of Christians!', he said as he withdrew, 'they are everywhere inexorable'.
>
> (ibid. 26:229)

The more institutionally well-established the Jesuits became, the more they were able to secure for themselves central positions which others had to take cognizance of in their day to day lives, the more successful they became in imposing their understandings of sexuality/pleasure and in confining sexual expression to the conjugal (and thus the reproducing) couple. Women, potentially filled with sexual energy, potentially capable of pursuing sexual pleasure as an end in itself, had to be frightened into containing their sexuality and into denying its expression anywhere but in the marital relationship and in the service of having children.

In the Jesuits' view, women's sexuality, their capacity to seek out pleasure for itself, was something dangerous; left uncontrolled it was capable of undermining the higher morality of men. It was the responsibility of Christian women, therefore, not only to refuse the advances of men, but to never make any themselves. While men who sought intercourse outside marriage behaved contrary to the rules of Christian morality (but not to the more base aspects of their natures) women who sought intercourse outside marriage behaved contrary to human nature. These women tempted men, but because such activity was outside of their true natures, it was temptation from Hell. Women were especially susceptible to the influence of the Devil, and in the Jesuits' view the Devil was extraordinarily active among the native peoples.

Jesuit attempts to redefine male/female relations did not stop with sexual expression and marital relations; they also sought to extend their control into the realm of emotional life. The trained ear of the confessor strained to hear, not just about actions, but also about thoughts and feelings. In all areas of life women were exhorted to pattern their emotions into a submissive, patient understanding of, and compliance with, their lot in life. Many interpretations of women's emotions appeared in the pages of the *Jesuit Relations*. The Jesuits were especially concerned with monitoring both the feelings women had and the way in which they expressed them. This concern is particularly evident in their reporting on Christianized women's responses to news of the capture and torture of their male relatives by the Iroquois.

During the Jesuits' mission both the Huron and Montagnais were at war with the Iroquois. Battles usually resulted in both men and women being taken prisoners, and male prisoners were frequently tortured to death and then eaten in ritualistic feasts. As the Huron and Montagnais began to convert to Christianity the Jesuits devoted pages of the *Relations* to discussing the emotional responses of women to the torture and death of their spouses.

The women who were made to express themselves in the pages of the *Relations* did so with a certain consistency which reflected the Jesuits' views of proper Christian sentiments of love. Women's emotional responses were carefully monitored to make sure they represented a submission to the will of the 'Supreme Being'. Women who submitted without complaint, or even joyously could also be counted on to submit to the church and to their husbands. In one example, the Jesuits reported on a group of Christian women who heard that their husbands had been captured and tortured by the Iroquois. The Jesuit Superior began by contrasting the response that would have occurred if old customs had been followed:

It is the Savages' custom, when such casualties occur, to make the air resound with doleful lamentations, cries and groans – women calling their husbands by name in pitiful accents, children their fathers, uncles their nephews. As this sad ceremony is enacted not for one day merely, or two, but throughout the entire year, nothing but weeping and lamentation being heard, every morning and evening, in the whole village that has suffered some great loss.

(ibid. 40:61)

Instead, the Christian women came to the chapel

with tears in their eyes, indeed, and sobbing bitterly, but with such inward peace and such entire resignation to God's decrees that they themselves were astonished there at, and could not sufficiently marvel at the efficacy of prayer, which made them find consolation in extreme anguish.

(ibid. 40:61)

One such woman claimed to feel no grief at the news of her husband's torture and subsequent death. The man had reputedly wished to be captured and tortured as compensation for the sins he committed before his baptism, and his widow was content that God granted her husband what he had asked. Another woman, on hearing of her husband's murder, claimed that the first thought that came to her was 'he who is the master of it has thus arranged it; what could we do in the matter' (ibid. 21:149). According to the Jesuit Vimont, 'she afterward so bore herself in her affliction that I do not know how anyone of the best Christians in our Europe could have done better' (ibid. 21:149).

For the Jesuits, love was only properly expressed through the happiness felt when God's will had been done, or when the will of the Devil had been thwarted. Thus mothers were taught to treat the pain and suffering of their children as a trial sent by God to test them or by the Devil to cause them to give up Christianity. In 1647 the Jesuits were able to report on a woman who had left her children at home unattended in order to be instructed in the Christian faith. She was told that during her absence one of her children had scalded himself very badly with boiling water, Although the child was gravely injured the mother did not show any sign of agitation fearing that 'the Devils were trying to make [her] hate instruction and prayer' (ibid. 44:253–5).

Another woman, described as a good mother, claimed that she no longer grieved on the death of a child. God in his wisdom, she claimed, caused the death, perhaps 'because he sees long beforehand that, if my child lived longer, he would no longer believe in him, and would be burned' (ibid. 27:241). Women, weeping in despair would suddenly stop their tears if a Jesuit affectionately reproached them for mourning at the 'happiness and glory of their children who were now in Heaven' (ibid. 31:201). The notion that the souls of their children were in Heaven, the Jesuit wrote, 'infinitely comforts them in their distress that they feel at their death' (ibid. 31:201).

Women who were 'extremely proud' prior to their baptism, now appear in the pages of the *Relations* as 'docile as little lambs' (ibid. 20:267). Asked by a dying relative to send for a shaman to cure her child, one woman was reputed to have said, 'I would rather see him die, than that God be offended through my instrumentality' (ibid. 20:267).

Baptism, burial and other Christian rites were a further point of contention between the Jesuits and the men and women they sought to convert. In the early days of the Jesuits' missions, most Huron and Montagnais who sought baptism did so as an aid to health (ibid. 4:13). When they regained their health, the converts most often also renounced their baptisms. Thus, the Jesuits had a difficult time holding converts who survived an illness to Christian practices. Many bitter disappointments occurred for the Jesuits when they baptised men and women, expecting to be able rely on their help in further conversions only to have those persons renounce their baptism. As a result the Jesuits soon established a policy of refusing baptism to all but the very few they felt they could trust or to those in obvious danger of dying, and who therefore would not get the chance to renege.

Yet once the Montagnais and later the Huron came under the influence of the Jesuits, as more and more converted to Christianity, it was still women and girls who continued to refuse to be baptised, even in the face of a concerted effort made by their Christianized husbands. Often the women claimed they were unable to promise to never be separated from their spouses. Only a very few women, close to death, would actually consent to baptism (ibid. 13:245). Women's and girls' refusal to be baptized in spite of pressure from husbands or fathers (or, in the opposite but much less likely instance, their determination to be baptized also in spite of opposition) suggests the extent to which women continued to be able exercise their free will.

In 1637 Brébeuf recounted the story of a man who was baptized and who tried to get his daughter to do the same. The girl refused to follow her father's example 'and he could not make her comply' (ibid. 12:139). In another instance a 5-year-old girl became a Christian, in spite of her parents opposition (ibid. 34:115). In yet another, a young girl of 7 or 8 years intervened physically to prevent a Jesuit baptising one of her adult male relatives. According to the father who was trying to effect the baptism of the dying man the little girl seized the vial of holy water he was about to employ and 'trampled it under her feet'. Claiming she would do everything in her power to prevent the father from finding more holy water, she turned to the would-be convert, telling him he would die if he consented to the baptism. 'This little fury of hell', the Jesuit concluded, 'is so eloquent that the sick man goes back on his word and will not be baptised' (ibid. 19:213). In still another case, the daughter of an 'infamous magician' defied her parents wishes and was baptised on her death bed (ibid. 23:119–21).

With conversion to Christianity and settlement in Christianized villages women only married Christian men approved by the Jesuits. They no longer divorced whenever they felt they had good reason, nor did they have sexual relations with whomever they pleased. They ceased to oppose their husbands' will, or even stand up to men, when they thought they had reason. Now they were fearful of being humiliated or beaten if they did not obey.

Now women who were chastised by their husbands for disobedience felt themselves guilty of a sin, and were compelled to confess as much to the Jesuits. A baptised women, for example, attended some public feast or game against the expressed wishes of her husband. When she returned home he upbraided her saying:

> If I were not a Christian, I would tell you that, if you did not care for me, you should seek another husband to whom you would render more obedience; but, having promised God not to leave until death, I cannot speak to you thus although you have offended me.
>
> (ibid. 18:135)

This woman felt compelled to ask for her husband's forgiveness, and appeared in the Jesuit's cabin the next morning to confess saying, 'My Father, I have offended God, I have not obeyed my husband;

my heart is very sad; I greatly desire to make my confession of this' (ibid. 18:135).

Young women began to behave as if their honour, virtue and standing in the community depended on their sexual comportment. One young Christian woman was brought before the Jesuits to face charges of behaving like a 'profligate who did not believe in God'. Her crime was to have allowed a non-Christian young man to talk to her in her cabin which scandalized the other Christians who accused her of being caressed by him. The young woman denied the charges, insisting that he had not touched her and that she had told him to talk to the Jesuit fathers about his interest in her.

One of her interrogators then told her that she would be made to swallow a potion to determine if she told the truth. If the young man had indeed touched her, the potion would immediately make her vomit. Assured that she would not vomit if in fact she had not been touched, she demanded to have the potion so that they all could see her innocence. She was then given a spoonful of a black syrup which 'she took with a very cheerful face' (ibid. 18:143). The action earned her praise for her firmness and her purity. Meanwhile, as the Jesuit noted, the girl had learned a valuable lesson about the harm that could be done if she scandalized her neighbours by continuing to place herself 'in danger of being deluded by the devil' (ibid. 18:143).

As a result of this young woman's trial, all of the other young girls of the village sent their suitors to the Jesuits, wishing to avoid a similar fate. Those men who persisted in seeing them were threatened with firebrands. The Jesuit Vimont happily concluded his account of these events with the observation that 'to be born in Barbarism, and to act in this manner, is to preach Jesus Christ boldly' (ibid. 18:143). Another young girl, a student at the Ursuline seminary, who had allowed a French man to take her hand to lead her in a procession was 'laughingly reproached because she, who wished to remain ever a virgin, had allowed a man to touch her hand' (ibid. 22:185). The effect on the girl was devastating. Weeping, she tried to wash the stain of contact with the man from her hand, in order, as Vimont tells us, 'to remove any evil that she might have contracted by such an innocent action, being greatly afraid that it would prevent her from being a Virgin' (ibid. 22:185).

Another Huron girl tried to prevent men from talking to her by adopting a 'melancholy air'. This girl claimed that she only showed happiness when she was alone with her parents and her sisters. If she went anywhere else she altered her expression. 'I keep my eyes down, and my forehead wrinkled, and I try to look sad', she said, 'so that no one is encouraged to accost me' (ibid. 23:71). A Huron women, who observed a man looking at her, reported to her confessor that she suspected 'some evil design', saying that she had refused even to look in his direction. She was afraid that the attention directed towards her by the man was some ploy by the Devil, 'who sought only to do her evil, and to tempt her to sin in order to make her afterwards lose the Faith' (ibid. 23:71).

Somehow, in a period of less than thirty years, the Huron and the Montagnais had gone from being as free as 'wild animals' to administering French-style justice to compel dissenters to obey impersonal and universally applicable rules and regulations. What is even more astonishing is that those rules and regulations, along with the kind of individual-centred corporal punishment that was meted out to offenders, had been, only a few years previously, abhorrent to the Huron and the Montagnais. The Jesuits report on a 'very good Christian woman', for example, who beat her 4-year-old son (ibid. 33:177–9). A young Montagnais girl who refused to go to attend to her father's fishing nets when ordered was denied food for two days as a punishment for her disobedience (ibid. 19:173). Previously such actions, especially the disciplining of children, would have been considered repugnant and unnatural.

Women were especially singled out for surveillance and punishment on the grounds that they posed the greatest potential threat to the collective well-being. They were taught that, in any domestic dispute, it was always they who were at fault, being susceptible to the temptations of the Devil. Christian 'captains' took it upon themselves to frighten newly married couples against separating (ibid. 22:69). The virginity of young girls became something of great interest to all Christians. Young girls, formerly allowed nightly visits by men, were cloistered together at night, guarded by bells and male relatives who were to watch out for their virtue (ibid. 22:233).

But what stands out as the greater curiosity, even more so than the need the Jesuits seemed to have had in seeing native women subdued, is the apparent sudden shift in the Huron and the Montagnais themselves: from resistance to compliance, and even more astonishing, to self-policing. Hierarchical relations came to permeate most aspects of the lives of the Huron and the Montagnais, where previously very little hierarchy had existed at all. Women and men became potential enemies; their relations, especially their sexual relations, were fraught with danger, distrust and distaste. Any contact between unmarried men and women was suspected of being influenced by the Devil.

Moreover, the exclusive division of men and women into the categories of good or evil, active or passive, submissive or dominant, so prevalent in western European thought of the seventeenth century had not originally been part of Huron or Montagnais experience. Yet, within a period of less than three decades members of Huron and Montagnais societies were behaving as if Jesuit views of men and women were true. Although the Huron and the Montagnais had recognized differences between individuals (the Huron, for example, appointed war and civil leaders to represent each of the clans), leadership positions conferred more honour than authority on their incumbents. And while there were clearly recognized differences between men's and women's work, knowledge and experiences, neither sex was judged to be superior to the other.

The native perception of the significance and meaning of differences between men and women was antithetical to the objectives of the French adventurers, merchants and missionaries who were intent on establishing colonies. Once the native people of New France were converted to Christianity and settled on agricultural land, once they were won over to French civilization, they were expected to intermarry with immigrants from France. The offspring of these marriages were to become productive agriculturalists and suppliers of raw materials. They were to become fitting subjects of the church and the state. Samuel de Champlain, in dedicating his diaries to Louis XIII, held out to his monarch the vision of a wealth producing, passive population, obedient to the king's authority and willing to fight for France. This vision of a new race of people created out of the merger of French and Indian populations in the New World was predicated on the destruction of existing social relations and, especially, on the subjugation of women to men.

In seeking to transform both Huron and Montagnais societies, the Jesuits acted from a body of knowledge (Christian theology) which viewed the proper ordering of relations between people as decidedly hierarchical, and which attributed specific and different natures and capabilities to men and women. This hierarchical ordering of human relations delineated the appropriate ways for both men and women to act as individuals and as members of family units and of society. In carrying out their missions to the Huron and the Montagnais the Jesuits sought to put that body of knowledge into practice by convincing the native peoples of New France that Christianity embodied the true expression of the nature of men and women. By the mid-seventeenth century Huron and Montagnais women were silenced, supervised and subdued. Viewed not just by the Jesuits or the men in their society, but also by themselves, as shrews and potential corruptors of men, women were singled out as the source of evil in society, in need of constant vigilance and supervision.

A new philosophy and morality was accepted that not only rationalized women's subordination and silencing but also gave men and women a new way to think, feel and experience themselves. The marriage of Charles and Marie stood as a ratification of the new relations between men and women and of the emotional life that accompanied those new relations. The marriage ceremony itself reflected what was rapidly becoming the true knowledge for native men and women about their different natures and about the rightful distribution of power between them.

The modes of expression of that new ordering of power, the categories used to make the divisions between men and women and the rationalizations employed to justify the need, naturalness and desirability of the new order all found their roots in Christian theology, as interpreted by the Jesuit missionaries. For the Huron and the Montagnais, the first language of subordination, the first rationalizations for the suppression of women, the first order for understanding women as weak and submissive or defiant and dangerous, came from contemporary usage and interpretation of that theology. The Christian version of the true nature of men and women required, above all, the recognition that women, more than men, were capable of bringing about misfortune and eternal damnation. Yet the Christian view of women was contradictory. At one and the same time women were seen as passive by nature and yet as capable of lewd, seductive or other evil behaviour. Women were dangerous. More susceptible to the influences Satan, women could tempt men to follow their example.

As their world began to fall apart, as Huron and Montagnais men and women lost their ability to make sense out of the world and relations within it, they adopted the Jesuits' view of men and women and their interrelations as the 'truth'. Huron and Montagnais men and women began to police themselves and each other, to look for 'sins' and faults, to seek out the Devil everywhere in their own hearts and actions, to punish themselves and others for their misdeeds and refusal to comply with new rules of behaviour. Punishment of the body was meted out to correct indiscretions of the spirit. Wilfulness, independence and the search for personal power, all important aspects of traditional native personality structures, were now to be expunged.

Huron women, formerly known for their 'bad tempers' now begged for instruction and baptism. The husband of one expressed his disbelief at his wife's determination, saying 'that is impossible, thou hast so bad a temper that nobody can endure it'. His wife's recorded response was 'they tame, indeed, their dogs. When they shall have taught me well, they will easily manage me' (ibid. 23:191–3).

Images of women presented in the writings of the seventeenth-century Jesuits were consistent both with Christian theology and with French intentions to transform native society. Under Jesuit direction that transformation was to be effected through changes in the family structure and marriage, as well as in morality, especially sexual morality. But to transform marriage and morality meant the introduction of new definitions of men, women and authority into native society. It meant the introduction of new behaviours and new ways of expressing emotions.

It was one thing for the Jesuits to write about the native women of New France using images that would be understandable to the French nobility of the day. It was another matter to be able to fix those images as part of a people's way of being in the world. Two things remain to be examined. First, what supported women in their egalitarian relations with men that the Jesuits found so distasteful? What allowed these women to resist Christianity? Second, by what means were new definitions and new behaviours successfully implemented? By what mechanisms did a discourse, based on a seventeenth-century Catholic interpretation of the long-standing tradition in western thought and practice that women were the inferiors of men, and that men were 'more fitted to rule', come to dominate previously egalitarian societies? How did the manner in which power circulated between men and women come be altered so quickly and so extensively? What new practices, mechanisms, rules and beliefs intervened to change the existing conceptualization of men and women and their interrelations to such an extent that new forms of behaviour were practised, new knowledge was created and 'truth' was altered? How were the old 'internal regimes of power' (which acted to inform and regulate behaviour, and on which truth and knowledge rested) (Foucault 1979:32) jettisoned and replaced by something new, by something recognizable to both the writers and the readers of the *Jesuit Relations* as proper behaviour, in short as evidence of a virtuous and pious Christianity?

Figures 1–4 are details taken from the *Novae Franciae Accurata Delineatio, 1657*. This map was most likely drawn by the Jesuit Bressani. Reproduced by courtesy of the Public Archives of Canada.

Figure 1

Figure 2

Figure 3

Figure 4

6

'WOMEN SUSTAIN THE FAMILIES'

In any society an individual's worth can be measured by the extent to which they are validated as full, participating members of the society. That validation takes many forms, including being considered capable of acting on their own behalf, being given the freedom to take whatever leeway is allowed in making decisions and in following them through, being held responsible for their own decisions, and being accorded the widest range of rights and privileges offered by that society. Huron and Montagnais women led a very different kind of existence than did men yet they were not less valued. Nor were they allowed fewer freedoms, permitted to make fewer decisions about their lives or subjugated to more onerous prohibitions. They did not serve men, do their bidding, or exist as diminished beings in male-dominated societies.

Women's freedom from men's domination in both societies was supported by a number of complex, interconnected factors. Institutional structures, the organization of the productive process and the distribution of the product of labour, combined with specialized knowledge, including ritualized social practices and myths, all contributed to this lack of domination. So did the very way in which Huron and Montagnais subjectivity was constructed and experienced. What then, were the factors creating, supporting, sustaining, reinforcing and continuing women's worth and lack of subordinate status?

THE MONTAGNAIS

The Montagnais were among the first peoples in New France proselytized by the Jesuits. They were one of the many groups of hunter/gatherers who summered on the shores of the St Lawrence

River and who spent the winter in small bands along the rivers that emptied into it. Their economy followed a seasonal cycle. In the summer and autumn they lived by fishing, gathering and trapping small game. In the winter they dispersed into small bands to hunt caribou, moose and beaver (Leacock 1980:29). Once the French arrived in New France the Montagnais participated in the fur trade, both on their own accord and as intermediaries for other groups in the interior.

The social division of labour among the Montagnais assigned different economic tasks to men and to women. Women transported the game that men killed, gathered wood, made household articles, skinned and prepared hides, caught fish and hunted small animals, made canoes and set up tents (Thwaites 1896–1901, 2:77). The men hunted and waged war. Marriages were sometimes polygamous and tribal leaders often had more than one wife, they claimed, to help with the extra tasks that such an office required (ibid. 5:101). Defending their practice of polygamy to the Jesuits, one Montagnais pointed out that since there were more women than men, if a man only took one wife many women would have to suffer (ibid. 12:165).

The largest unit of production, consumption and residence among the Montagnais was the extended family. During the winter the tribe broke up into small bands, the members of which comprised several nuclear families. About ten to twenty persons lived together for the entire winter in conical lodges that served as a base camp from which the men left to hunt. Residence rules were flexible and people moved on the basis of personal choice and the need to keep a balance in the working group between young and old, men and women (Leacock 1980:129). Ideally, though, a man resided with his wife's kin after marriage (Thwaites 1896–1901, 31:169).

While the Montagnais experienced changes similar to those experienced by the Huron after their encounter with the Jesuits, it is the Huron society which we will examine in detail in the following chapters.

THE HURON

When French explorers, missionaries and traders arrived at the turn of the seventeenth century they found a society of semi-sedentary slash and burn horticulturists living on a strip of land, about 35 miles long and 20 miles wide, bounded on the west by the Georgian Bay and on the east by Lake Simcoe (Trigger 1976, 1:27).[1] The French called these people the Huron, a word meaning a crude or little civilized person (Dubois (ed.) 1977:875). The actual name of these people for themselves was 8endat (pronounced Wendat) and possibly meaning 'the one island' or 'one land apart'.[2] The term 8endat, in any case, referred, not to a single tribe, but to a confederacy and was analogous to the Iroquois *Hodenosaunee* – meaning people of the longhouse – which referred collectively to the five nations making up the Iroquois confederacy (Trigger 1976, 1:27).

The major objective of the Huron confederacy was most likely, as the Jesuits observed, protection against common enemies (Thwaites 1896–1901, 17:15). By the first decade of the seventeenth century that confederacy was composed of four or five 'nations' or 'tribes' – the Attignawantan, the Arendarhonon, the Attigneenongnahac and the Tahontaenrat.[3] A fifth group, called the Ataronchronon, has been identified as most likely being a division of the Attignawantan.[4] Each of the four or five 'tribes' that made up the confederacy had a different history as each was resident in 'Huronia' for varying periods of time. Each 'tribe', too, occupied its own territory.

The largest, the Attignawantan, comprised half the total Huron population, occupied a territory in the extreme west of Huronia and were the oldest residents of Huronia (Thwaites 1896–1901, 10:77). Members of both the Attignawantan and Attigneenongnahac tribes told the Jesuits that their ancestors had inhabited the area for over two centuries (ibid. 16:227–9). Archaeologists have determined that the area was continuously occupied by horticulturists for several hundred years. It is possible that some of the many prehistoric sites found there can be attributed to the ancestors of the Attignawantan (Trigger 1976:156). It is also possible that the Attigneenongnahac were resident in the northern part of Simcoe County for over two centuries.

The Arendarhonon and the Tahontaenrat, on the other hand, both appear to have moved into Huronia only after the mid-sixteenth century. In 1634 Le Jeune claimed that the Arendarhonon had moved into Huron country fifty years previously, while the Tahontaenrat had been resident in the area for only thirty years (Thwaites 1896–1901, 10:229). The exact origins of these two 'tribes' is not certain, but Huron tradition maintained that the Arendarhonon came from the Trent Valley about 1590 while the Tahontaenrat may have developed in the Humber and adjacent valley and moved into northern Simcoe County as late as 1610 (Trigger 1986:157). The relocation of these two 'tribes' into an already settled area of approximately 810 square miles, helped to create a relatively dense settlement pattern that was maintained until 1649 when the Huron were finally dispersed by the Iroquois.

Contemporary observers, including Samuel de Champlain, the Recollect lay brother Gabriel Sagard and various Jesuit missionaries all estimated the Huron population to be around 30,000 prior to the mid-1630s (Biggar (ed.) 1922–36 III; Thwaites 1896–1901, 6:59; 7:225; 8:115; 10:313; Wrong (ed.) 1939). Between 1634 and 1640, due to their exposure to European diseases including smallpox and influenza, the Huron population was greatly reduced. In a letter addressed to Cardinal Richelieu, and dated 28 March 1640, the Superior of the Jesuit missionaries to the Huron, Jérôme Lalemant, wrote that the population of the Huron had declined from 30,000 to 10,000 (Thwaites 1896–1901, 17:223). Modern-day estimates of the Huron population, however, call these figures into question, and suggest that the pre-epidemic Huron population was between 18,000 and 21,000 persons, while the post-epidemic population probably stood at around 9,000.[5]

Between 1609 and 1649 this population was distributed among eighteen to twenty-five villages ranging in size from 300 to possibly 1,600 in the largest village of Teanaostaiaé (called by the Jesuits, St Joseph II) (Biggar (ed.) 1922–36 III:122; Thwaites 1896–1901, 8:115; 10:313; 19:125–7; Wrong (ed.) 1939:91). Huron villages were made up of a clustering of longhouses, often surrounded by a palisade of wooden stakes, and were separated from each other by cultivated fields and by forest (Heidenreich 1971:125). They were strategically located, often in naturally defensible locations, near streams for canoe travel and well-drained sandy soil that was preferred for corn cultivation (Trigger 1976, 1:52).

By the time the Huron were directly contacted by the French in 1609, their economy had already undergone a number of important changes. Sometime between AD 500 and AD 1000, in what archaeologists call the Late Woodland Period, the Iroquoian peoples of the St Lawrence lowlands had adopted horticulture, thus laying the basis for later cultural changes that would eventually characterize the Iroquoian peoples which included the ancestors of the group historically known as the Huron.

There is growing evidence that in the fourteenth century certain important changes occurred, once again, that affected the lives of the Iroquoian people throughout most of the St Lawrence lowlands. This period, known as the 'Middle Iroquoian Period', was characterized by the consolidation of smaller populations into larger communities and a concurrent increase in dwelling size, with dwellings now being arranged according to a village plan, close together and parallel to each other. Horticulture provided most of the food for these increasing population concentrations, although fishing and hunting camps continued to be associated with villages (Trigger 1986:91–2).

The trend towards population concentrations was the result, not of a sudden natural increase in population, but of the coalescence of previously separate groups, due, most probably, to the increased incident of warfare (Ramsden 1978:101–5). Underscoring this conclusion are the observations that dwellings were more sturdily built, and often surrounded by more elaborately constructed palisades, indicating both that villages were inhabited for longer periods of time and that defence was an important consideration. The discovery of bone fragments in refuse dumps attests to the fact that cannibalism was added to the repertoire of warfare practices during this period (Wright 1966; 1967).

New burial customs appeared centred around the Feast of the Dead, in which the remains of all who had died during the tenure of a village were dug up and reinterred in a common pit. New forms of pottery also were developed, and vessels were apparently made especially for boiling corn soups. Smoking pipes became more elaborate in style, possibly indicating the development of more 'formal political deliberations' in which pipe smoking became part of a ritual of decision-taking (Trigger 1986:95).

The push towards consolidation of populations into larger and larger villages for defence, however, seems to have been balanced by countervailing factors having, in part, to do with the administration of larger populations, particularly with an apparent lack of suitable mechanisms for dispute settlement. It appears that villages did not exceed 1,500–2,000 inhabitants. After this point fractionalizing disputes were settled through fission of the village (ibid.:101). Another important factor, however, in limiting village size was the rapidity with which local resources were used up by large populations. Larger populations exhausted soil and sources of firewood more quickly than did smaller ones. Moreover, the larger the population the farther individuals had to travel to reach cultivated fields and wood supplies. Because of this large villages were compelled to move more frequently than small ones (Trigger 1976, 1:158)

Prior to their direct contact with the French the people who became known historically as the Huron and who were living in northern Simcoe County traded for various luxury and subsistence goods with the Algonkian peoples, especially the Nipissings and Petite Nation bands (Biggar (ed.) 1922–36 I:164; Heidenreich 1971:227; Trigger 1986:160). Most likely, beginning in the sixteenth century, that trade also included a very small number of European-made items. After 1580 larger amounts of trade goods begin to appear in southern Ontario, including axes, knives and glass beads (Trigger 1986:152). It is quite possible that the proto-Huron confederacy moved into the Simcoe County region to be close to major trade routes with Europeans.

When the French explorer/adventurer Samuel de Champlain first met them in 1609, the Huron were far from being a 'stable' society, untouched by currents of change for many generations. Far-reaching changes had occurred, even within the life-time of the adult members of the society. Those changes included, most importantly, increased concentrations of population, increased frequency of warfare and the practice of prisoner torture and cannibalism, the appearance, most certainly of tribes, and most likely of a pan-tribal confederacy. As well, new forms of political organization must have been developed to deal with intra- and inter-tribal relations, and to co-ordinate day to day living, as well as defence and offence against common enemies. Finally, as the seventeenth century unfolded, involvement in the fur trade, directly with the French rather than through intermediaries, became more and more prevalent. Indeed, the Huron proper, as referred to in records left by Champlain, the Recollect lay brother Gabriel Sagard and the Jesuit missionaries, had only just emerged as an identifiable group on the eve of their contact with the Europeans.

KINSHIP AS SOCIAL RELATIONS OF PRODUCTION

Using the information left by seventeenth-century observers of the Huron we can construct a description of social, economic and political life during the period 1610 to 1649. Each member of Huron society was embedded in a series of ever-widening social relations which began with the domestic unit, extended outward to the confederacy and, finally, to foreign nations. We can distinguish six key organizational points at which the life of any one Huron intersected with that of other Huron: the domestic unit or household, the longhouse, the clan, the village, the tribe and, finally, the confederacy. At each of these points the individual's life space came into contact, in an organized and regularized way, with those of others. At each point of intersection individual Hurons oriented themselves towards others in terms of differing sets (depending on the nature of the inter-relation) of rights and obligations based on one or another form of kin alliance.

We can visualize these relations as a series of ever-widening and more extensively connected networks, contained one within the other, and moving from the smallest number of ties, the domestic unit, to the largest, the confederacy. An individual was born into a domestic unit, and immediately connected, through birth, to a matrilineally reckoned descent group. Marriage, adoption, trading partnerships and even special ties of friendship brought linkages to other longhouses, clans, tribes and even to other nations.

On a day to day basis the most significant social unit appears to have been the longhouse, composed of three to six matrilineally related households or domestic groups. Each longhouse served as the most basic unit of both production of food staples and their consumption; contemporary observers noted that members of the same longhouse stored food in common. Residence patterns within the longhouses were usually matrilocal, and descent was reckoned through one's mother. A married man would most likely reside with his wife's kin, although there were exceptions to this practice, especially if the man was a clan leader. Children received their clan membership through their mother and not through their father who remained tied all his life to his own clan.

It is probable that the Huron had eight matrilineal clans;[6] turtle, bear, deer, beaver, wolf, sturgeon or loon, hawk and the fox (Steckley 1982:32; Thwaites 1896–1901, 33:243, 247; 38:283, 287). These clans may have been divided into three phratries – the bear, the turtle and the wolf – with the bear phratry containing the bear and deer clans, the turtle phratry containing the turtle and beaver clans and the wolf phratry containing the wolf, hawk, sturgeon or loon, and fox clans.[7] Members of each clan were found in most Huron villages. Clan leaders, organized on a village basis into councils, were assigned the role of managing public affairs and of administering public policy. Moreover, each village had both 'civil' and 'war' leaders who served to co-ordinate all the clan representatives on the village council in their area of jurisdiction. Although the clan leaders were male, they were appointed by the matrons of their clan. They held their positions as long as their clan members felt they were adequately fulfilling their duties.

Regardless of the aspect of Huron life we look at, then, we find some form of kinship organization. But if we take a closer look at those kinship relations we can immediately perceive another more basic social division, the division into male kin and female kin. The world of the seventeenth-century Huron was divided into male lives and female lives, and dominated by kinship and political structures which co-ordinated all social relations. Moreover, it was characterized by a large degree of autonomy at all levels of social organization; between the sexes, among kin and among the political allies that made up the villages, 'tribes' and the 'confederacy'.

Most anthropologists who study pre-capitalist societies recognize the importance of kinship relations in structuring and co-ordinating social life. Many make a point of noting that the social division of labour between men and women is a fundamental aspect in the organization of kin relations. Different authors, however, emphasize different aspects of kinship in constructing their analyses of relations between men and women in such societies. Some point to purely demographic considerations, arguing that women's subordination to men is a result of the existence of rules of exogamy, which in turn are necessary for the existence of culture and society. Others point to the productive process and to the relations that women bear both to the means of production and to the product of their labour, organized through kin relations, to demonstrate the basis of the relative statuses of men and women. Still others add the issue of property-holding and residence patterns to round out the picture of relations of production and distribution.

The significance of kinship structures in so-called 'primitive' societies has been stressed at least since the beginning of anthropology's appearance as a social science. Lewis Henri Morgan (1871; 1975) made some of the first observations of the Iroquoian system, and the study of kinship structures soon became an essential part of American and British anthropology. The interest in kinship – both with mapping kinship structures, and with constructing explanations of the meaning of the structures – has continued into the present.

The concern of earlier anthropologists who studied kinship was to establish a universally applicable and unilinear account of human history. For nineteenth-century theorists, kinship relations were understood in terms of the regulation of human sexual relations, and changes in those regulations in turn marked the passage from one level of social development to another.[8] As the search for evolutionary stages in human development was abandoned, many anthropologists began to argue that establishing genealogies was a less important task than establishing the concrete reality of who lived and worked with whom.[9]

Later, certain anthropologists developed an operational view that placed kinship in the context of political economy. Kinship was understood as a 'way of committing social labour to the transformation of nature through appeals to filiation and marriage and to consanguinity and affinity' (Wolf 1982:89). Employing Marx's concept of modes of production and social relations of production, these scholars discovered that kinship, in certain societies, functioned as social relations of production. Kinship provided the criteria and the structures on which people's productive lives were arranged. Not only was kinship a means of organizing the physical reproduction of new members of society, it was also a means of organizing adults into units of production and consumption. The capacity for social labour, in Eric Wolf's terms, was 'locked-up or embedded' in specific kin relations between people. Such labour capacity could be released only through symbolically defined access to kin.

Even though they focused on kinship as social relations of production, many anthropologists continued to see women as passive, or at best unwilling pawns in the life and death struggle waged by men to make sure that the society produces enough workers to survive. Claude Lévi-Strauss (1969), Maurice Godelier (1981) and Claude Meillassoux (1981), for example, have all concluded that women's reproductive role consigns them to a subordinated status, in which they are controlled and dominated by men.

It was the feminist scholars of the 1970s and 1980s who radically altered the focus of anthropology and, more specifically, the way in which women had been studied. As part of a more general trend in western scholarship, American and British feminist anthropologists began the task of reassessing the role of women in non-capitalist societies. Draper (1975), Leacock (1978; 1980), Reiter (ed.) (1975), Rogers (1975; 1978), Rosaldo (1980), Rosaldo and Lamphere (1974), Sacks (1975; 1976), Sanday (1973; 1974; 1981), and many more made women worthy and important parts of their analyses of pre-capitalist society. Some of these researchers discovered that in pre-capitalist societies women and men frequently occupied egalitarian positions of status, worth and ability.

Among the Huron, kin ties served as the basis on which all social relations were established, ordered and given their content and their signification. Kinship ties provided the structures through which relations between the two sexes were regulated. They provided the sets of relations through which production of the material means of subsistence was undertaken, and by which it was distributed and consumed. Finally, they acted as a framework through which almost all relations within units of residence, and between household group-ings were regulated. Kinship, social relations of production, family and sexuality as well as political life in Huron society were barely separated at all.

To look at kin relations (however they were constructed) means to look at the entire set of social relations in the society and, thus, to look at the field in which power relations operated. To look at kin relations means to consider what constitutes the social body itself. Kinship relations, as relations of parentage formed the basis – the shell – through which kinship as a set of social rights and obligations operated. But as a shell, or structure, kinship based on parentage remains devoid of any meaning unless the potential ties that it pro-vides are imbued with specific social content – with sets of rights and obligations, with shared understandings, and with what passes for knowledge – all of which tie individuals together into operating units. For the Huron the sets of rights and obligations, understandings and knowledge that activated the kinship structures did so in ways that both divided and united men and women. It divided men and women into two mutually exclusive groups whose productive and emotional lives differed significantly. It united them into family units, long-houses and clans and gave them a basis on which to anchor their political relations with 'non-kin'. It regulated their access to spouses, to the labour and the products of the labour of others, to social support in sickness and in need as well as to membership in resi-dential units, and political collectivities.

In analysing social relations within a society such as that of the seventeenth-century Huron, the concepts of mode of production and social relations of production are useful to the extent that they draw attention to a series of social practices out of which the everyday lives of all men and women were fashioned. These concepts are used here to indicate historically-specific constructs within Huron society through which flowed certain knowledge, truths, and forms of power – including knowledge and truth about men and women, and forms of power that acted on each gender differently, but that pro-duced, as a consequence, a single social body.

110

LONGHOUSE, HOUSEHOLD AND KINSHIP

Among the Huron, the largest unit of day to day life, which subsumed familial, economic and political institutions and relations, was the village. Each Huron village was essentially a collection of longhouses, often surrounded by a palisade. Around the village were cleared fields in which Huron women planted and tended crops during the spring and summer months. Although the village was the maximal unit of organization affecting subsistence production it was within longhouses and the natal and conjugal families (referred to here as 'households') that most activities were organized. On a day to day basis the longhouse and its 'household' components formed the units of production and consumption and served as a unit of residence.

Huron longhouses varied in length between 30 and 180 feet and in width between 25 to 30 feet. They contained a varying number of medial fireplaces, each one serving two families. Depending on its size, a single longhouse could contain anywhere up to twenty-four separate 'households' around twelve medial fireplaces. The size of any given longhouse and the actual number of people it sheltered therefore fluctuated widely. If we can speak of anything approaching an 'average' size and household composition for a longhouse of the period between 1615–1648, it would be about 80 feet long and contain three medial fireplaces, or about six families or households. About 45 per cent of the interior space of the longhouse would have been taken up by storage space while another 5 per cent would have been devoted to fireplaces (Heidenreich 1971:23). The Recollect lay brother Gabriel Sagard recorded this impression of the interior of a Huron longhouse in 1624:

> In one lodge there are many fires, and at each fire are two families, one on one side, the other on the other; some lodges will give as many as eight, ten or twelve fires, which means twenty-four families. Others fewer, according as they are long or short. There is smoke in them in good earnest, which causes many to have very serious trouble with their eyes, as there is neither window nor opening except the one in the roof of the lodge through which the smoke escapes. At each end there is a porch and the principal use of these porches is to hold the large vats or casks of tree-bark in which they store their indian corn after it has been well dried and shelled. In the midst of the lodge are suspended two big poles which they call *quaronta*; on them

111

they hang their pots and put their clothing, provisions, and other things, for fear of mice and to keep them dry. But the fish, of which they lay in a supply for winter after it is smoked, they store in casks of tree-bark which they call *acha*, except *leincha-taon*, which is a fish they do not clean and which they hang with cords in the roof of the lodge, because if it were packed in any cask it would smell too bad and become rotten at once.

(Wrong (ed.) 1939: 194–5)

Here is how the Jesuit Paul Le Jeune saw them:

If you go to visit them in their cabins... you will find there a miniature picture of Hell, seeing nothing, ordinarily, but fire and smoke, and on every side naked bodies, black and half roasted, mingled pell-mell with the dogs, which are held as dear as the children of the house, and share the beds, plates, and food of their masters. Everything is in a cloud of dust, and, if you go within, you will not reach the end of the cabin before you are completely befouled with soot, filth, and dirt.

(Thwaites 1896–1901, 17:13–15)

Together, the resident members of each of these longhouses formed a unit of production and consumption, sharing both labour tasks and the product of their labour in the two major subsistence activities, agriculture and fishing. Hunted food circulated on a wider basis, most often according to clan rather than household membership, while goods for personal use produced by individuals were exchanged on a more intimate basis or were acquired through trade with foreigners. Trade goods usually circulated through a series of elaborate exchange rituals, often between members of the same clan.

Agricultural products and fish provided the staples of the Huron diet. Access to agricultural land was open to anyone and the continued use of a particular field constituted the right of possession. Sagard observed that:

It is their custom for every family to live as they need for all the forests, meadows and uncleared land are common property, and anyone is allowed to clear and sow as much as he [*sic*] will and can, and according to his [*sic*] needs: and this cleared land remains in his [*sic*] possession for as many years as he [*sic*] continues to cultivate and make use of it.

(Wrong (ed.) 1939:103)

Most of the tasks involved in growing, maintaining and harvesting crops, such as weeding, and keeping growing crops free of birds, rodents and other pests, were undertaken, on a day to day basis, by single household units, usually consisting of a woman and her children (biological or classificatory). Other tasks, especially those requiring intensive labour inputs over a short period of time, required workers drawn from and organized on a much wider basis. Chores such as land clearing, planting and harvesting were likely to be accomplished by age and sex specific work teams composed of longhouse members. Each household within any given longhouse contributed their share to the common larder, although daily cooking was usually carried out on a per family basis.

Like corn and other agricultural products, fish provided another foodstuff that was stored and used in common by each longhouse. Access to fishing grounds, like access to agricultural land, was open to all. Fishing was most likely done by only some of the members of each longhouse, and the men, women and children who participated each contributed their own specialized labour to the activity. Most of the fish taken was stored in common for use by all longhouse members, although small portions were probably given by the married men to their mothers' households, by way of discharging obligations. Unlike fish and corn, however, hunted meat was not daily fare and was procured and distributed differently from other staples. Men owed a part of the game they hunted to their wives and children (Lafitau 1839:141). They also owed a part to the members of their own natal families, especially to their mothers and sisters. In the case of communal hunts organized on the village level, as sometimes took place, large feasts were given by each clan, as a means of redistribution of meat among its members.

MAKING A HOUSEHOLD: MARRIAGE AND DIVORCE

The Jesuits were impressed (unfavourably) with the ease at which Huron men and women married and divorced. The matrilineal, and matrifocal, nature of their kin relations, and the implications this had for the organization of work teams and the distribution of the products of labour certainly facilitated the ease with which marriage partners were changed. While both men and women were necessary to make up any given economic unit, as they contributed different kinds of labour, the kinship structure gave the two sexes access to the labour of members of the opposite sex on more than one basis. Women, for example, were not dependent on their husbands for hunted foods, or for a share of trade goods. Those goods came to them through exchange networks that they had access to on the basis of their clan membership. Men, on the other hand, relied more on their wives, given that the majority of them went to live in their wives' mothers' longhouses, and thus were dependent, on a day to day basis, on foodstuffs produced by women who were not members of their own clan. Men, though, usually had the option of returning to their mothers' or sisters' longhouses and of gaining access to agricultural foodstuffs there. Huron marriages, therefore, often appear to have been temporary arrangements. Moreover, at least until they had their first child, most Huron did not form recognized unions, but lived together, in sort of trial 'marriages'.

Although information on the exact ages at which Huron men and women married, and the age differences between spouses is not available from the historical record it is most likely that men married later than did women. Seventeenth- and eighteenth-century observers make it clear that there were more women available for marriage than there were partners for them, a good indication of age differences between men and women in marriage. One of the consequences of men being significantly older than their wives at marriage, especially in a society where neither female infanticide nor polygyny was practiced, is that there is usually a greater supply of women available for marriage than there is men.

Lafitau (1724), who studied the early eighteenth- century Iroquois, concluded that women married at a younger age than did men. The reason for this difference, he speculated, was because 'women sustain the families' and therefore had an interest in obtaining a husband as soon as possible. Once married a woman gained rights to the product of her husband's hunt; in Lafitau's view she thereby also gained a new means of support. Young men, on the other hand, 'showed no haste to get married'. Married men, Lafitau reasoned, incurred extra responsibilities towards a wife and children, responsibilities which they tried to avoid as long as possible (Lafitau 1724:340).

Of those who observed the Huron directly the Recollect lay brother Gabriel Sagard had the most to say about sex and marriage. Sagard commented that the Huron began sexual relations 'as soon as they are capable of doing so' but that they did not immediately marry. Sagard's observation that greater numbers of women were available for marriage than men, replicates the one made by Lafitau for the Iroquois. Prior to marriage, according to Sagard, young Huron men and women set up households together, although not necessarily with their future spouses. In these relations the women were called *Asqua*, i.e., companion as opposed to *Atenoha* or wife. The *Asqua's* role in these relations, according to Sagard, was to supply firewood and to do the cooking tasks that she would later have as a wife. During this period either member of the couple was free to have sexual relations with another person 'without fear of reproach or blame' (Wrong (ed.) 1939:122). Commenting on this practice, Sagard observed that 'without this liberty of seeking male friends I believe that many girls would remain virgins and unmarried, the number of them being greater than that of the men.' (ibid.:122).

While any young man could have an *Asqua*, it was not until he had proven himself 'bold in hunting, war and fishing' that he was considered fit to have a wife and children. According to Sagard, there were two steps to formalizing a Huron marriage. In the first, presents were given to a prospective wife. If she accepted the gift, the couple became lovers. After a period of time a second ceremony, a wedding feast, took place on the condition that both members of the couple, and their parents, agreed to the match. If anyone objected the feast was not given, and the relationship dissolved.

One point on which the historical record is quite clear is divorce. All contemporary observers agree that divorce was a relatively simple matter for the Huron. Prior to having children a couple could separate freely and easily. This action could be initiated by either husband or wife and little was done by others to prevent it or to bring about a reconciliation. After the couple had children, however, divorce was a more serious matter and was only undertaken for some important reason (Wrong (ed.) 1939:124).

WOMEN'S AUTHORITY

A Huron longhouse most likely consisted of what Kathleen Gough has called a 'matrilocal grand family'.[10] Longhouse membership would have centred around classificatory sisters, their husbands and their married daughters and their married daughters' husbands. Each classificatory sister would head her own household which might contain not only a husband and unmarried children, but also aged and/or widowed parents, widowed and/or unmarried siblings and, possibly, the children of a deceased sister (either biological or classificatory). Additional 'households' may have been composed of the sexually active but as yet unmarried daughters of these women, living in companionate relations with men. It is possible, in the case where the household had produced an important clan leader, that a married son, his wife and children would also reside in the longhouse, producing what Gough has called a matrilocal extended kinship unit with a sororilocal resident male head (Gough 1961:497). Most unmarried and married women resident in the same longhouse would have been members not only of the same clan, but also of the same lineage, while most of the married men would have belonged to different clans than did the women.

These residence arrangements, combined with the fact that most men were absent during the summer months, and that women who were kin worked together during the summer to produce most of the food stocks for the entire longhouse, helped to support the powerful place women held within Huron society. Moreover, women's ability to direct the dynamics within the longhouse, or at least to manage those dynamics to produce outcomes which were satisfactory to them, had far-reaching implications. Nowhere is this better illustrated than in the Jesuits' discussion of the fate of certain 'poor Christian' men, who incurred the anger of their mothers-in-law and who were on the verge of being expelled from their place of residence.

The freedom that all Huron, but especially women exercised in expressing and acting on their personal convictions was troublesome for the Jesuits. This was particularly true when women successfully interfered in the conversion of certain men to Christianity. Traditionally Huron and Montagnais women and men approached marriage not as a contract of subjugation of a wife to a husband but as a working relationship in which both partners had the right to expect satisfaction. In the early years of the Jesuits' mission to the Huron and Montagnais it was not usually a question of a newly converted man making his wife obey him but of whether or not the convert's family (usually his wife and mother-in-law) would be able to force him to renounce his conversion and resume his traditional roles. Even when clan leaders converted, their wives and children often refused to follow their example, fearing that baptism would cause them to die, or bring on calamities (Thwaites 1896–1901, 17:97).

The conviction that baptism caused misfortune and even immediate death continued to be a major theme in the resistance of Huron and Montagnais women to conversion and a major force that they used to try to get their husbands to abandon the 'Faith'. Writing about one Christianized Huron man who had been pressured to renounce his Christianity by his wife after the death of several of his children but who had later found the strength to resume his faith, Le Jeune implores: 'God grant that his wife be not again an Eve to him; for this unhappy woman is not brought down to her duty' (ibid. 19:245).

Far from being able to bring their wives and other female relatives 'down to their duty' Huron men who had converted to Christianity in the earlier years of the Jesuits' missions were susceptible to being strongly influenced by their wives, and (more significantly) by their mothers-in-law. Because a married man usually lived in his wife's mother's longhouse, his presence was often not completely secure and he ran the risk of expulsion if he continually offended the matrons of that longhouse.[11] Many Huron matrons considered conversion to Christianity to be unconscionable behaviour, and relied on ostracism to force recalcitrant men to behave in what they considered to be a more socially responsible fashion (ibid. 13:245).

A man's conversion to Catholicism often brought the severest kind of rejection, not only by members of his wife's longhouse but, even more disastrously for him, by his own clan members as well. A Jesuit missionary, for example, reported on the 'plight' of a 'poor Man, the only Christian in all his Family' who refused to renounce his faith in spite of all efforts to make him comply. Not only was he 'driven' from his wife's longhouse, but he was even refused admittance to the longhouses of members of his own clan.

> They drove him away from their Cabins, and refused to give him anything to eat; they reproached him with the death of one of his nieces, who had been baptized. He was left without means of support, and was compelled to do what is usually the work of Women. He was mocked at, and spurned from every Company; and quarrels were picked with him. If at any time he was invited to a feast, some insolent persons present would call out that he should not have been invited, because he was a Christian, and because he brought misfortune wherever he went; that he might certainly make up his mind to die sooner than he expected; and that he would be clubbed to death as a Sorcerer.
>
> (ibid. 23:67)

Or, take the case of the good 'Christian man' who was about to be abandoned by his wife and children 'in consequence of the persecutions of his mother-in-law, who could not bear to have him in her house when she found that he was a Christian' (ibid. 23:127). The man and his wife had lived together for fifteen or sixteen years and had five children. They had both been baptized and had promised never to separate. Yet, at the insistence of her mother, or so this convert told the Jesuit, his wife intended to leave him.

> Now she has abandoned the Faith, or at least, to please her mother, she no longer has the courage to profess it. She still loves me, and I also love her; and nevertheless her mother compels her to leave me, if I do not abandon the Faith.
>
> (ibid. 23:127)

Men who had converted to Christianity and whose wives refused to follow their example earned the Jesuits' sympathy. Being saddled with 'ill humored', 'jeering' or 'scornful' wives was hardly a just match for the 'courage', 'firmness' and 'gentleness' of the soul of a Christian man (ibid. 22:77). Even as late as 1645, in spite of the Jesuits' best efforts, the majority of women could hardly be described as 'lambs', willing to live 'in utmost obedience' with their husbands.

The Jesuits who wrote at length about these traditionalist women called them 'shrews' and 'Hellish Megeras', as in the case of the mother-in-law of the 'good Christian', described above. This man's 12- or 13-year-old son had also embraced Christianity, and the Jesuit observer reports that he faced his grandmother's ire:

> Everything that could be done was tried, to make him desist from the Faith. They endeavored to corrupt him by kindness, by threats, and by such rigorous measures as were within their power. At last, when he saw himself tormented by his grand-mother, who allowed him no rest by night or by day, hoping to prevail upon him to give up the Christian practices as his mother had done, the child said to this Hellish Megera: 'Know that they may burn me alive, – here are my arms, my feet, and my body, all ready to suffer it; but never will I abandon the faith.
>
> (ibid. 23:69)

Even clan leaders could not compel obedience, nor were they immune from the wrath of their female relatives when they made unfavourable decisions. In one village the Jesuits had some success in converting four of the village clan leaders, but their wives and children refused to follow their example, fearing that 'baptism causes death'. In yet another case, a clan leader who had converted to

Christianity, and had subsequently renounced his position and all the duties that it entailed suddenly found:

> [h]is mother, his wife, his relatives, all his village leagued against him; but nothing of all this has shaken him. 'Poverty', he said to us, 'will not frighten me. God shall take the place of my relatives and of my mother, and he alone shall be my support. Let my wife leave me and deprive me of my children.... My heart is prepared for everything.'
>
> (ibid. 26:271)

Women's power, then, derived in large part from the actual structure of kin relations and residence patterns. In a society where residence patterns are matrilocal, where women work together with their female kin to produce a major part of subsistence goods, and where women have a certain degree of control over the distribution of necessary foodstuffs, men do not control domestic space. Moreover, that domestic space intrudes into, is connected with, has influence over, all other aspects of an individual's life. To be expelled from a longhouse carried with it a certain degree of difficulty for men. It meant returning home to a biological or classificatory mother or sister if she could be persuaded to take him back in.

Although a very young woman might have been in a less secure position than an older woman, who was in charge of her own longhouse, women as a whole wielded a great deal of power. That power, moreover, extended well beyond the longhouse. A further indication of the respect given to women was that they were considered as capable as men of occupying prestigious positions as healers and foreseers of the future. Up until their mass conversion both Huron men and women equally practised curing, as well as what the Jesuits labelled the 'supernatural arts'. The Huron recognized three sources of illness, each with an associated type of cure. Illness with natural causes were subjected to 'natural' remedies. Illnesses caused by 'desires of the soul' – which were revealed in dreams – were cured by meeting those desires in real life. Finally, illnesses caused by witchcraft were cured by counteracting and neutralizing the sorcerer's spell (Thwaites 1896–1901, 33:191–7; 17:155–215; Tooker 1964:83). Women and men equally gained reputations as healers, performing in aid of the sick certain songs, dances and rituals which they obtained through personal visions. Pregnant women were especially valued in certain types of healing rites. Arrow wounds, for example, were reputed to heal only if the arrow was withdrawn in their presence (Thwaites 1896–1901, 17:213).

Not only were men and women of equal value as healers, they also received the same quality of attention during illness. When sick, both women and men had curing ceremonies performed for their recovery. If the individual was important the ceremonies became elaborate affairs in which the entire village participated (ibid. 17:165–87; 23:45). In one case, the Jesuit missionary reported that no less than three village leaders tried to persuade the Jesuits living in their village to participate in the curing ceremony for a sick woman (ibid. 23:45). In another instance, during a curing ceremony for a young girl who had fallen ill, all the women of a village danced while the men 'struck violently against pieces of bark'. Some women then took live embers in their hands and passed them over the girl's stomach (ibid. 13:189).

Certain Huron occupied more important positions in society and were highly valued as shamans. In 1636 Le Jeune reported on one incident in which three male shamans[12] had attempted to summon a 'manitou' in order to help heal a sick woman. When they failed a powerful woman shaman entered their tent and 'began to shake the house and to sing and cry so loudly that she caused the devil to come who told them more than they wanted' (Thwaites 1896–1901, 9:113). Le Jeune found this woman particularly galling because she made a habit of travelling from village to village, trying to incite the Huron to think only about going to war. When one of the Jesuit missionaries tried to take her to task for her 'maliciousness', she drew a knife and threatened to kill him (ibid. 9:117).

Both Gabriel Sagard and Samuel de Champlain noted that women, much more than men, had curing ceremonies performed for them as a result of their adverse dreams (Wrong (ed.) 1939:75; Tooker 1964:91). There are many indications, too, that women participated regularly in curing ceremonies for others. At times these ceremonies required that women and men dance naked together (Thwaites 1896–1901, 17:81; Wrong (ed.) 1939:147). Women, especially older ones, often took central roles during these curing dances, receiving presents on behalf of the afflicted person, and leading that person in the dancing (Biggar (ed.) 1922–36, III:148–50; Tooker 1964:107).

Women, too, acted as predictors of the future, using such methods as pyromancy. Paul Le Jeune mentions one 'old woman, a sorceress or female soothsayer' who predicted that certain men of her village who had gone to war would return with prisoners. She made this prediction using a number of fires to represent the Huron warriors and their enemies (Thwaites 1896–1901, 8:125).

Indications of the relative worth of men and women to the Huron themselves can be taken from information concerning compensation paid to the families of murder victims. While few Huron were ever murdered by other Huron, when this happened it was customary that the relatives of the murderer compensate the relatives of the victim through gift giving. In the case of reparation for murder, according to one Jesuit's report, 'women are considered more valuable than men', commanding forty as opposed to thirty presents because 'they cannot so easily defend themselves' and because they 'people the country so their lives are more valuable to the public' (Thwaites 1896–1901, 39:283). The birth of a daughter, too, was apparently more desired than that of a son for similar reasons. As the Jesuit François Du Peron wrote to his brother: 'they rejoice more in the birth of a daughter than of a son, for the sake of the multiplication of the country's inhabitants' (ibid. 15:181–3).

POLITICS AND POWER

So far we have seen that Huron women were able to maintain relatively egalitarian positions within society, and to exercise a certain degree of authority within the longhouses, managing to influence the behaviour of their male kin. But did that authority extend beyond the longhouse, that is beyond the so-called domestic or private sphere, and into public life?

At the village level, the existence of 'localized clan segments' was of central importance for the organization of relations between the members of different longhouses (Heidenreich 1971:78). Clan membership played a central role in organizing village and tribal political life, and political representation at the village and tribal levels was on the basis of clan membership. At the village level of organization, the members of each clan segment – made up of all those who were resident in the village and who traced their descent from a common female ancestor – were represented on civil and war councils by two different clan leaders. While small villages may have been made up of only a few clan segments, according to Jesuit observers each large village had 'several captains both of administration and of war who divided among them the families of the village into so many captaincies' (Thwaites 1896–1901, 10:213; 15:43). Councils were held almost daily and on almost all matters. In council, civil leaders were assigned the role of managing public affairs and administering public policy. These leaders were responsible for dealing with those aspects of social and political life that affected people outside of the longhouse, including public feasts, ceremonies, games and projects, as well as the care of strangers and orphans. The role of a civil chief was to 'exhort' the members of the village, or more likely, of the clan that each represented, to carry out the decisions made in council meetings.

The Jesuit Bressani described what he called 'the government of the Canadian Barbarians' in the following way:

> These peoples have neither King nor absolute Prince, but certain chiefs, like the heads of a Republic, whom we call Captains, – different, however, from those in war. These hold office commonly by succession on the side of the women, sometimes by election. They assume office at the death of a predecessor (who, they say, is resuscitated in them). This is celebrated with certain ceremonies. These Captains have not *vim coactivam*, which even the Fathers do not exercise over their sons in order to correct them, as they use words alone; and, thus brought up, the more the sons increase in age, the more they love and respect their fathers. Therefore both the former and the latter obtain everything *precario* by eloquence, exhortation, and entreaties.
>
> (ibid. 39:265)

Occasionally there were 'captains to whom matters of government were referred to on account of their popularity, intellectual superiority, or wealth and other qualities which rendered them influential' (ibid. 17:265; 10:231). The Jesuits tell us that those Huron who were accorded 'first rank' held that position by virtue of their intellectual pre-eminence, courage and wise conduct, and not by election (ibid. 10:231). Father du Peron, for example, wrote that 'they have no government at all; such power as the captains have is little more than that of criers and trumpets; they make their announcements in loud voices in the public places' (ibid. 15:157).

It would appear that Huron clan leaders had little ability to control the behaviour of either women or men who chose to disobey or to not follow the decisions that had been taken in council. The election of a clan leader, however, was always an occasion of great ceremony because the election was, in fact, a type of resurrection or resuscitation of the deceased who had previously occupied that position. In the ceremony creating a new clan leader, the incumbent took over the name and responsibilities of his immediate predecessor (ibid. 23:167).

Leadership of a clan segment was gained partly through succession and partly through the election of a new leader, chosen from among the nephews and grandsons of the former leader (ibid. 10:231). Jesuit missionaries reported that 'children only get the position if they are suited to it and accept it and are accepted by the whole country' (ibid. 10:231). The leadership of a clan segment seemed to the Jesuits to have been more of an honorific position than one of power. According to one observer, the positions were 'servitudes more than anything else'. Clan segment chiefs were responsible for attending tribal assemblies in both winter and summer, which often took place in other villages. Sometimes they had to travel great distances to reach these councils. It was the clan leader's duty to make decisions public. Yet at the same time they exercised 'small authority' over their clan's members. Thus, clan leaders were unable to govern by command or to use absolute power, and had 'no force at hand to compel their people to their duty' (ibid. 10:233). They merely made known what was decided on in council as being for the good of the village or the country. 'That settled', wrote Le Jeune, 'he who will takes action'.

The Jesuits only mention of women's role in political life of the Huron was to note that the clans were matrilineal. Information on the Iroquois, who had the same social, economic and political structures, points to the important role that women played in political life. While women never held public office among the Iroquois they did exercise considerable influence over public policy through their ability to appoint and depose matrilineage leaders (Lafitau 1839:84–5). The power of Huron matrons to depose unpopular clan leaders is at least indirectly confirmed by the Jesuit reference to the problems that clan leaders faced when they converted to Christianity against the wishes of their families.

Although the immediate impression gained from the *Relations* concerning Huron political life is one of complete *laissez-faire* there is another side to consider – that of public or general opinion. If an individual persisted in a course of action that was contrary to deeply and widely held opinions, beliefs and practices, they were subjected to ridicule, ostracism or even killed outright, depending on the nature of their offences. In 1642–3, for example, when the French were busy trying to negotiate a peace with the elusive Iroquois, they attempted to persuade both their Algonkian and Huron allies to release some Iroquois captives to go and convince their fellow countrymen to make peace. Although the Algonkian complied with this request, accepting the presents offered by the French in exchange, the Huron refused. According to the Jesuit present at this meeting, the reason for their non-compliance given by the Huron was that they were warriors, and not traders, that their 'glory' did not come from bringing back presents, but prisoners. One of the Huron war chiefs was reputed to have offered the French this rationale:

> It is not through disobedience [to the Governor who made the request] that we act thus, but because we fear to lose both honor and life. Thou seest here but young men; the elders in our country govern its affairs. If we were to return to our country with presents, we would be taken for grasping traders, and not for warriors. We have given our word to the Captains of the Hurons that, if we succeeded in capturing any prisoners, we would deliver them into their hands. Just as those soldiers around thee obey thee, so must we perform our duty toward those who are over us. How could we endure the blame of a whole country when, knowing that we have taken prisoners, they would see only axes and kettles. [Our actions] will be condemned, and we shall be looked upon as persons without sense for having decided a matter of such consequence without consulting the elders of the country.
>
> (Thwaites 1896–1901, 26:63–7)

The question of power of the elders or captains of the villages, however, brings us full circle back to the complaints voiced by the Jesuits that, in fact, these clan leaders had little or no real authority. Although it was the older men who had control over the councils, anyone who wanted to be present had the right to attend and be heard (ibid. 10:213). Women could and did address public assemblies especially on matters considered to be of importance to the entire nation. Many Huron women did not want the Jesuits in Huronia and frequently expressed this opinion. The Ursuline nun, Marie de l'Incarnation, sent to Quebec by the Jesuits to educate Indian girls, was an ardent writer of letters. In a letter written in 1640 she remarked on the response of a Huron matron, 'one of the oldest and most important of that Nation' to the Jesuit presence in Huronia. According to the letter, the Huron matron had announced to a public assembly that:

> It is the black robes who make us die by their spells: listen to me and I'll give you incontrovertible proof. They arrive in a certain village where everyone is healthy. As soon as they are

established there, everyone dies, except for three or four people. Then they change places, and the same thing happens again. They have only to enter a cabin to bring sickness and death with them. Don't you see that when they move their lips, which they call praying, they are really casting spells. It's the same thing when they read their books. Moreover, they have big wood (fire arms) in their cabins and they use these to make noise and to send their magic everywhere. If we don't put them to death immediately, they will ruin the country and leave no one alive.

(Oury 1971:117–18) [my translation]

Marie de l'Incarnation added that 'when the woman stopped talking, everyone agreed that what she had said was true and that they would have to do something about the problem'. Women, it seems, numbered among the most vocal and adamant enemies of the Jesuits in Huronia and were not denied a public forum in which to express their opposition.

THEORIZING KINSHIP AND WOMEN'S STATUS

Some interesting propositions concerning egalitarian relations between the sexes in pre-capitalist societies, and focusing on kin groups, property-holding and residence patterns, have been made by Stephanie Coontz and Peta Henderson (1986a). Coontz and Henderson attribute the existence of such relations in pre-capitalist societies to the interplay of residence rules and systems of kin corporate property-holding. They begin their argument by distinguishing between 'corporate kin groups' and communal societies in terms of the way in which resources are accessed and used. In societies founded on corporate kin groups people live together and share because they are related. Strangers and visitors must make special arrangements if they are to either consume or produce in territory belonging to some corporate group. In communal societies, by contrast, 'people consider themselves related because they live together'. Here strangers and visitors have unquestioned access to resources and are equally expected to contribute labour (Coontz and Henderson 1986a:17). Moreover, in kinship corporate societies 'resources are assigned to distinct kin groups units, and kinship organizes the tasks and mutual obligations that can no longer be left to informal good will' (ibid.:118). Formalized, 'balanced' reciprocity in gift-giving replaces free exchange.

Coontz and Henderson enumerate six consequences of this kin corporate property-owning system for the potential of introducing hierarchical relations, especially between men and women. First, emphasis is placed on unilineal descent, and with this emphasis seniority becomes a relation of production, situating each individual with respect to others. Moreover, each individual worker no longer controls the product of their labour; that control is now in the hands of an intermediary – the head of a lineage (ibid.: 119).

Second, the sexual division of labour becomes codified. Under certain conditions the male sphere can come to dominate if it is expanded at the expense of the female sphere. Third, there is a new concern among each corporate kin group for their biological perpetuation. Group boundary maintenance becomes 'vital', as each local kin group must perpetuate itself in order to maintain its social existence. Coontz and Henderson, however, are careful to disassociate themselves from Meillassoux's arguments about demographic crisis and women's subordination. Patriarchy cannot be explained by the threat of extinction. Rather, 'in general the increased emphasis on descent and marriage were the result of a social rather than a demographic imperative, an imperative flowing from property relations and the kin corporation' (ibid.: 120).

Fourth, Coontz and Henderson claim that kin corporate property holding tends to increase the possibility of conflict between communities over resources or labour. Fifth, differential access to resources make marriage and adoption more elaborate processes. It also leads to more elaborate networks for exchange of people and food. Finally, there is a tendency to develop a formal standard of balanced reciprocity and exchange. This implies both the existence of discrete social units and at the same time reinforces their separate existence, even though it is designed to compensate for this (ibid.: 126).

Within these exigencies Coontz and Henderson find important differences between kin corporate societies based on matrilocal and patrilocal residence. Within matrilineal, matrilocal kin corporate societies women's social product is produced by a group of related women who live together. It is most likely therefore to be locally shared, and immediately consumed among members of a household or a local group (ibid.: 130). The product of a woman's husband's labour, on the other hand, has to be parcelled out to members of both his wife's kin corporate group and his own natal kin corporate group. Thus while the product of women's labour is shared locally, and with little elaborate redistribution ceremony involved, that of men is subjected to wider distribution networks and more ritual.

Coontz and Henderson conclude that 'this need for broader distribution of male products between his wife's household and his own provide less opportunity for the local matrilineage to concentrate male wealth, or for differentials to emerge among lineages in the amounts accumulated' (ibid.: 131). Matrilineal/matrilocal societies have different structural and ideological characteristics than do patrilineal ones. These differences stem from the interaction of marriage patterns, rules of residence and forms of property exchange. In matrilineal societies women do not come to dominate because, while they may control domestic affairs, they do not control external ones. On the other hand, men cannot dominate either. Of importance here is the fact that while an adult woman is entitled to a share in male produced goods, simply by being a member of a kin group, an adult man is entitled to goods produced by women, only by virtue of being married. In such societies, they point out, women need husbands far less than men need wives (ibid.:132).

The relatively egalitarian status of Huron men and women, it can be argued, was at least in part the outcome of a delicately balanced distribution of power between the two sexes and was based on a kinship system which distributed men and women both spatially and in terms of mutually held sets of rights and obligations in relation to each other. Women and men appeared to dominate decision-making processes in different, and apparently separate spheres: women in the longhouse, men in the political councils. Yet, as we have seen, in Huron society relations between the 'domestic' and the 'public' were fluid. Men's authority extended into the longhouse, through the decisions they made in council. Women's authority, based on their domestic location and kin relations within the longhouse, extended into political life. Women sometimes refused to comply with men's political decisions. They made political statements of their own, and they directed the election and impeachment of clan leaders.

The power of Huron women, however, did not only arise from their domestic arrangements. It also had a basis in public life – where women could comply with, or refuse to follow decisions made by men in council and where women could send authoritative messages to male councillors regarding what they saw as their interests. Once we stop thinking of power flows between the domestic and public spheres in terms of 'binary' relations, with one side dominating and the other being dominated, we can cease to see women's power as being tied to their role in the reproductive process, or to their role as domesticating nurturers of children and men. Institutions which organize production, the reproductive processes, political and other social relations are most usefully conceptualized as instances of social interaction, where strategies of power may act on and through the entire society. The result of such a way of thinking about relations between different bearers of power is a search not for binary structures of domination/submission (which too often result in a reference back to women's roles as bearers of children and men's roles as hunters and warriors) but for a 'multiform production' (Foucault 1979:55) of relations of domination and subordination.

7

'AMONG THESE TRIBES ARE FOUND POWERFUL WOMEN OF EXTRAORDINARY STATURE'

SUBSISTENCE, TECHNOLOGY AND THE SOCIAL DIVISION OF LABOUR

The activities of any adult Huron engaged in day to day work were structured by three interrelated factors: the material-technical aspects of production, kinship alliances and gender. Both material and technical aspects of each given labour process set limits to the types of organization necessary to carry out production. Kinship alliances, functioning as social relations of production, assigned individuals to units of production which carried out labour tasks, and to units of consumption. Finally, the social division of labour determined the particular types of tasks to be performed by the individual within the unit of production in conjunction with complementary tasks performed by members of the opposite sex. Of all the divisions between people within the productive process the most fundamental was the division between men and women. The relationship between the two sexes in the productive process was regulated by a series of rules, delineating rights and obligations, and based on kin relations.

The subsistence economy of the Huron was based on slash and burn horticulture, supplemented with fishing, and some hunting and gathering (Wrong (ed.) 1939:96–103). Other economic activities included gathering wild foods, collecting hemp to manufacture twine and armour, gathering firewood and domestic manufacture of clothing, mats, pottery and household articles. Corn, the major food staple, was eaten raw, roasted, as a bread or as a type of porridge called sagamite (Biggar (ed.) 1922–36 III:125; Wrong (ed.) 1939:80; Thwaites 1896–1901, *passim*). In addition to corn, beans, squash and pumpkins some sunflowers and tobacco were also cultivated. Gathered food accounted for a relatively small portion of the

Huron's caloric intake – about 5 per cent (Heidenreich 1971:160). Hunted meat was relatively unimportant in supplying daily caloric needs, especially after the Huron came to reside in Huronia, which was poor in large game.

This lack of meat was noted by most contemporary writers, who pointed out that at best game was usually only available during the late autumn and the spring (Wrong (ed.) 1939:107). The reports of contemporary observers are borne out by archaeological evidence: few animal bones are found in Huron middens dating from after European contact (Heidenreich 1971:161). Fish bone outnumbered all other classes of bone by at least 5:1, while domesticated dogs outnumbered all other mammal species by 10:1 at one historic site (Latta 1976:142). By the turn of the seventeenth century, it would appear, fish and dog had become increasingly important as sources of protein, replacing hunted meats.[1] Several contemporary writers indicate that small quantities of fish 'rank with internal rottenness' were added to the sagamite to give it flavour.[2]

Just as the range of economic activities available to the Huron was limited, so were the technical means of production. Tools of native manufacture, constructed from stone, twine, wood, bone and clay, and European trade goods of iron and copper made up the entire repertoire. Tools of Huron manufacture included stone hoes and wooden digging sticks, used mainly by women for agricultural work, flint arrow heads for hunting, hemp nets and wooden spears for fishing, bone needles, awls, sinews and guts for sewing, bark baskets and clay pots for storage and cooking, and stone axes and knives for chopping, cutting, scraping and clearing new land for cultivation. With the exception of guns, the European trade items used by the Huron were also simple. They included steel-edged iron axes, knives and hatchets used for forest clearing, wood chopping, hunting and food preparation, metal awls and needles for sewing, copper kettles for cooking and textiles for clothing. Often, the Huron transformed the metals they received from the European traders. Worn out kettles, for example, were reworked into arrow heads and cutting edges.

Together, these items formed the major part of the technical means of production available to the Huron. The use of any one of these means of production required no complicated social division of labour, and little co-operation between workers in order to put it to use. While the technical aspects of Huron subsistence economy required little or no social division of labour, the seasonal nature of their economic activities did require that tasks be divided. The fact that the Huron engaged in several different kinds of economic activities during the same season (e.g., hunting, fishing and agriculture during the summer months) provided a basis on which the division of labour could develop. Agricultural tasks, moreover, could be divided by the seasons, each task following another as the seasonal cycle progressed. Land clearing, for example, was followed by planting, which was followed in turn by weeding and then harvesting. The Huron assigned each of these tasks differentially to men and women: men did certain types of work to clear the land, women performed the rest of the agricultural labour. In cases where anything more than the simple labour of one individual was called for in order to bring some product into existence, the basic unit of co-operation, and of redistribution, remained the longhouse for most subsistence activities undertaken by the Huron.

GENDER AND THE SOCIAL DIVISION OF LABOUR

Contemporary writers marked a pronounced social division of labour based on gender among the Huron and noted that women occupied an important place in the economy, often doing more arduous work than the men. Champlain wrote that:

> Among these tribes are found powerful women of extraordinary stature; for it is they who have almost the whole care of the house and the work; for they till the soil, sow the Indian corn, fetch wood for the winter, strip the hemp, and spin it, and with the thread make fishing nets for catching fish, and other necessary things they have to do: likewise they have the labour of harvesting the corn, storing it, preparing food, and attending to the house, and besides are required to follow and accompany their husbands from place to place, in the fields, where they serve as mules to carry the baggage, with a thousand other kinds of duties and services that the women fulfil and are required to carry out. As to the men, they do nothing but hunt deer, and other animals, fish, build lodges and go on the war-path.
>
> (Biggar (ed.) 1922–36, III:136)

Champlain's comments are echoed by those of the Recollect lay brother Gabriel Sagard, who noted that women and girls did more work than men 'although they are not forced or compelled to do so':

> They have the care of the cooking and the household, of sowing and gathering corn, grinding flour, preparing hemp and

tree-bark and providing the necessary wood. And because there still remains plenty of time to waste, they employ it in gaming, going to dances and feasts, chatting and killing time, and doing just what they like with their leisure: this is no trifle since their whole household arrangements amount to but little, in view furthermore of the fact that among our Hurons they are not admitted to many of the men's feasts, nor to any of their councils nor allowed to put up lodges and make canoes.

(Wrong (ed.) 1939:102)

Women were responsible for processing and preparing grain for food, for cooking, making pottery, mats of reeds 'which they hang in the doors of their lodges', bowls for eating and drinking and 'the sashes, collars and bracelets that they and the men wear'. Of the men Sagard noted the following:

The occupations of the savages are fishing, hunting, and war; going off to trade, making lodges and canoes or contriving the proper tools for doing so. The rest of the time they pass in idleness, gambling, sleeping, singing, dancing, smoking or going to feasts, and they are reluctant to undertake any other work that forms part of the women's duty except under strong necessity.

(ibid.: 96)

During the winter men made nets, and snares for fishing with the twine twisted by women, went ice-fishing, made arrows out of copper trade kettles, wooden clubs for warfare and shields for armour as well as bow strings and snow shoes out of animal gut.

Agriculture

The subsistence activities of the Huron took place in nature and were regulated by the cycle of the seasons. For the residents of any Huron village, the cycle began in the early spring, when fields had to be prepared for planting the year's crops. Both men and women participated together in this task, organized in work teams based on longhouse residence. Here labour was undertaken on the basis of simple co-operation within work teams: men used axes to clear the fields while women gathered the brush together and burned it. Men also hunted deer in the spring months because it was the yarding season and large groups of the animals congregated together, making hunting an easier task. The task of replenishing wood supplies depleted during the winter months fell to the women, who had some free time because their attention was not yet taken up with planting and tending fields. In both cases either individuals or sex-specific co-operating groups, often drawn up on the basis of clan membership, performed the necessary labour.

During the summer months Huron villages were virtually abandoned. Men left during the early months for fishing, trading or warring. Some set out in small raiding parties against the Iroquois. Others went to trade with the French on the St Lawrence River or with native groups in the interior. The rest remained near the village to protect the women against Iroquois raiders and to go fishing. Women and children left the village to work in the fields, beginning in the late spring, taking up residence in small cabins near their fields. They remained there from late May to August, planting the crops in May, and then hoeing, weeding and keeping animals and birds out of the fields during the growing season. Children often helped with this work and with gathering berries and fruit. Late in the season women also gathered hemp. Near the end of August they harvested, dried and stored their corn in bins especially designed for that purpose. Male relatives began returning from raiding and trading expeditions, to leave again for hunting and fishing. Some women, now freed from agricultural work, accompanied their male relatives to clean and prepare whatever fish and game was taken.

In the winter, men from each village would occasionally go ice fishing, or hunting. Winter, however, was the most important time of socializing and many feasts were given, especially after hunting expeditions returned. Both men and women had some time free during the winter months to engage in domestic industry. Women wove mats, made pottery, spun twine and did decorative arts. Men made nets and snares and manufactured implements for war, hunting fishing and agriculture. Finally, the lives of village members were also structured by a less frequent cycle of events. Every eight to twelve years, when agricultural land and firewood sources were depleted, the entire village would be relocated, and the event marked by the great 'Feast of the Dead'.

Of all the subsistence activities undertaken by the Huron, horticulture was both the most important, in terms of the caloric input it provided, and the best documented in the historical record. Corn, combined with beans and squash, provided over 65 per cent of the

Huron's dietary needs. While men did a certain amount of work clearing the fields it was the women of each village who were the major contributors to this subsistence activity. Contemporary descriptions of Huron horticultural practices are consistent with modern day descriptions of slash and burn horticulture. According to Sagard:

> Clearing is very troublesome for them, since they have no proper tools. They cut down the trees at the height of two or three feet from the ground, then they strip off all the branches, which they burn at the stump of the same trees in order to kill them and in the course of time they remove the roots. Then the women clean up the ground between the trees thoroughly, and at distances of a pace apart dig round holes or pits. In each of these they sow nine or ten grains of maize, which they have first picked out, sorted, and soaked in water for a few days, and so they keep on until they have sown enough to provide food for two or three years, either for fear that some bad season may visit them or else in order to trade it to other nations for furs and other things they need; and every year they sow their corn thus in the same holes and spots, which they freshen with their little wooden spade, shaped like an ear with a handle at the end. The rest of the land is not tilled but only cleansed of noxious weeds, so that it seems as if it were all paths, so careful are they to keep it quite clean.
>
> (Wrong (ed.) 1939:103–4)

The Huron practised a form of extensive, rather than intensive cultivation, in which a period of long fallow, rather than fertilization, plowing or irrigation, was used for soil regeneration (Bender 1975:13). This form of cultivation required large amounts of land per capita. Land was left fallow for longer than it was cultivated and new lands had to constantly be brought into cultivation to make up for declining fertility on already cultivated lands.

The introduction of steel-edged axes would certainly have had an effect on the rate at which Huron men could fell trees. In 1967 William Townsend conducted a study among the Heve of New Guinea to determine the effects of the introduction of steel axes. The Heve, who lived in large communal houses, engaged in horticulture, hunting, gathering, fishing, and raising pigs, had received steel axes only in 1950 (Townsend 1969:169–205). Comparing the rates at which trees could be felled using stone as opposed to steel axes,

Townsend found that it took a man using a stone axe approximately four times as long to fell a tree as it did a man using a steel one.

Within any given longhouse, any of the married women would have had access to the labour of men from three different categories of kin to help provide her with cleared land to cultivate. First and most important, she would have relied on the labour of her own husband, and, in addition, on that of her real or classificatory sisters' husbands. It was these men who formed the majority of adult males resident in any given longhouse. Second, she could rely on the labour of her own father, and of the husbands of any of her mother's sisters if they were still living and could work. Her unmarried sons, as well as those of her sisters, would have provided some labour, although most likely, being children, they would have only helped with the lighter chores such as weeding and chasing birds and animals out of the fields. If she had any married daughters (real or classificatory) she would have also had rights to the labour of those daughters' husbands. As long as a woman had living kin organized into a functioning longhouse, she was assured access to cleared land, even if she had never married, was divorced or widowed.

The married women of a Huron longhouse could have counted on the assistance of their 'sisters' and their 'mothers' in performing agricultural chores, gathering firewood, with child care and in carrying out other domestic duties. Most assistance would have come from 'sisters', whether married or not, since it was these women who would most likely be of the same age group and in the productive years of their lives.

Married men in any given longhouse depended first and foremost on the labour of their wives and their wives' sisters to provide them with their subsistence needs, clothing, armour and decorations. Young men could rely on the labour of their wives' mothers (biological and classificatory) and their wives' mothers' sisters, if they were still living, while older men had the labour of their daughters and their wives' sisters' daughters. Young unmarried men, on the other hand, could count on the labour of their mothers, mothers' sisters and their own 'sisters' to provide them with a large portion of their subsistence requirements. As well as owing labour to his wife and her longhouse, a married man retained ties, through clan membership, to his own mother's longhouse. Thus, men not only had both rights and obligations to and from their conjugal families, they also maintained a set of relations with their natal families.

Fishing

Next to the crops they grew, fish provided the Huron with the most substantial portion of their diet (Heidenreich 1971:163). Like corn, fish was stored in common for use by all members of a given longhouse. As in horticulture, men, women and children contributed labour time to fishing, although men's may have exceeded that of women's. Fishing was carried out in all seasons, although there were two peak seasons, late September to early December and late winter to early spring (ibid.:209). As with horticulture, the means of production were simple and easily acquired, consisting of canoes, made by individual men, nets made by the co-operative labour of women (who spun the twine during the winter) and men (who made the nets themselves), hooks acquired either in the fur trade or made from bone, knives for gutting the fish (either trade knives or made of flint), wracks for drying and baskets for storing the dried fish (made by women). Co-operation in fishing was minimal and was based on a simple division of labour. Fishing grounds and rights to take fish were open to all.

Fishing was done in a number of ways, depending on the season and the type of fish caught. Fish were netted from canoes or in weirs, taken by line or seine net pulled through holes cut in the ice in winter, and caught with line and hook or with wooden spears. By far the greatest portion of fish were taken during the late autumn to early winter. During this season a number of people undertook expeditions to fishing camps on Lake Huron. Gabriel Sagard accompanied four Huron men in a small canoe to an island in Lake Huron which served as base for a village fishing camp. At the base camp they built a lodge 'in the Algonkian fashion' which housed 'four chief men in the four corners, and the others after them arranged side by side, rather crowded together' (Wrong (ed.) 1939:185).

Life in the fishing camp, which went on for two months, consisted of a limited number of activities. Each evening the men carried the nets in their canoes out into the lake. Each morning they brought the nets in full of fish. During the day the fish were gutted, spread on racks and set to dry in the sun, or, if it was raining, smoked and then 'packed into casks, for fear of dogs and mice'. Some of the fattest fish were boiled in large kettles to make oil, which was skimmed off the top and put into 'bottles like our calabashes'.

Other camp activities included keeping birds, squirrels and chipmunks away from the drying fish, gathering firewood, preparing feasts and 'preaching to the fish'. This latter activity took place every evening in each lodge where the 'fish-preacher' as Sagard called him, had everyone lie down on their backs and then delivered a speech.

> His subject [writes Sagard] was that the Hurons do not burn fish-bones. Then he went on with matchless sentimentalities, exhorting the fish, conjuring them, begged them and entreated them to come, to allow themselves to be caught, to take courage, to fear nothing, since it was to be of service to some of their friends who respected them and did not burn their bones.
>
> (ibid. 1939:186–8)

It is most likely that, except for setting nets and 'preaching' to the fish, the women and children contributed to all activities in camp. While Sagard never explicitly mentions women, he does mention children. Moreover, since Iroquois women accompanied men fishing, it is reasonable to assume that Huron women also went on these expeditions. Unlike horticultural production, however, all members of a given longhouse did not contribute labour time to fishing. It is probable that certain households within each longhouse attended the large annual fishing camps each autumn and their catch was shared with other members of the longhouse. Any individual, therefore, who was a member of a functioning longhouse had, by right of residence, access to a source of protein.

Hunting and Gathering

Hunted foods provided a much smaller portion of the Huron's dietary needs, and its production and distribution differed significantly from that of fish and corn (Heidenreich 1971:163–4). Hunted meat was usually killed by men, although women helped butcher the animals and transport the meat back to the village (Thwaites 1896–1901, 33:83–5). Butchered meat was distributed among men's natal and conjugal families. Instead of forming part of the daily diet, hunted meat was consumed when taken, at irregular intervals, and in large, clan-based feasts. Because participation in these feasts was on the basis of clan membership men did not attend the same feasts as did their wives or children.

Deer were taken either in communal hunts or by individuals using bows and arrows (Biggar (ed.) 1922–36, III:60). Communal hunts were undertaken by warriors as a means of feeding themselves while on raiding expeditions, or by groups of men from a village in order to provide food for a feast (ibid.III:83). While large game animals, such as white tail deer and bear, were the most common meats in the Huron diet, other game animals were hunted for food. These included squirrel, fox, hares, marten, mice and beaver (Wrong (ed.) 1939:222–7). The smaller animals, however, did not account for any large portion of the diet and archaeological evidence indicates they were not often used as food (Heidenreich 1971:208). Beaver were rapidly depleted in Huronia, and by 1634 the Jesuits noted that the Huron 'have not a single Beaver, going elsewhere to buy the skins they bring to the storehouse of these Gentlemen [i.e. the French fur traders]' (Thwaites 1896–1901, 8:57).

Like all of the Huron's production activities, hunting required simple tools and simple forms of co-operation. Arrows, knives for butchering and, in the case of deer, a corral constructed in the course of the hunt into which deer could be driven, constituted most of the means of production required. Hunted meat could be produced by individuals or by groups of men engaged in co-operative labour. In either case, little prevented an individual from gaining access to the necessary means of production or from the social relations necessary to hunt. Hunted meat was often consumed as it was taken, and what was brought back to the village was distributed to wives as well as to 'mothers' and 'sisters' to be made into clan feasts. According to the Jesuits:

> As game is very rare and very difficult to get they are exceedingly greedy for meat ... of the little that they bring back they make a feast. As a token of great affection a father will give his son a bone to gnaw with that has been given him at the feast.
>
> (ibid. 8:57)

There were four kinds of feasts which involved the communal redistribution of hunted foods (mostly on a clan basis): the *Athataion* feast of farewell given by a person who knew he or she was dying, the *Enditewhua* feast of thanksgiving and gratitude, the *Atouroi Aochien* feast for 'singing and eating' and the *Awatawrohi* feast 'for deliverance from sickness' (ibid.36:177). These feasts were frequently extended over several days and often all the members of a clan within a village would participate, consuming twenty or thirty deer, bear and a large number of fish (ibid. 36:179–81).

Thus, access to hunted meat, while not necessary for survival, was an important basis on which social life was carried out. While obligations existed between a man and his conjugal family, the most important sets of rights and obligations for the redistribution of hunted meat were between members of the same clan, and links to natal families provided the basis on which ties to clan members were established and perpetuated. It was through feasting that inter-long-house relations were reconfirmed and that clan alliances asserted themselves as a basic form of social and political organization. Clan membership, therefore, gave each resident of any Huron village, whether male or female, access not only to hunted meat but also to a set of social relations which organized an important part of social life around feasting.

Next to fish, dogs, the only domesticated animals kept by the Huron, provided the largest source of high quality protein, and were most likely fed on fish scraps and what they could scavenge and hunt (Biggar (ed.) 1922–36, III:129; Wrong (ed.) 1939:226). While some Huron dogs were kept as pets and for hunting, skeletal evidence indicates that most Huron dogs were slaughtered before one year of age, strongly suggesting that they were raised as a food source. Although women were reputed to have fed puppies on corn gruel, little labour was involved in raising dogs and it would appear that neither men nor women bore any special relation, as producers, to them. As scavengers, dogs more or less took care of themselves, coming and going freely. They apparently had the run of the long-house, and even ate out of the same dishes as their masters. Like hunted meat, dogs played an important part in the feasting surrounding the Huron's social and ritual life. Dogs were most often eaten in curing feasts or on other ritual or ceremonial occasions. Their use, therefore, would most frequently have been associated with clan membership.

Gathering was usually done by women and their children. The most important gathering activity in which women participated was the collection of firewood, which took place between March and April. Women and girls from each village often travelled great distances to obtain dry hardwood for their fires. They sometimes felled trees with dry branches and cut them into lengths which they transported back to their village using a tumpline (Wrong (ed.) 1939:92–3). Wood gathered by all the female members of a longhouse was then stored within that longhouse and used for the benefit of all its residents. Women also gathered hemp, sometimes in groups of up to forty (Thwaites 1896–1901, 26:203–5). Hemp was later spun into twine by the women and then used by the men of the longhouse to make snares and fishing nets, as well as armour. Finally, women gathered berries, nuts, fruits and other wild foods and herbs in season, although these gathered foods provided a small portion of Huron subsistence needs.

GENDER, POWER AND SOCIAL RELATIONS OF PRODUCTION

While the village was the largest unit affecting subsistence production and consumption, longhouses and their component 'households' constituted the more usual units of production and consumption in which day to day living was carried out. The overall subsistence needs of village members were provided for by the labour of both men and women, and women made substantial contributions to the village economy. The labour of men and women, in all subsistence activities, was organized into sex-specific tasks, co-ordinated within each longhouse. Most of the subsistence needs of each individual, therefore, were satisfied within that unit of organization. Longhouses, in turn, were linked to each other through two kinds of connections: those which were the results of common matrilineally reckoned clan membership, and those which resulted when men married and came to reside with their wives in their wives' mothers' longhouses. Finally, each clan was represented at the village level of political organization through membership on a village council which discussed matters affecting the well-being of all village residents. Intra- and inter-clan relations unified the Huron into units larger than those in which the product of social labour circulated.

While the work of each subsistence activity was usually mostly done either by men or women (e.g., women did most of the work in horticulture, men in hunting) not all tasks in any subsistence activity were assigned exclusively to one gender. Furthermore, in all subsistence activities, tools were relatively simple, easily procured and usually employed by only one person. There was little need for extensive co-ordination among individuals performing a single economic task. However, no one individual could perform all the subsistence activities necessary to Huron life, and it was kin relations, functioning as social relations of production, which co-ordinated men's and women's economic rights and obligations. As producers and as consumers, men and women equally gained access to the means of production and to the product of their own and of other's labour through both natal and conjugal kin relations. It was these relations, for example, which made men responsible for providing wives, wives' sisters, sisters and mothers with cleared land on which corn could be produced. It was these relations, too, which made women responsible for providing husbands, children and other kin with their daily meals.

Because the Huron usually practised matrilocal residence the kin composition of the longhouse in which they resided as married adults differed for men and women. For women, whose economic activities were confined almost exclusively to subsistence production, social relations of production rarely extended beyond their natal and conjugal ties. Moreover, matrilocal residence gave women ties to both natal and conjugal families that often did not go beyond the longhouse. Men, on the other hand, usually did not reside with their natal families once married. Because their rights and obligations in subsistence production and consumption were divided between natal and conjugal families, married men's economic ties in subsistence often extended beyond the longhouse in which they lived with their wives to other longhouses where they had natal kin ties. Moreover, married men were often born in villages other than the ones in which they lived with their wives. Unlike their wives, then, they were often not spatially near their own natal kin.

As Coontz and Henderson (1986a) have pointed out, this difference in access to kin affected the ways in which men and women gained access to the products of each other's labour. In matrilineal, matrilocal societies with a kin corporate group organization such as the Huron's, the product of women's labour was the result of the co-operative work undertaken by a group of matrilineally related women. The product of their labour in subsistence horticulture provided the greater part of the daily subsistence requirements of all members of the longhouse (the unit of residence and consumption) and was stored in common. Each woman and her 'household' (i.e., her husband and children) had access to the common food store. The products of women's husbands' labour, however, were shared more widely, part going to the members of the husband's own natal group, and part going to the members of his wife's longhouse. Adult women had access to the products of men's labour directly through clan relations. Adult men on the other hand needed a wife (or an *Asqua*) in order to access their daily subsistence requirements which were largely the product of women's work.

The corporate nature of the organization of economic life meant that economic success and even renown within the society was more a collective matter than a matter of individual achievement. The

Jesuits, for example, noted that there were differences between families, some being of higher standing in the community than others, some, too, commanding more wealth than others. Lafitau, who observed the Iroquois in the early part of eighteenth century, recorded what he thought to be three 'great social classes', the noble families, the common people and the captives and their children (Lafitau 1724:341). He noted that 'some households are shunned (as a source of marriage partners) because they are not numerous and consequently are poor'.

A prominent Huron was a member of a prominent longhouse, and a longhouse became prominent through the demographic success of all its members. The more economically active members a longhouse had the more likely its members were to have connections to other longhouses. The wider those networks were drawn the more likely it was that its members could expect to be able to rely on assistance in times of need (famine, disease, war) as well as generally enjoying security on a day to day basis.

Both Huron men and Huron women were tightly enmeshed in extensive kinship structures. These structures provided each Huron, male or female, with a set of social relations – a concrete assemblage of people – with whom day to day productive life was carried out. Kinship structures, too, provided other sets of social relations within which all aspects of economic, social, political and sexual life were enacted. In short kinship structures provided the institutional settings in which men and women lived almost all aspects of their day to day existence. They provided the basis on which men and women interacted and the rules by which they conducted those interactions. It was, at least in part, through socially organized and sanctioned kinship relations, which structured and rationalized male/female relations, that both men and women found a basis for their 'power' within Huron society.

TRADE, WARFARE AND WOMEN'S STATUS

When we turn to look at commodity production and exchange and the effect it had on the seventeenth-century Huron two things about it immediately spring to attention. First, it was an activity that was exclusively the province of men; men and not women traded. Moreover, not all men traded – only a limited number made the journey to Quebec each year to trade with the French. It is most likely that certain men, representing their clans, traded on behalf of the members of those clans just as certain men, representing their clans, attended village councils on behalf of their clan members. Second, an analysis of the trade cannot be separated from an understanding of warfare, for a number of complex and intertwined reasons. Warfare like trade was a men's activity. Like trade it was carried on during the summer months, and like trade only a portion of all men were engaged in it at any one time. Furthermore, while engaging in warfare certainly brought honour to a young man, its objective first and foremost was the fulfilment of social responsibilities, especially clan responsibilities. A young man went to war not so much to kill enemies but to bring captives back for the use of members of his clan. In much the same way, designated traders went to trade on behalf of their clan members and brought back trade goods for redistribution. It is not unusual, therefore, to find trade and warfare side by side for reasons other than the fact that trade engendered conflict between groups who were competing for limited resources. Trade and warfare were young men's activities, undertaken as clan and not individual enterprises, whose results affected many more people than were directly involved. From the moment of first contact between the French and the Huron, trade and warfare proceeded hand in hand.

Huron involvement in the fur trade spanned only forty years, beginning in 1609 with their first contact with the French and ending in 1649 with their dispersal by the Iroquois. Yet even during this short period both the extent of their participation in the trade and the strategies they used for trade and defence changed so rapidly and extensively that we can divide the forty years into four distinct sections:

1609–15   During this period the Huron made direct contact with the French but continued to trade through their Algonkian trading partners.

1615–33   This marks the beginning of direct trade with the French rather than trade through intermediaries. These were relatively good years for the Huron as few Iroquois either raided into Huronia or were able to prevent them from travelling on the St Lawrence, the major trade artery. Between 1627 and 1632, moreover, it was the English and not the French who momentarily controlled the trade on the St Lawrence.

1634–9   During this period the Huron suffered greatly from virulent and frequent outbreaks of epidemic diseases.

As a result the Huron were often unable to travel down the St Lawrence to trade at Quebec.

1640–9   In this last period the Iroquois were relatively effective in blockading the St Lawrence and thus preventing the Huron from reaching the French at Quebec. In response the Huron attempted to reorganize their methods of transportation and defence, coming to Quebec in one large group, rather than in several smaller ones, as they had previously done. But by 1649, the Iroquois had succeeded in destroying them as a people.

As we have already seen, it was only in the late sixteenth century that the French actively sought to colonize what was to become New France. At the turn of the seventeenth century, monopoly trade holders had established a small post at Tadoussac to promote good relations with the Montagnais living in the area. At the same time three young relatives of Montagnais chiefs were sent to France (Trigger 1986:172–3). Although the Montagnais had tried to prevent the French from trading directly with other tribes to the west they also needed help in their struggles against the Iroquois and their most important allies in this struggle were other Montagnais and Algonkian groups living both to the north and to the west of Tadoussac (ibid. 8:41). In this way the Kichesipirini Algonkian were introduced to the French at Tadoussac in 1603.

As early as 1602 the French had realized it was to their advantage to trade with native peoples living north of the St Lawrence than with those to the south. Furs coming from the north were of superior quality to those from the south, and they could be had in greater numbers. French traders wished both to cement their alliances with the Montagnais/Algonkian people who came to Tadoussac, and to expand that trade further west, to include other Algonkian-speaking people living in the interior (Trigger 1976, I:229–31).

In 1608 Samuel de Champlain's employers benefited from his establishment of a post at Quebec. The location of this new post allowed the legitimate monopoly holders to intercept illicit traders going up river to trade with the Montagnais and afforded them some added protection against the Iroquois (Trigger 1976, I:229; 1986:174). In that same year, Champlain agreed to participate in a raid with the Montagnais and the Petite Nation Algonkian against the Iroquois. Some of the Algonkian who spent that winter with their Huron trading partners in turn invited some of the Huron to participate in the fighting.

In 1609 French trader/adventurers and Huron trader/warriors met for the first time to battle against their common enemy, the Iroquois. The 'Battle of Lake Champlain', as Champlain himself dubbed it, was fought by about sixty Huron and Algonkian warriors and a few French gunmen (Biggar (ed.) 1922–36, II:104–5). Champlain described the battle in detail and it is worth examining this description as it illustrates native warfare practices and objectives. According to Champlain, a mutual sighting took place between the Iroquois and the Montagnais/Algonkian/Huron contingent late in the evening of 29 July 1609. Both sides immediately began shouting at each other, preparing their arms and setting up barricades. While they were doing this the Huron sent out two canoes of men to learn whether or not the Iroquois intended to fight. The answer was affirmative, but because it was already night no fighting would take place until dawn, so that combatants could distinguish one another.

> Meanwhile [says Champlain] the whole night was spent in dances and songs on both sides, with many insults and other remarks such as lack of courage on our side, how little we could resist or do against them, and that when daylight came our people would learn all this to their ruin. Our side too, was not lacking in retort, telling the enemy that they would see such deeds of arms as they had never seen and a great deal of other talk.
>
> (ibid. II:104–5)

When daylight broke both sides lined up and shot arrows at each other. Champlain and his men were kept hidden until the right moment when they stepped out and shot at the Iroquois. The use of guns, something which the Iroquois had never experienced before, threw them into confusion. They fled after two of their leaders were killed and another wounded. Ten or twelve prisoners were captured, fifty others killed and the Huron and Algonquian took the corn and war shields left behind by the fleeing Iroquois as booty.

The 'Battle of Lake Champlain' and Champlain's subsequent conclusions about the Huron are significant for a number of reasons. The battle was the Huron's first encounter with the French. It served as a first introduction to an important alliance between the Huron and the French as trading partners. But more importantly, the battle and Champlain's subsequent remarks illustrate how trade, Christianity and colonization were closely intertwined in Champlain's mind. In his description of the 'Battle of Lake Champlain', Champlain records for us a number of his reactions to what he considered to be irrational or stupid practices on the part of his Indian allies.

To Champlain war meant the attempt to utterly defeat, if not exterminate, the enemy. For his Indian allies, however, it was another matter. When they encountered each other in battle, the two sides lined up facing each other. Champlain was frustrated by this, as it was clear the objective was not mass extermination, but fighting. Had he directed the battle, Champlain was certain he could have used tactics that would have allowed for the complete routing of the Iroquois. As it was, he was forced to face the enemy, and to fight directly with them, with as much courage as possible. Moreover, once the Iroquois had broken ranks and had fled, Champlain's allies showed no interest in pursuing them and in killing them but were satisfied with the prisoners they had already taken. Finally, Champlain reported he was disgusted with the torture of prisoners and with the ritual cannibalism that followed their deaths.

But by 1613, in spite of his feelings about their warfare practices, Champlain had come to the conclusion that if more fur was desired, it would be necessary for the French to further aid the Huron in their wars, in order, he noted,

> both to engage them more to love us, and also to produce the means of furthering my enterprises and explorations which apparently could only be carried out with their help and also because this would be to them a kind of pathway and preparation of embracing Christianity.
>
> (ibid. III:31–2)

From 1616 onwards, when they began to act as intermediaries in the French fur trade network, the Huron's experiences with warfare were irrevocably changed. In addition to traditional 'mourning' raids,[3] warring with the Iroquois had became a contest between the Huron and the Iroquois over whether or not the Iroquois raiders could despoil the Huron traders of their goods. It had also become an attempt, on the part of the Iroquois, to push to the limits one of the traditional functions of warfare: providing new members for them through prisoner capture. Moreover, European technology, including the increased use of guns, as well as the making of arrow heads out of copper and the purchase of ready-made iron ones, rendered useless traditional armour and other similar defences against stone-tipped missiles. Pitched battles, like the one described by Champlain in 1609 became impossible, and stealth and ambushes which involved killing the enemy on the spot and despoiling them of trade goods became more and more common.

Champlain died in December 1635, and was replaced by Charles Huault de Montmagny who adopted an even more aggressive policy towards the Huron to induce them to trade with the French and to forgo any alliance with the Iroquois which might divert furs to the Dutch. Pressing an advantage in view of the setbacks suffered by the Huron at the hands of the Iroquois, Montmagny told them that French assistance against the Iroquois depended on their acceptance of Christianity. By becoming Christians the Huron would learn to become French citizens, and, as such, would have a right to military assistance from French soldiers (ibid. III:40–51).

In August 1637 the Iroquois were again active on the St Lawrence. Approximately 500 were camped on the northern shore of Lake St Peter to intercept those coming to trade with the French (Thwaites 1896–1901, 12:207). In 1638 rumours of an impending Iroquois attack circulated, once again, in Huronia. The Huron themselves mounted a retaliatory raid against the eastern Iroquois, to avenge the previous year's attacks. Although they brought home a number of prisoners, this raid was to be one of their last successful ventures. Many Iroquois raiders on the St Lawrence meant that few Huron were able to trade at Quebec.

During the 1630s the Huron had managed to hold their own against the Iroquois. But the balance of power was tipped in the Iroquois's favour, however, and in 1642 they began a series of raids both on the St Lawrence and into Huronia itself that ended with the destruction of Huronia in 1648–9.

THE POWER OF TRADERS

Between 1609 and 1649 Huron participation in the fur trade had three facets: trade with the French for European goods; trade with other native groups for fur and tobacco which was then re-traded to the French; and trade with other native groups for goods which were not re-traded to the French but were consumed by the Huron themselves. Different types of social relations co-ordinated the first and the last two aspects of the trade.

It was Champlain's acceptance of an invitation to accompany some Montagnais and Petite Nation Algonkian warriors on a raid against the Iroquois that first brought the French and the Huron together. Some of the Petite Nation Algonkian passed the winter of 1608–9 in their customary fashion, living near one of the Huron tribes, the Arendarhonons. Their reputed chief, Iroquet, invited his Arendarhonon trading partner, whose name was Ochasteguin, to join him in the raid planned for the following summer. Ochasteguin's acceptance of this offer brought him and a small group of other Arendarhonons into contact with the French. Because Ochasteguin was the first to make contact with the French, Huron custom dictated that he and his family were the owners of the trade. According to one Jesuit observer 'several families have their own private trade and he is considered master of one line of trade that was first to discover it. Children share in their parents' rights as do those who bear the same name' (Thwaites 1896–1901, 10:223–5). Control over a particular line of trade meant that no one else had the right to enter except with permission of the owner which was always 'given for a few presents'. Illicit trade existed, but anyone caught participating in it was treated as a thief, beaten and deprived of all his possessions. Such an important trade connection as that with the French, however, was not left in the hands of one individual and his family for long. By 1611, Atironta, the principal spokesman for the Arendarhonons, had taken over responsibility. Moreover, the trade was to be shared with all Hurons, although Atironta 'was recognized as the principal Huron ally of the French and as the spokesman for all the Huron in high-level negotiations with them' (Trigger 1986:178).

An official alliance with the French was concluded when Champlain visited the Huron in 1615, wintered at the village of Cahiagué and was accompanied on his return to Quebec the following spring by Atironta (Biggar (ed.) 1922–36 III:168–72, Thwaites 1896–1901, 20:35; 23:167). Thus, between 1608 and 1615 the French had managed to extend direct trading relations to the Huron. Although the Montagnais and the Algonkian were not pleased by this they did not have the means to prevent it (Trigger 1986:181). The Kichesipirini Algonkian, for example, would stop the Huron going down the Ottawa River and charge them tolls for passing through their territory.

Huron men were organized for trade and war on a basis that was different from the way in which they were organized for subsistence production. Men undertook both trade and war on the basis of clan, village, tribal and pan-tribal affiliation. Those relations assured that all members of Huron society, whether they traded or not, would have some access to the goods brought back by the traders. In each village only a small number of men acted as traders, and it is most likely that the organization of and participation in the trade (except for the last few years) was done on a village by village basis, and within that by clan membership. Although originally the Bear clan had nominally controlled the trade with the French because it was they who first made contact, that trade was quickly shared with the other clans.

There is no direct reference in the historical record either to exactly how traders were chosen or whether or not they represented themselves or some larger corporate group. Nor do we know for certain if the furs the Huron traders bartered for belonged to members of the entire clan, some portion of it, the trader's immediate family or to the trader himself. We do not know, either, how the trade goods that the Huron traders brought back were redistributed within each village. We have good reason to conclude, however, that the goods were redistributed and that no one individual or family or even clan hoarded more trade goods than others, or grew wealthy at others' expense. There were powerful social forces at work within Huron society to enforce the redistribution of goods. While a certain number of traders converted to Christianity, ostensibly to get better terms of trade, they also used their conversion as an excuse to cease participating in traditional rituals, many of them involving redistribution (Thwaites 1896–1901, 23:129, 173). When they did this, however, their traditionalist kin, especially women, put a great deal of pressure on them to resume their former duties and obligations.

A study of the distribution of European goods in a number of longhouses from a site that may have been contemporary with Champlain suggests that goods were not evenly distributed, yet in itself this is not conclusive evidence of a systematic unequal distribution of goods during the period that the village was occupied. Gabriel Sagard, moreover, noted that each village often kept a store of goods in one place, under the control of the village leader for use in cases of public need:

> In all towns, boroughs and villages of our Hurons they lay in a kind of stock of wampum necklaces, glass beads, axes, knives and in general all that they gain or obtain for the community, whether in war, by treaty of peace, exchange of prisoners, tolls from the other tribes which cross their territory, or by any other means and method. Now all these things are placed and deposited in the hands and under the care of one of the captains of the place, appointed for this purpose, as treasurer of the

republic; and when it is a question of making some present for the common benefit and safety of all, either to be released from making war and to secure peace, or for any other service to the public, the council meets, and there, after having expounded the pressing necessity obliging them to draw from the treasury, and having determined the amount and quality of the goods which should be withdrawn, they notify the treasurer to search his coffers and produce from them all that has been resolved upon; and if he finds his finances exhausted, then every man taxes himself freely with what he can pay, and without any compulsion gives of his means according to his convenience and goodwill. They never fail to get what is necessary and has been agreed upon for the common security, so generous and rightly placed a heart have they.

(Wrong (ed.) 1939:266–7)

The trade goods brought back into Huron villages were largely intended for use in production – knives, axes, awls, iron arrow heads (Garrard 1969:3–15; Latta 1971:116–36; Trigger 1986:209). They also brought back brass and copper kettles, 'glass beads, metal bracelets, and other ornaments, as well as occasional novelties such as scissors, magnifying glasses (used to start fires), and keys' (Kidd 1953:359–79). At least one Huron brought home and planted some peas that he had seen being grown at Quebec, while the Recollects found that domestic cats were very welcome presents to chiefs (Wrong (ed.) 1939:91, 118, 270).

If an individual traded for himself, all the items he brought back to the village would have been stored in the longhouse in which he lived. It seems most unlikely, given the communal nature of a Huron longhouse, that goods as useful as kettles, axes and knives could have been kept under the control of a single individual for very long, especially as men most often resided with their wives' kin. Moreover, given the inter-clan links which existed between longhouses (married men and women of any given longhouse were from different clans and maintained primary relationships with their own natal families), it is most unlikely that a trader could have prevented his store of trade goods from disappearing.

Nor is it likely, given the nature of Huron domestic arrangements, that any one man could have used his position as a trader as a means of becoming an authority figure who wielded power by controlling access to valued trade goods. Men who traded were not clan chiefs.

Even more important, however, is the fact that subsistence production continued to be the most important part of Huron economy and Huron social organization reflected that importance. The trade goods brought back into Huron villages were, for the most part, metal tools, useful to the Huron in subsistence production. One of the most frequently found trade items on historic sites is iron axes. It is most likely that iron axes were largely women's tools, used by them to cut firewood and underbrush in land clearing. Iron trade axes have been found associated with women in Seneca and Neutral burials, further indicating that these were women's tools.[4]

Over and above the immediate relations between close kin, longhouse co-residents and clan members were involved in a number of formal and informal mechanisms which served to circulate goods not just within a village, but also between villages. By the seventeenth century beaver pelts, wampum and European trade goods had become important factors in a number of ritual activities and exchanges in Huron society. Burials, gambling, dream-guessing and fulfilment, ritual curing ceremonies and payments for crimes all involved the circulation of trade goods, sometimes on a very wide basis (Ramsden 1978:36). Seventeenth-century burial practices, for example, reveal extensive use of European goods. The Ossossané ossuary contained over 534 European as compared to sixty-one Huron made artefacts (Kidd 1953:364–7; Ramsden 1978:37). Gambling, which was often done as a ritualized activity, either in aid of someone's recovery to health, to change the luck of an entire nation or simply as some form of entertainment involving a number of villages and even tribes, often entailed large-scale transfers of goods. In one recorded instance an entire village lost thirty wampum collars to another (Ramsden 1978:37).

Dream-guessing and dream-fulfilment (to be discussed in the following chapter) as well as crime repayment were other ritualized ways in which goods changed hands. Cures were to be had if a dream of the sick or 'mad' person was acted out or if his or her secret desires could be guessed by another person, who would also fulfil the desire. Finally, redistribution was effected through crime payments which sometimes amounted to a substantial number of European trade goods. Often, payments for some crime, committed by an individual, would be made by the entire clan or even by the entire village to which the criminal belonged. If a crime had been committed by some Huron against some non-Huron, the entire confederacy could be held responsible for making restitution.

Certainly the fur trade had profound effects on Huron society and their destruction by the Iroquois cannot be understood outside the context of the effects that participation in the trade had on traditional warfare practices. The fur trade, however, did not alter property relations to any significant degree. Traders, as we have seen, had little opportunity to hoard European goods, let alone to use that hoard as a means of exercising power over either men or women. Huron men could not use access to scarce trade goods as a means of dominating or exercising control over women.

WOMEN, COMMODITY EXCHANGE AND SUBJUGATION

A number of theorists, concerned with the issue of women's sub-jugation to men, have looked to the material conditions of life, and to access to means of production and the product of social labour, as the basis either for egalitarian relations between the sexes, or for women's domination by men. This approach is informed by a sort of humanism which sees human nature as being expressed in the labour process: freedom or domination lies in the relations that each individual bears to the means of production and the product of their own labour. The domination of women by men is not a natural condition, but is brought about by some force which changes their essential relationship to the means of production.

This line of reasoning may be traced to Engels, who proposed that the introduction of commodity production led to the appearance of private property and the monogamous family. Concurrent with this introduction, Engels reasoned, was a decline in the status of women, as their work in the domestic sphere was relegated to an insignificant part of the economy and as their sexuality and reproductive capacities came under the control of their closest male relatives. Engels believed that in 'primitive communist' societies the original division between men and women was a 'natural' one. The division of labour, he stated, 'was a pure and simple outgrowth of nature: it existed only between the two sexes' (Engels 1972:17). This natural division of labour between the sexes has nothing to do with differences in status attributed to men and women. While the division of labour had 'natural' causes, differences in status were the result of social causes, specifically the development of private property and the state.

The importance of Engels's work has been recognized by many theorists, and excellent summaries as well as critiques may be found elsewhere.[5] A summary of the major points of Engels's arguments is useful here in order to show their continuity with a number of more recent feminist theorists' thinking on the question of women's equality with and subjugation to men as it relates to the social division of labour and women's roles in the processes of production and of the distribution of the social production. Moreover Engels's work is of particular relevance as he drew on Morgan's work on the Iroquois in formulating his thesis.

Morgan, Engels and the Iroquoian People

Engels's work on the 'world historic defeat of women' was influenced by the work of not only Morgan, but others such as Bachofen and McLennan. The work of all these writers centred around several assumptions: that an understanding of the regulation of sexual relations was the key to understanding all social relations within society, and that a clear line of evolutionary development could be discerned leading from the most primitive stages of human social organization up to the apex of industrial society, and the monogamous patriarchal family (Coward 1983:48–9). To one degree or another Morgan, Bachofen and McLennan all postulated an early stage of human society in which women ruled.

Bachofen, for example, proposed a stage in human society of 'gynocracy', or 'mother-right' (Bachofen 1968:1). Women initiated this stage when, reacting in disgust to a previous period of sexual promiscuity, they seized control of religion and were able to establish a new form of society (ibid.:2). Then, turning their attention to the advancement of civilization, they invented agriculture. Men, meanwhile, began to acquire military power. Eventually they used this power to overcome women, establish their own dominance and, with it, the patriarchal family.

Engels praised Bachofen for being the first to seriously consider the existence of a stage of human society in which unrestricted sexual freedom prevailed within the tribe. But he criticized him for introducing 'into his extremely important discussion the most incredible mystifications through his notion that in their historical development the relations between men and women had their origins in men's contemporary religious conceptions, not in their actual conditions of life' (Engels 1972:97). Thus, it was to the work of L. H. Morgan that Engels turned in developing his own thesis about the 'actual conditions of life' in which the historical development of the relations between men and women was based. In *Origins*, Engels hailed Morgan's 'rediscovery of the primitive matriarchal gens as the earlier stage of the patriarchal gens of civilized peoples' as having the same importance for anthropology 'as Darwin's theory of evolution has for biology and Marx's theory of surplus value for political economy' (ibid.:71). According to Engels's assessment, Morgan's rediscovery of the matriarchal gens was the pivot point 'on which the whole science turns', it shows us 'what to look for in our research and how to arrange our results' (ibid.: 71). Morgan's 'discovery' was crucial for Engels because it allowed him to postulate that the first social form to exist was the collective household practising a form of collective marriage. When prohibitions against sexual relations with certain people are introduced, it follows that they must be introduced on the basis of relation to mother. Female lineages are the result, mainly because with group marriages it is impossible to know who fathered any given child. The matriarchal gens emerge – a group in which common ancestry is recognized, but which is not based on individual or pairing families (Coward 1983:144).

In *Origins*, Engels embarks on a twofold task; to establish the successive forms of social organization in human society that led to the appearance of 'Civilization', characterized by the monogamous family, private property and the state, and to establish the mechanisms whereby the transition from one stage to another was accomplished. In this work Engels maintains that the position of women in society is ultimately the outcome of the form of property ownership that characterizes the society. There is a direct correspondence, moreover, between property ownership and form of family organization. Together, property ownership and family organization structure the nature of women's contribution to the economy, their relations with men and, ultimately, their status.

Engels begins his assessment of the conditions which brought about a change in the position of women with Morgan's work on the Iroquois. The Iroquois represented a lower stage of barbarism characterized by the 'pairing family'. The 'pairing family' was too weak to establish itself outside of the 'communistic household' that had previously contained the members of a group marriage.

> Communistic house keeping, however, means the supremacy of women in the house; just as the recognition of the female parent, owing to the impossibility of the recognition of the

male parent with certainty, means that the women – the
mothers – are held in high respect.

(Engels 1972:113)

The communistic household 'in which most or all of the women
belong to one and the same gens, while the men come from various
gentes, is the material foundation of the supremacy of women which
was general in non-capitalist times' (ibid.: 113).

Although women in these societies work hard, Engels tells us that
we should not let that lead us to believe that they occupy the position
of drudges or that they are overburdened with work. It is the very
fact that they do work that causes them to be held in such high regard.

Among people where women have to work far harder than we
think suitable there is often much more real respect for women
than among our Europeans. The lady of civilization, surrounded by false homage and estranged from all real work, has
an infinitely lower social position than the hard-working
woman of Barbarism, who was regarded among her people as a
real lady ... and who was also a lady in character.

(ibid.: 113–14)

Engels argues that with the introduction of commodity production
and exchange each man becomes a property-owner while his wife,
and other female relatives who might reside in his household, being
propertyless become his wards. What Engels appears to be proposing
as the end to barbarism is some form of class society in which all men
constitute a property-owning class, while all women constitute a
class of dependants whose major purpose is to reproduce heirs.
Referring to the end of the stage represented by the Iroquoian people,
Engels wrote: 'The man took command in the home also; the woman
was degraded and reduced to servitude, she became the slave of his
lust and a mere instrument for the reproduction of his children'
(ibid.:120).

Here, then, we have the first basis for the appearance of the
monogamous, patriarchal family, and, possibly, an explanation of the
force behind social change, from sex in the transition from savagery
to barbarism, to property in the transition from barbarism to civilization. To Engels, and indeed to most other Victorian thinkers, sex
and motherhood seemed to be *natural*. Blood alliances through birth,
only really knowable, given the technology of the day, by the fact of a
particular birth to a particular mother, appeared to Morgan, Engels

155

and many others as the natural basis of a society. It was the introduction of something quite unnatural and very far removed from the biological processes of birth and the naturally occurring filiation – the introduction of private property and its inheritance – that allowed men to take over as heads of families and assign themselves the role of patriarch. Maternal filiation can be seen as natural because it has a clear biological basis. Paternal filiation, on the other hand, has to be sustained by belief, reinforced by property and requires the active subjugation of mother and child (Badinter 1989:19).

As ethnographically flawed as Engels's work is it contains, none the less, three basic propositions which continue to be addressed by modern theorists:

1   In the past societies have existed, prior to the development of commodity exchange, in which women were not subordinated to men. It is possible, moreover, to reconstruct that past.
2   Women's position in past societies can best be explained by the relation between sexuality and the resulting family arrangements which structured both the social and sexual freedoms that women enjoyed and the nature of the economic contributions that they made.
3   The introduction of commodity production and exchange, of necessity controlled by men, led to the development of private property. This, in turn, undermined women's importance in the family. Men, in control of property, wanted to assure that their property was passed on to their own heirs. It was impossible for men to 'know' who their own children were in a society where women mated with many men. The 'need' of property-owning men to 'know' who was and who was not a legitimate offspring led to the undermining of women's importance in the family (change from matriarchy to patriarchy) and to their economic, social and sexual subordination to men.[6]

Although the historical sequences envisioned by Engels have largely been relegated to the category of flights of imagination, uninformed by modern anthropological knowledge, many of the propositions of historical materialism continue to be employed. What is useful to consider is how Engels's ideas about the basis of egalitarian relations between men and women and the causes of their undermining have affected feminist thinking about women and men and their relationships in the process of producing and reproducing their material and social lives. It is particularly important because contemporary feminist theorists who use Engels's work continue to rely on the idea of the separation between the domestic and the public spheres of existence as central to their formulations.

Probably the most explicit endorsement of Engels's ideas can be found in *Women and Colonization*, edited by Mona Etienne and Eleanor Leacock (1980). The contributors to this volume locate the mechanisms that bring about women's subjugation in the processes that occur as the result of colonialization and the introduction of commodity production. The various chapters which make up *Women and Colonization* all keep to this single theme. In their introduction, Etienne and Leacock develop a theme of a position of independence and high status for women prior to the introduction of commodity production and exchange, followed by women's subjugation to male authority and their economic dependence on men. As pre-capitalist societies began to produce commodities for exchange with Europeans the sexual division of labour developed to the extent that:

> adults of each sex were producing or procuring significant quantities of different things (rather than virtually the same things) creat(ing) the possibility for ties of economic dependence that had not previously existed. Therefore it laid the basis for inequalities both among women and men and between women and men.
>
> (Etienne and Leacock (eds) 1980:13)

In her study of seventeenth century Montagnais–Naskapi women who were subjected to the 'civilizing' programme of Jesuit missionaries, for example, Leacock found that women became subordinated to men once their economic base had been undermined (Leacock 1980:38). In an article on the Bari of Columbia, Brown and Buenadventura-Posso argue that the recent (1964) transition among the Bari from collective horticulturalists to wage-labourers produced 'the forced break-up of the collective living unit and its replacement by the patriarchal nuclear family' in which females became 'dependent upon a wage earning male for subsistence items which are now purchased with cash' (Brown and Buenadventura-Posso 1980:125). Similarly, Etienne points out that with the destruction of traditional male/female relations surrounding cloth production and exchange among the Baule of the Ivory Coast women became wage-labourers. This in turn produced a great deal of antagonism between men and

157

women (Etienne 1980:230–1). Finally Gailey's contribution to the volume concludes that Tonga women of the South Pacific lost authority and autonomy as a result of the introduction of trade with Europeans. Colonization and ultimately state formation redefined women's roles as wives 'in such a way as to transform what was simple deference behaviour towards husbands into structural and economic dependency' (Gailey 1980:381).

This same phenomenon has also been found by several authors who have written, elsewhere, on African women. Patricia Draper (1975), for example, has illustrated the way in which the introduction of commodity production precipitated the breakdown of relations between men and women among a small number of !Kung hunter-gatherers who became settled pastoralists after European contact. Among those !Kung who became settled, cattle emerged as the private property of men, and the position of the wives and daughters of cattle-owning men declined from one of autonomous, fully participating members of society to one of dependence and subordination.[7]

The point on which women's independence from male domination turns, according to Leacock, is whether or not women 'control the conditions of their work and the dispensation of the goods they produce' (Leacock 1978:161–2). Women, she argues, are not the 'literal equivalents of men'. Rather they are seen as 'female persons, with their own rights, duties, and responsibilities, which were complimentary to and in no way secondary to those of men' (ibid.: 252). This opinion is reinforced by Moore, who has argued that women's status depends on whether or not they have access to and control over the means of production, the product of their own labour and the conditions of their work (Moore 1988:31–2). European contact and the subsequent introduction of commodity production, of necessity, undermines this.

The case of the Huron, however, suggests that another explanation is called for. During the period between 1609 when they were drawn into the French fur trade network and 1649, when they were destroyed by a combination of lack of resistance to fatal epidemics and the depredations of Iroquois raiders, Huron women maintained a strong basis of resistance against Christianization and its consequential subjugation of women to men. Certainly direct trade with the French altered the face of Huron society. To begin with, trade introduced material goods that rapidly replaced goods of native manufacture and became indispensable within Huron society.

Second, trade altered the scope and meaning of warfare, and drew the Huron into networks of social relations with foreigners beyond anything they had experienced. But it did not, in and of itself, result in the diminution of women's status. Well after commodity exchange had become a central facet of Huron existence, the Jesuits continued to struggle against powerful women as they attempted to convert the Huron to Christianity right up to the defeat of the Huron in 1649 (Anderson 1985:48–62).

However trade also had adverse effects on women. Women were affected because they prepared the corn meal the traders ate *en route*, and used as a trade commodity. Women, too, were responsible for dressing the skins that were traded. Both of these activities would have increased women's workloads. Second, as the century progressed, Iroquois raiders made frequent incursions into Huronia, killing or abducting women as they worked in their fields. Finally, the Jesuits' presence in Huronia, tolerated because of the trade, offered a constant challenge to women's position. Jesuits encouraged men to subjugate their wives, and the conversion to Christianity of men in important positions presented women, especially matrons, with a number of difficulties.

Yet neither European trade goods, brought back into Huronia by men, Iroquoian raids nor Jesuit intervention undermined the women of Huronia. As long as the fundamental principles of Huron social organization remained intact, as long as kinship functioned as social relations of production to organize people into units of production and consumption in which women had the right of access to the means of production and to the product of their own and other's labour, commodity production and exchange could not undermine their status. The existence of commodities, and even the exclusive role of men in the actual process of their exchange, was not a sufficient condition to bring about women's subjugation.[8] It brought with it no new means of organizing rights of access to or use of trade goods. As long as the kinship structures remained intact, even the introduction of commodity exchange, exclusively in the hands of men, was not sufficient to create new institutions to control access to trade goods even when those trade goods rapidly began to replace ones of native manufacture in day to day usage.

Probably the best illustration of the relative distribution of power between Huron traders and the women of their clans is to be found in the Jesuits discussion of their own attempts to obtain Huron boys for their seminary at Quebec. The Jesuits were convinced that beliefs,

159

values and loyalties were set in early childhood, and could be greatly influenced by the proper education. It was imperative to separate the boys from their families so that they could be educated apart from any familial influences (Thwaites 1896–1901, 6:169). The Jesuits intended that once instructed in Catholicism the boys could be returned to their own people to act as missionaries among them. A two year absence from parents was considered necessary, so that the child would become accustomed to Jesuit ways and remain loyal to them once he was returned to his own people.

Huron traders, persuaded that trade with the French depended on some of their children attending the Jesuits' seminary, consented to the Jesuits' request for boys. The Jesuits, however, were soon to learn that it was not the fathers who exercised control over the children. The mothers of the promised children interfered in the arrangements and refused to permit their children to leave. As one Jesuit reported, when it came time for everyone to leave the village for the journey to Quebec, the mothers 'and above all the grand-mothers' would not allow it. The fathers, who had made the original promise, then offered 'a hundred excuses' and the Jesuits had to content themselves with 'the grandson of a captain'[9] as their sole pupil (ibid. 9:283). A similar occurrence was recorded a few years later, when 'the extraordinary tenderness which the savage women have for their children stopped all proceedings and nearly smothered our project in its birth – only one went and he was nearly full grown' (ibid. 12:39–41).[10]

The refusal of Huron women to allow their children to live among the Jesuits is remarkable, considering that exchange of children was a common enough practice, especially among trading partners. One reason for their actions in this regard may have been their intense mistrust and dislike of Jesuit child-rearing methods. Neither Huron nor Montagnais beat their children as a means of punishment, a method frequently used by the Jesuits and other French. Commenting on Huron child-rearing practices Le Jeune noted:

These Barbarians cannot bear to have their children punished, nor even scolded, not being able to refuse anything to a crying child. They carry this to such an extent that upon the slightest pretext they would take them away from us, before they were educated.

(ibid. 5:153)

As long as the very powerful longhouse-based, matrifocal kinship structure continued in existence it was Huron women, and not Huron men – particularly not the traders – who were able to exercise control over the fate of the young children of the longhouse. Men could make what promises they would with their trading partners; those promises simply were not kept unless women also agreed.

8

'DEATH OVER
A SLOW FIRE'

We have seen how Huron and Montagnais women were able to exercise a great deal of power; how, although formally excluded from what has come to be called the 'public' sphere, they were not dominated by men who occupied public positions. We have also seen that women held important positions within the productive process and how the introduction of commodity exchange with Europeans in itself did not undermine their status even though women did not participate directly in the trade.

What is astonishing, however, is how quickly women's status was changed once Christianity was established. It is difficult to comprehend the rapidity with which behavioural changes occurred; how men began to dominate women by chastising them, physically punishing them and by controlling their decisions. This is all the more puzzling because it took place in a society where, even a few years previously, the majority of the people had been dedicated to individual freedom for both men and women. When the change came, it came suddenly and thoroughly. What is even more curious is the sudden acceptance by women of their inferior status and their apparent passivity. Women, before Christianization, are portrayed as angry, demonstrative, aggressive and vocal. After Christianization they are meek, compliant and fearful. How could this happen? Clearly, it took more than the introduction of commodity exchange, or more than an entire revamping of economic, social, kin and political relations within Huron society to create, so quickly, a situation in which women's sense of self was so radically altered, and in which men felt justified in expressing aggression towards their wives. What made men capable of blaming women for their troubles, of keeping them under constant supervision and control? And just as importantly, what made women accept this?

162

The struggle that the Jesuits were engaged in with the Huron and the Montagnais was nothing short of a struggle over redefining the subject and subjectivity. The Jesuits sought to change both the individual's self-definition, experience, self-knowledge and will to act *and* the institutional and social knowledge basis that helped to form and reproduce the individual's identity. The subjugation of Huron and Montagnais women should, therefore, also be understood in the context of the reformation of individuals, and the redirection of aggression.

Without doubt the subjugation of Huron and Montagnais women would not have taken place without widespread changes in the economy, the disruptive effects of epidemic disease, famines and warfare, and the 'civilizing' efforts of the Jesuits. But these events, social processes, and catastrophes only provided the groundwork to allow something else, something much more profound, to take place. What ultimately brought about the subjugation of Huron and Montagnais women was a momentous change in the expression of self and in the institutional structures and knowledge basis that supported such a change. Women became the objects of fear and aggression.

The Jesuits saw their struggle with the 'Savages' of New France in particular terms: as a pitched battle between the forces of good and salvation, which they represented, and the forces of evil and damnation which the Devil had unleashed in the New World. The battle against these evil forces had to be waged on several fronts – instilling lawfulness and the fear of God, imposing Christian marriages and rooting out all 'diabolical ceremonies' that the Huron and Montagnais used to mark, order and regulate their relations with each other, their enemies and nature.

The answer to questions about why this all could have happened lies along two related axes. In the first place we need to consider cultural representations of women, men and their powers. For example, how were women and men viewed in Huron mythology, and in other representations of their 'nature'? As we will see, through the Huron mythology available to us in the *Relations*, women were portrayed in an ambiguous fashion. They were seen as aggressive, dangerous, vengeful and capricious at the same time as they were also valued for being the source of all life. Second, we should consider the ways in which anger and aggression were traditionally handled in Huron society. With Christianization a great deal of anger was directed towards women. Women were identified as responsible for any unpleasantness, insecurity or danger that the members of society, especially men, found themselves in. A great deal of energy was then directed towards controlling women and they became the legitimate brunt of hostility – both of their own self-loathing, and of men's loathing and mistrust. Traditionally, feelings of fear, mistrust, anger and aggression, and the actions that they inspired, had been directed away from women and outwards, either towards 'enemies' or expressed through ritualized 'insane' behaviour. It was these feelings that the Jesuits were finally able to tap, to reformulate, give new direction and meaning to, and thereby provide an organized framework for steering the Huron and the Montagnais towards entirely new modes of self-expression, and subjectivity. It is here that the subjugation of Huron and Montagnais women was finally accomplished.

ANGER, AGGRESSION AND FEAR

The seventeenth-century French, in dealing with their own fear and aggression, had created a world-view in which Satan and God were locked in combat for the future control of the world. Drawing on the misogyny already present in western thought, theologians, moralists, medical writers, educators and jurists all placed increasing emphasis on women's incapacities, and feebleness, as compared to men's abilities and strength. Women, along with Jews, Turks, heretics (for the Catholics), the pope (for the Protestants) and pagans were all identified as potentially or actually the allies of Satan. One of the consequences of this identity, as we have seen, was the increasing subjugation of women, including the close identification of women with witchcraft and the worship of Satan.

Like the French, the seventeenth-century Huron had their share of aggression, fear and anger which was expressed in culturally and socially sanctioned ways. But an important difference between the two societies is immediately apparent. Whereas women were considered legitimate objects of fear and aggression in seventeenth-century France, and could be tortured, burned at the stake, incarcerated or at least kept under the watchful eye of male relatives, women were assigned no such place in Huron society. To talk about the mechanisms supporting women's equality with men is to talk about the diverse forms that expression of aggression and domination took. Domination is expressed not only through material means (such as the regulation of access to means of production) but also through emotional, and ideological, venues.

In his study of the sex segregation and male dominance among the Baruya of New Guinea, Godelier (1982) describes the social mechanisms whereby boys become men and learn to dominate women, and girls become women and learn to accept being dominated by men. Godelier shows how much of the sex role behaviour and comportment towards members of the opposite sex is learned through the different male and female initiation processes. Initiation, which lasted ten years or so for boys, and fifteen days for girls, instils in boys, and reinforces in girls, the belief in male power and domination.

The ethnohistoric record left to us by seventeenth-century missionaries strongly suggests that no such elaborate ceremonies existed among the Huron to mark the initiation of boys into men's world and to separate them so clearly from that of women. This is not, however, to say that there were no rites of passage for boys into manhood, girls into womanhood; no means of segregating men from women. Huron society, like other Iroquoian societies, was clearly divided into men's world and women's world. Men's tasks, duties, rights and obligations were quite different from those of the women. Life experiences of members of the two sexes were quite separate: rarely did a man venture to undertake women's responsibilities or vice versa, even under the most trying of circumstances.

The feelings of mistrust of women, and the desire on the part of men to control them, to subjugate them and to humiliate them, and generally to see them diminished that emerged as more and more Huron and Montagnais were converted did not really begin with the introduction of Christianity. Such feelings could hardly have arisen spontaneously in adult people over the course of a few months. Although the Huron may have valued women above men because of their contribution to peopling the country, they also found them dangerous, capricious and without scruples. Yet the Huron, unlike the French, tended to see things less as either good or evil, and more in terms of the potential for several qualities to exist simultaneously in one person, or even in a Divinity. But even more importantly, the Huron, unlike the French, had an overwhelming commitment to individual freedom. There were no institutional mechanisms available to limit that freedom from extending to women as well as to men. As we have already seen, the organization of the productive process and the redistribution of subsistence goods helped establish women in their egalitarian positions.

AATAENTSIC AND IOUSKEHA

The Huron creation myth illustrates a certain ambiguity towards women. The Jesuits recorded the myth as part of their attempt to come to understand whether or not the Huron had any natural grasp or knowledge concerning the existence of God. Finding a creation myth, the Jesuits concluded that '[i]t is so clear, so evident that there is a Divinity who has made Heaven and earth, that our Hurons cannot entirely ignore it' (Thwaites 1896–1901, 8:117). However, because

> the eyes of their minds are very much obscured by the darkness
> of a long ignorance, by their vices and sins ... they misappre-
> hend him grossly, and, having the knowledge of God, they do
> not render him the honor, the love, nor the services which is his
> due. For they have neither Temple, nor Priests, nor Feasts, nor
> any Ceremonies.
>
> (ibid. 8:117–19)

It was the Jesuits' task to change that.

Central to the Huron creation myth were two beings, a woman called Aataentsic, who is said to have made 'earth and man', and Iouskeha, her son, and assistant. Together these two govern the world.

> This Jouskeha [sic] has care of the living, and of the things that
> concern life, and consequently they say that he is good. Eat-
> aentsic [sic] has care of souls; and, because they believe that she
> makes men die, they say that she is wicked ...
>
> This God and Goddess live like themselves, but without
> famine; make feasts as they do, are lustful as they; in short, they
> imagine them exactly like themselves.
>
> (ibid. 8:117)

Another, and more detailed version of this myth appeared a few years later in the *Relations*. Aataentsic, who lived in Heaven, was working one day in her field when she saw a bear. Her dog gave chase, and she followed her dog. The bear fell into a hole and the dog followed. In despair Aataentsic threw herself after them, landing in water without being hurt, in spite of her pregnancy. After she landed the waters surrounding her began to dry, little by little, until habitable earth appeared.

In another version of this fall, Aataentsic went out to cut down a tree for her sick husband who was convinced that if he could eat its fruit he would be cured. Taking her husband's axe Aataentsic went to get him the fruit. But as soon as she dealt the first blow to the tree, it split and fell to earth. Astonished, Aataentsic went and informed her husband, then returning she threw herself after the tree.

> Now, as she fell, the Turtle, happening to raise her head above water, perceived her; and, not knowing what to decide upon, astonished as she was at this wonder, she called together the other aquatic animals to get their opinion. They immediately assembled; she points out to them what she saw, and asks them what they think it fitting to do. The greater part refer the matter to the Beaver, who, through courtesy, hands over the whole to the judgement of the Turtle, whose final opinion was that they should all promptly set to work, dive to the bottom of the water, bring up soil to her, and put it on her back. No sooner said than done, and the woman fell very gently on this Island.
>
> (ibid. 10:129)

In one version of this story Aataentsic is pregnant and delivers a daughter, who herself immediately becomes pregnant; in another version she delivers two boys, Tawiscaron and Iouskeha. In the latter version Iouskeha eventually pursues and kills Tawiscaron. In this version, Iouskeha is the sun, Aataentsic, the moon, whose home is located at the ends of the earth (ibid. 10:133). According to legend, four young men went to visit these two, and finding Iouskeha alone in his cabin, they were well received. Iouskeha, however, warned the four young men to hide themselves in preparation for Aataentsic's return, because she 'was sure to play them a bad trick if they did not keep on their guard'.

> This Fury arrives toward evening, and, as she assumes any form she sees fit, perceiving that there were new guests in the house she took the form of a beautiful young girl, handsomely adorned, with a beautiful necklace and bracelets of Porcelain, and asked her son where his guests were. He replied that he did not know what she meant. There upon she went out of the Cabin, and Iouskeha took the opportunity to warn his guests, and thus saved their lives.
>
> (ibid. 10:135)

Iouskeha was reputed to have given humans water, fire and corn. Aataentsic, on the other hand, spent her time trying to undo all her son's good works. In charge of the souls of the dead, she caused humans to die, and spread epidemics and famine. Iouskeha, however, is not all good, nor Aataentsic all powerful in her evilness. Iouskeha, for example, apparently took great delight in putting on disguises and going to insult his mother at village feasts (ibid. 10:135).

It is interesting to note here that although a man can be a murderer, even commit fratricide, it is the woman who is attributed with causing potential harm to all; it is Aataentsic who brings death, Aataentsic who tries to dupe the young men, Aataentsic who goes around trying to undo all the good done by her son. The Huron, it would appear, were no strangers to the idea that at least a part of the true nature of women was capricious and dangerous. While women gave life, they could also take it away, not by murdering, which after all is a single act of violence done to a particular person, but by causing all people to die. The source of all life was also seen as the source of all death. Indeed, Iouskeha could not have killed his twin brother if it were not for the fact that Aataentsic caused humans to die in the first place.

Women's destructiveness, however, is equally balanced by their capacity to create. The Huron made no clear-cut distinctions between good and evil, nor did they assign men to the side of good, and women to the side of evil, as did the French. An important consequence of this egalitarian division of the capacity for good and evil between men and women was that the expression of fear and aggression was not directed, within the society, by one sex against the other as was the case for the French. Rather, there were general institutionalized forms of expression of aggression and fear within the society, and means of externalizing that aggression and fear towards others, either outside of the society or internally in ritualized form, that were equally open to men and to women. While it was true that women in Huron mythology were more capable of evil, and men were more capable of good, the institutional structures available which shaped the expression of anger and aggression, and the knowledge base which was available to identify and deal with dangerous or evil components directed the expression of any negative feelings either outside of the society, or else gave them expression through the amorphous 'desires of the soul'. Thus no category of Huron, whether men or women, was singled out for special treatment as dangerous members of society.

DEALING WITH AGGRESSION AND FEAR IN HURON SOCIETY

Like the Europeans, the Huron also experienced fear and aggression. They chose targets for their aggression and socially sanctioned means of discharging their feelings against those targets. Three ways of dealing with fear and aggression stand out: ritualized warfare and prisoner torture practices, dream-guessing rituals for satisfying 'desires of the soul', and what the Huron called the *Ononharoia*, or 'brain turned upside down' – that is to say, a form of ritualized insanity. In each of these instances women and men expressed fear, hostility, longings and needs through socially sanctioned, regularized and 'safe' means.

Torture and Cannibalism

Gabriel Sagard, who had the opportunity of living with the Huron in the 1620s, observed that when war was to be undertaken:

> two or three of the elder or more daring captains who will undertake to lead them ... go from village to village to explain their intention, giving presents to some in these villages in order to persuade them and procure their aid and support in the war.... These captains ... have authority not only to choose the places [to go to], to assign quarters and form battalions, but also to dispose of the prisoners taken in war and to settle everything else of great consequence. It is true that they are not always implicitly obeyed by their soldiers.
>
> (Wrong (ed.) 1939:151)

Gabriel Sagard's observations underline one of the major points of conflict of interest among the Hurons – a conflict which existed between younger and older men. One sure route to praise and honour for a young man was to give a feast to celebrate a decision to go to war, and even to supply the food and other needs of those who would accompany him (ibid.:151–2). Often participation in a war party, especially a successful one, influenced a young man's stature with members of his clan and village by increasing his chances of obtaining a position of leadership, a good marriage or important alliances (Ritcher 1983:530). On the other hand, Huron chiefs, both political leaders and war leaders, were selected from among older men who had already achieved their social standing through earlier exploits. At times the older leaders of the village or tribes would promote a policy of peaceful relations with another group, only to have that policy overturned or ignored by younger men.

But most importantly, warfare was a socially sanctioned outlet for the expression of rage, grief and anger that was not permitted to be displayed in Huron society in any other way. Warfare, almost exclusively undertaken during the summer months, was also frequently undertaken as a response to the desire of specific families to have the death of one or more of their members avenged. When a certain amount of support for the idea was gained within a village, war chiefs set out for other villages to recruit young men, often with gifts, to follow them to war. Although only young men went to war, their objective was not so much to kill enemies as to take prisoners and to bring them back to their villages. The honour which accrued to anyone who took a prisoner was enough to kindle intense rivalries among the warriors. Sagard tells a story which if not 'true' at least illustrates the competition in parable form:

> Now since there is rivalry as to who shall have the prisoners, this very rivalry or envy also brings it about sometimes that these prisoners set themselves free and escape, as the following example shows. Two or three Hurons were desirous each to have the credit of taking prisoner an Iroquois, and when they could not come to an agreement themselves they made their own prisoner decide it, and he very cleverly used the opportunity and said: 'So and so took me and I am his prisoner', but what he said was purposely untrue in order to make the man whose prisoner he really was feel justly dissatisfied. And this man in fact, being indignant that another should unjustly receive the honour which was due to himself, spoke in secret to the prisoner the following night, saying to him: 'You have given and adjudged yourself to another instead of to me who had taken you, and for this reason I would rather set you free than that he should have the honour due to me', and thus untying his bonds he made him escape and take to flight secretly.
>
> (Wrong (ed.) 1939:160–1)

But any prisoner brought into Huronia was not the property of the man who took him. Once inside a Huron village the prisoner became the property of a certain household, those who had requested, and often financed the war party in the first place, and who were given the right to decide the prisoner's fate.

The Huron, like the other Iroquoian peoples with whom they shared a common culture, went to great lengths both to suppress feelings and to give them indirect channels for expression. They tried to avoid any expression of anger or even annoyance towards anyone within their society. Should one of them become enraged enough to act aggressively towards another Huron his or her actions were immediately subject to an elaborate system of social accountability that extended well beyond the aggressor and his or her victim. The French were astonished to learn that whatever the nature of the injury done to a member of one's own society, even if it was murder, seldom was any revenge sought directly against the perpetrator. Again Sagard:

> if one among them has injured, killed, or wounded another of the same nation, he gets off by means of a present, and there is no corporal punishment (because they do not use it against those of their own nation), unless the relations of the man wounded or slain take it upon themselves to revenge him, which seldom happens; for they rarely do wrong to one another.
>
> (ibid. 1939:163)

Only those Hurons who were convicted of using a poison or of 'bewitching' another, or who were traitors and thus threatened the security of the entire society were executed immediately 'without any form of trial and there is no disturbance about it' (Thwaites 1896–1901, 14:47). But often even a minor offence committed by a non-Huron was cause enough to go to war against an enemy tribe.

While no Huron could express rage or grief over the actions of someone from within the society who had offended them, anyone who had a family member killed by the enemy was allowed full expression of grief. This expression, however, was channelled in socially approved ways. Mourners were expected to blacken their faces, neglect their appearance as much as they could and to disregard social niceties. Others were expected help assuage the grief with gifts, feasts and condolence rituals. If the person who had been killed or who had died was an important member of society, sometimes transmogrification ceremonies were held. In these ceremonies some living person went through a ceremony and when it was over emerged, not as himself or herself, but as the deceased, with all that person's honours, status and responsibilities (ibid. 1896–1901, 16:201–3).

The ultimate means of assuaging grief, however, was to bring a prisoner back to the relatives of someone who had been killed. Raiding parties were often instigated at the wish of the *female* relatives of the deceased. They were often small, and composed of young men who were 'related by marriage to the bereaved women but who lived in other longhouses and were obliged to form a raiding party or face the matrons' accusation of cowardice' (Ritcher 1983:532). When an enemy prisoner was brought home to them it was up to the deceased man's relatives, especially the matrons of the household, to decide whether or not the prisoner would be adopted into their household permanently, or whether they were to be ritually tortured, executed and then eaten.

The most detailed descriptions of this come from the Jesuits themselves, in particular from Father Jogues, who was captured by the Iroquois, and later adopted into a family. Although the description is of the Iroquois, the Huron engaged in similar practices, as we shall see. According to Jogues's account, he was first tortured by having his finger cut off at the request of a woman who had 'presented a brasse of Porcelain to enforce her request' (Thwaites 1896–1901, 40:131). As Jogues himself describes it:

> The One-eyed man, who had approached our scaffold with a purpose which he did not execute at the time, took my right hand and examined my fingers; and, just as I was thinking that the fingers of that hand were a little more necessary to me than those of the left, he took the latter and dropped the right. Then calling a child, from four or five years of age, he gave him his knife, took the index or forefinger of my left hand, and made the child cut it off . . . . The finger cut off, that man hung around my neck a part of the Porcelain beads which the woman mentioned above had given; and with the rest he encircled my severed finger, and carried it to my captor.
>
> (ibid. 40:131–3)

Jogues's amputated finger was cauterized with a burning coal 'applied to it by the same child who had done the cutting'. The following day Jogues and other captives were taking to another village 'where there was to be held a great Assembly of the Notables of the country' (ibid. 40:135). There the prisoners were taunted, ridiculed, insulted, hit and burnt for three days and two nights. 'In a word', Jogues wrote, 'everyone did us some injury, according to his fancy.' The torture continued when the prisoners were very rigourously bound... the cords around our hands and feet being made fast at such a height, and in a manner so extremely uncomfortable, that we were half suspended in the air; we suffered, in consequence, a pain of such excruciating severity that a good old man, seeing plainly that it was unbearable, loosened our bonds and relieved us a little.

(ibid. 40:137)

After two days, Jogues was given to 'a good old woman in place of a brother of hers, who had been captured or killed by those on our side'. This woman then was given the right to decide Jogues's fate, and could have made him die 'in all the torments that could have been suggested by revenge'. She decided instead to adopt Jogues.

As soon as I had entered her cabin, she began to sing a song of the dead, in which two of her daughters accompanied her. I was near the fire during these doleful chants and was made to sit down on a kind of table slightly raised from the ground; and then I became aware that I was given in return for a dead man, the last mourning for whom these women were renewing, – causing the departed to become alive again in my person, according to their custom.

(ibid. 40:137–9)

Jogues's finger was treated, he was given a blanket, some stockings and shoes 'after their fashion' and an old, greasy shirt,

all that with so much savage kindness and so great affection, that I have not experienced more cordiality among the Savages who are friendly to us. Moreover, they went to my captor, and paid him for my life with several thousand Porcelain beads.

(ibid. 40:139)

Jogues was finally returned to the French through the auspices of a 'captain', the brother of the woman who had adopted him as her brother.

As in Jogues's experience, prisoners who were brought back to a Huron village were beaten, tortured and then adopted into a family. There they were given the status of the person whom they were replacing, and addressed as uncle, brother, nephew, etc. It was only after a certain length of time that their final fate was decided. If the prisoner was to be put to death, he was usually allowed to give a farewell death feast, a custom that was the right of any Huron who knew he or she was dying. At that feast the prisoner was expected to entertain the gathering by telling about his war honours and other acts of bravery. On the appointed day he was taken out into the open, where the sun could be witness. The Huron viewed the torture both as an act of revenge, and as a sacrifice to the sun, and there were certain restrictions to follow, as a result. No one should engage in sexual intercourse the evening before. The torture itself was to proceed in an orderly manner, beginning with the prisoner's legs. The prisoner was to suffer as much as possible, for as long as possible, and was to die in view of the sun.

It is difficult not to be struck by the combination of kindness and cruelty, the exquisitely painful techniques used and by the sexual innuendos, both covert and overt, which accompanied the torture. The fact that the torture victim became someone's uncle, brother, cousin or father only serves to underscore the intensely emotional and incestuous/sadistic nature of the practices.

One of the most detailed accounts of the torture of an Iroquois prisoner by Huron captors, was recorded by François Joseph Le Mercier in 1637. Early in September of that year Huron warriors had returned with eight Iroquois prisoners and had divided them up among the members of the three different tribes that had participated in the raid. One of the prisoners came to the village of Onnentisati, where the Jesuits were staying. On the prisoner's arrival in the village, the old men 'to whom the young men on their return from war leave the disposition of their spoils' held a council to decide who should get to adopt the prisoner 'for it is customary, when some notable personage has lost one of his relatives in war, to give him a present of some captive taken from the enemy, to dry his tears and partly assuage his grief' (ibid. 13:37–9).

It was decided that the prisoner be given to a man called Saouandaouascouay, whom the Jesuits identified as 'one of the chief men of the country'. The gift was made 'in consideration of one of his nephews who had been captured by the Iroquois' (ibid. 13:37–9). The prisoner was dressed in fine beaver robes, and given strings of porcelain beads to wear around his neck and head. Although the prisoner had previously been beaten and was made to sing, Le Mercier noted that, 'I will say here that, up to the hour of his torment, we saw only acts of humanity exercised towards him'. The villagers all brought him food, and treated him only 'as a brother and a friend'. Speaking to him at the beginning of his stay in the village, one of the village clan leaders said 'My nephew, thou hast good reason to sing, for no one is doing thee any harm; behold thyself now among thy kindred and friends' (ibid. 13:41). 'Good God, what a compliment!', was Le Mercier's response. 'All those who surrounded him, with their affected kindness and their fine words, were so many butchers who showed him a smiling face only to treat him afterwards with more cruelty' (ibid. 13:39).

A few days after the prisoner's arrival in the village, Saouan-daouascoüay fixed the day of his death. Addressing the prisoner with 'incredible gentleness' he announced:

> My nephew, thou must know that when I first received news that thou wert at my disposal, I was wonderfully pleased, fancying that he whom I had lost had been, as it were, brought back to life, and was returning to his country. At the same time I resolved to give thee thy life; I was already thinking of preparing thee a place in my cabin, and thought that thou wouldst pass the rest of thy days pleasantly with me. But now that I see thee in this conditions, thy fingers gone, and thy hands half rotten, I change my mind, and I am sure that thou thyself wouldst regret to live longer. I shall do thee a greater kindness to tell thee that thou must prepare to die; is it not so!? It is the Tohontaenras[1] who have treated thee so ill and who also cause thy death. Come then, my nephew, be of good courage; prepare thyself for this evening, and do not allow thyself to be cast down through the fear of the tortures.'
>
> (ibid. 13:53)

During the speech the sister of the deceased entered the cabin bringing the prisoner some food. She is so solicitous of his well being that Le Mercier comments:

> You would almost have said that he was her own son, and I do not know that this creature did not represent to her him whom she had lost. Her countenance was very sad, and her eyes seemed all bathed in tears. This Captain often put his own pipe in the prisoner's mouth, wiped with his own hands the sweat that rolled down his face, and cooled him with a feather fan.
>
> (ibid. 13:55)

At noon the prisoner prepared his farewell feast, called his *Athataion*. He addressed the people who came as brothers, and told them that he would soon die, inviting them to 'amuse yourselves boldly around me, – I fear neither tortures nor death' (ibid. 13:57). He was then taken to the cabin of a war captain, called the 'house of cut-off heads', where the torture began with each person in the cabin trying to burn him with a firebrand. 'Meanwhile', Le Mercier reports, 'he shrieked like a lost soul; the whole crowd imitated his cries, or rather smothered them with horrible shouts.' They broke his hands, pierced his ears with sticks. He was made to sit on hot ashes and burning coals. This torture continued throughout the night, and when he fainted from pain, he was revived and tortured again. As Le Mercier recounts the scene:

> One thing, in my opinion, greatly increased his consciousness of suffering – that anger and rage did not appear upon the faces of those who were tormenting him, but rather gentleness and humanity, their words expressing only raillery or tokens of friendship and good will. There was no strife as to who should burn him, – each one took his turn; thus they gave themselves leisure to meditate some new device to make him feel the fire more keenly .... No one spared himself, and each one strove to surpass his companion in cruelty. But, as I have said, what was most calculated in all this to plunge him into despair, was their raillery and the compliments they paid him when they approached to burn him. This one said to him, 'Here, uncle, I must burn thee'; and afterwards this uncle found himself changed into a canoe. 'Come', said he, 'let me calk and pitch my canoe, it is a beautiful new canoe which I lately traded for; I must stop all the water holes well', and meanwhile he was passing the brand all along his legs.
>
> (ibid. 13:67–9)

The torture victim was made to indicate some part or other of his body that he would prefer to have burned. Asked 'uncle hast thou had enough', and replying that he indeed had, the prisoner was then told he had not had enough. Given food to eat, he refused and was asked 'dost thou think thou art master here' (ibid. 13:71). Le Mercier marvelled that in the midst of all the taunts, jeers and torture 'not one abusive or impatient word escaped his lips'. The next morning the prisoner was taken outside, tied to a tree and again burned over his entire body. Firebrands were forced down his throat, and even 'into his fundament' (ibid. 13:77). They burned his eyes, they applied red-hot hatchets to his shoulders, they hung some around his neck; he was not allowed to sit. While he was still barely alive, and 'fearing that he would die otherwise than by the knife', they cut off his foot, his hand, and then his head.

Cannibalism played a central role in the ritual of prisoner torture. To begin with, while the victim was being tortured, the torturers would often cut or bite off a finger, an ear or some other body part and force the victim to eat it. Describing another torture which took place the previous year, Le Jeune writes:

As soon as the [prisoner] who had been brought to the three Rivers had set foot upon land, the women and children fell upon him, each one trying to see which could strike the hardest blows. Meanwhile the prisoner sings, and continues on his way without turning around to see who strikes him. A wretched cripple, seeing him entirely naked, took a heavy doubled rope, and lashed this poor body, upon the back, upon the stomach, and upon the chest, so that he staggered and was about to fall, his flesh becoming quite livid and dead. Others put fire in his mouth, others thrust firebrands at him from different directions, to roast him; then he was given a little respite, and was made to sing and dance; a woman came and bit into his finger, trying to tear it off, as a dog would do; not being successful, she finally took a knife and cut it off, then put it in his mouth, to make him swallow it; he tried to do so, but could not. Having restored it to this Tigress, she roasted it, to give it to some children to eat, who continued to suck it for some time.... Another time two young men took this poor wretch by his two arms, and bit into them as greedily as rabid Wolves, shaking him as an angry dog shakes a carcass to get a piece off.

(ibid. 9:257)

There are several points to note about the torture of prisoners. The Jesuits observed that women participated in the activities with as much or more vigour than men. Not only were Huron women capable of the most aggressive acts, but they were not prevented from expressing that aggression as long as they did so in socially acceptable ways. Second, in torturing their prisoners the Huron continued to address them as uncle, brother, cousin, and they pretended their actions were helpful, and not cruel and murderous. In doing so they were able to mock all the constraints placed on them by a society in which they were never permitted to express anger against anyone, no matter what the offence. Finally, the ritualized torture had both an oral-aggressive and a sexual-sadistic component to it equally expressed by women and men. To eat a tortured prisoner was to show how much contempt you had for that person. A dead, tortured prisoner ceased to be brother, cousin, uncle, and became an object of derision, less than human. An Algonkian was reputed to have given the following information to the Jesuit Jacques Buteux concerning the possible fate of the Jesuit Isaac Jogues after his capture by the Iroquois:

> This time we will see whether or not the Hiroquois fear you.... As soon as thy Brother reaches their country, the Captains will assemble, and, if the French name frightens them, they will speak thus: 'Let us not eat the flesh of the Frenchmen: that flesh is not good food, – it is a poison, that will kill us if we taste it. Let us take them back to their brothers and country-men.' That is what they will say, if they fear you; and in the Spring they will bring back thy Brother and the two Frenchmen whom they hold captive. If, on the contrary, they despise you, they will call out, on the arrival of thy Brother and of the Frenchmen who accompany him: 'Now let us eat, let us see how the flesh of the French tastes; let us swallow them all whole'. Thereupon they will burn them; they will make them suffer a thousand torments; they will cut them in pieces and throw them by quarters into great kettles; they will eat them with pleasure; every one will want to taste them. And when they are full to repletion, they will say 'That is good meat, that flesh is delicate; we must eat some.'
>
> (ibid. 22:283–5)

For the Huron, warfare had really only one purpose: to bring home a prisoner who could act as the cipher for everyone's aggressive impulses. But, as in the case of all acting out of aggressive impulses, when not discharged against the real objects of aggression, the relief is at best only temporary. The Huron and their traditional enemies were locked into ritualized practices that they were compelled to repeat, season after season.

Desires of the soul

Fears and aggression were not only dealt with as directly and as cruelly as in prisoner torture and cannibalism. The Huron had other, less vicious means of dealing with emotional issues. They believed, for example, that there were two orders of desires – those which were generally voluntary, and others 'inborn and concealed'. The inborn desires came from the depths of the soul, 'not through any knowledge, but by means of a certain blind transporting of the soul to certain objects' (Thwaites 1896–1901, 33:189).

For the Huron, dreams were the language of the soul. It was through dreams that the soul made its desires known. When the desires were fulfilled, the soul was content. When they were denied the soul became angry. Operating entirely beyond the consciousness of the individual, a soul whose desires have been denied might refuse to give the body 'the good and happiness' it needed, and in revolt against the body cause various diseases and even death (ibid. 33:189).

Le Jeune took great pains to emphasize the importance of dreams to the Huron:

> They have a faith in dreams which surpasses all belief; and if Christians were to put into executing all their divine inspirations with as much care as our Savages carry out their dreams, no doubt they would very soon become great Saints. They look upon their dreams as ordinances and irrevocable decrees, the execution of which it is not permitted without crime to delay .... The dream is the oracle that all these poor Peoples consult and listen to, the Prophet which predicts to them future events, the Cassandra which warns them of misfortunes that threaten them, the usual Physician in their sickness, the Esculapius and Galen of the whole Country, – the most absolute master they have. If a Captain speaks one way and a dream another, the Captain might shout his head off in vain, – the dream is first obeyed. It is their Mercury in their journeys, their domestic Economy in their families. The dream often presides in their councils; traffic, fishing, and hunting are all undertaken usually under its sanction, and almost as if only to satisfy it. They hold nothing so precious that they would not readily deprive themselves of it for the sake of a dream. If they have been successful in hunting, if they bring back their canoes laden with fish, all this is at the discretion of a dream. A dream will take away from them sometimes their whole year's provisions. It prescribes their feasts, their dances, their songs, their games, – in a word, the dream does everything and is in truth the principal God of the Huron.
>
> (ibid. 10:169–71)

Le Jeune mitigates this somewhat by telling us that not all dreams are treated equally. Certain people's dreams are ignored, while others are heeded. There are some people, he wrote, 'who dream in vain; for

179

these no one will stir a step' (ibid. 10:171). If someone is without resources, for example, his or her dreams attract little attention. Even people who have a reputation for 'dreaming well' did not attach the same importance to all dreams, recognizing 'some of them as false and some as true, – the latter, they say being quite rare' (ibid. 10:171).

One of the major points of conflict between the Huron and the Jesuits centred around the conduct of moral life. A large part of that conflict was focused on the question of fear – both on what was to be feared and what one did to appease and control the forces that caused one fear. While the Jesuits and the Huron might have shared some of the same fears and some of the same aggressiveness, they expressed these emotions very differently. For the Jesuits, the Huron's attempts to control their fears and to diffuse their aggressiveness were serious moral transgressions. Not only did the Huron not fear God, but the very things that they did to mitigate their own fears contravened what the Jesuits felt were God's laws. Indeed the very things the Hurons did to restore balance within themselves, such as dream interpretation, in the Jesuits' view put them in league with or under the influence of the Devil – the source of all evil.

Interpreting dreams was a delicate business, often entrusted to a specialist – the *ocata*, who went into a self-induced trance to analyse the meaning of a particular dream. Men sometimes had dreams about success or dangers in warring, which could be fulfilled or averted only if certain gifts were given. Sometimes, particularly frightening or dangerous situations had to be enacted in symbolic ways. For example, one young man dreamed that he would be captured and tortured by enemies. A council was held to discuss the matter, where it was decided that the ill fortune of such a dream must be immediately averted. To this end, the clan leaders had twelve or thirteen fires lit on the spot where prisoners were usually tortured and burned. Le Jeune described the events that followed:

> Each one armed himself with firebrands and flaming torches, and they burned this Captive of a Dream; he shrieked like a madman. When he avoided one fire, he at once fell into another. In this manner, he made his way three times around the Cabin; and, as he thus passed, as naked as one's hand, each applied to him a lighted torch, saying: 'Courage, my Brother, it is thus that we have pity on thee.' At the conclusion, they left him an opening by which he might issue from captivity. As he went out, he seized a dog that was held there ready for him, placed it

at once on his shoulders, and carried it among the Cabins as a consecrated victim, which he publicly offered to the Demon of war, begging him to accept this semblance instead of the reality of his Dream. And, in order that the Sacrifice might be fully consummated, the dog was killed with a club, and was singed and roasted in the flames; and after all this, it was eaten at a public feast, in the same manner as they usually eat their Captives.

(ibid. 23:171–3)

Sometimes men and women desired, and were allowed to perform, or to have performed for them, usually unsanctioned sexual acts. Older men might request to have some form of sexual activity with young women. Young people might be asked to dance naked, or invited to have sexual intercourse while the patient looked on (ibid. 17:179). One woman requested that a young man urinate in her mouth (Wrong (ed.) 1939:118, 120).

It was during sleep that the rational, as opposed to the sentient soul left the body, venturing out to places where dreams took place. In response to these dreams the Huron took great care to give their souls what they asked for. A secret desire of the soul, made manifest through a dream was called *Ondinnonk* (ibid. 33:191). The Huron held that there were some among them who were more skilled in discovering the hidden desires of the soul, even if these desires had not yet been made known through a dream. These people were called *Saokata*, and were called in to diagnose people who fell sick. The Huron believed that one of the most effective means of restoring a sick person to health was to discover and fulfil the secret desires of their soul.

The Jesuits, of course, were quite disparaging about the entire process of divining the secret desires of the soul, and the curing ceremonies that surrounded them. They could see only trickery, deceit and faulty reasoning on the part of all involved. In a society, however, where the individual was often forced to submerge himself or herself in a collective identity, almost from birth, where even criminal acts were a collective and not individual responsibility, where everyone was expected to be brave, uncomplaining and above all else cheerful and generous, the acting out of individual and forbidden desires was understandable. Huron life was often short, precarious, full of danger and pain. Public and private ceremonies and practices which took individual needs into account and which allowed for the expression of 'irrational' or 'anti-social' longings, wishes, and desires played a central role in managing individual behaviour.

Consider how much care, preparation and concern for the individual was expressly demonstrated through the preparations for and execution of a feast to restore the health of someone suffering from a disease caused by a secret desire of their soul. To begin with, the sick person need not even be able to articulate what it was that their soul secretly desired. This was given over to an expert who not only determined what the desires were, but also prescribed the exact means of fulfilling them.

If the individual was of any consequence, the leaders of that person's clan would call a council meeting to decide on what they should do, and the issue was treated as a matter of public importance (ibid. 33:163). Once that happened, the entire village became involved in the proceedings necessary to effect someone's cure. Everyone was encouraged to contribute, and people competed with each other to show who could be the most generous. The sick person usually received all he or she wanted and more. Not only did the individual benefit, but the curing ceremonies, feasts and dances which usually took place during the winter, acted as a means whereby meat, fish and other foodstuffs, along with trade goods, were redistributed.

When anger and aggression were expressed within Huron society, it was usually done stealthily, through charms and spells which could only be broken by others trained to do so. According to Le Jeune:

> They say that the Sorcerers ruin them; for if any one has succeeded in an enterprise, if his trading or hunting is successful, immediately these wicked men bewitch him, or some member of his family, so that they have to spend it all in Doctors and Medicines. Hence, to cure these and other diseases, there are a large number of Doctors whom they call Arendiouane. These persons, in my opinion, are true Sorcerers, who have access to the Devil.
>
> (ibid. 8:123)

The belief that others, through jealousy or malevolence could cause disease and death was strong among the Huron. The Jesuits report, for example, on a man who, when he fell ill, was convinced that another had given him the disease. This was because the sick man had been angry with the other man 'and his fear that I would kill him induced him to bargain for my death with the Manitou' (ibid. 8:237). Although the Huron were not allowed to directly express hostility, jealousy or anger towards any member of the society, those feelings were clearly there, and were allowed expression through the indirect means of sorcery and accusations of sorcery. In the case of the man who fell ill and who attributed his illness to his rival, for example, the man seems to have projected on to his rival actions that he himself would have liked to have been able to take.

The *Ononharoia*

During the winter, when both men and women were resident in the villages and not out in the fields or on hunting, trading or warring trips, the Huron celebrated the *Ononharoia* ceremony, translated by the Jesuits as the 'turning round the head' or 'turning the brain upside down' ceremony (ibid. 17:167). This was the great soul-curing ceremony, lasting several days and held to cure anyone in the village who felt physically or emotionally ill.

In 1639 Le Jeune reported at length on one of these ceremonies, which came to be centred around a woman by the name of Angoutenc, who although born in Ossossané, the village where the Jesuits were staying, had married and gone to live in another village. During the Ononharoia ceremonies in the village where she was living, this woman happened to leave her longhouse carrying one of her small daughters when she saw the moon leave its spot in the sky and appear in front of her as a beautiful tall woman, also holding a young girl in her arms. As Le Jeune recounts the meeting:

> 'I am,' quoth this spector to her, 'the immortal seignior general of these countries, and of those who inhabit them; in testimony whereof I desire and order that in all quarters of my domain, those who dwell therein shall offer thee presents which must be the product of their own country'.
>
> (ibid. 17:165)

The spectre went on to name the presents that she desired from the various countries, including one from the French. Finding the feast currently being celebrated in the village agreeable, she commanded that many others like it also be celebrated in other villages. As for Angoutenc, she was told: 'I love thee, and on that account I wish that thou shouldst henceforth be like me; and, as I am wholly of fire, I desire that thou be also at least of the color of fire' (ibid. 17:167).

Angoutenc was ordered to wear a red cap, plume, belt, leggings, shoes and other clothing with red ornaments.

The vision over, Angoutenc returned to her longhouse. As soon as she reached the door she collapsed and her muscles contracted. Everyone concluded that she had fallen sick from a disease and the remedy for that disease would be the *Ononharoia*. The leaders of the village of Ossossané, where she had been born, declared that this affair was of vital importance to the welfare of the entire country and had the announcement made throughout the village. People from that village made the trip to fetch her from where she was living, and carried her back to Ossossané in a basket.

They gave Angoutenc the twenty-two presents that the moon/woman had commanded. That evening, fires were lit along the middle of all the longhouses. Angoutenc, whose muscles relaxed a bit was supported between two aides and walked through the middle of the longhouses, and thus through the middle of 200 or 300 fires 'without doing herself any harm, even complaining all the time how little heat she felt' (ibid. 17:177). Following this there occurred:

> a general mania of all the people of the village who, – except, perhaps, a few Old Men, – undertake to run wherever the sick woman has passed, adorned or daubed in their fashion, vying with one another in the frightful contortions of their faces – making everywhere such a din, and indulging in such extravagances ... [comparable to] the furies of Hell. They enter, then, everywhere, and having during the time of the feast, in all the evenings and nights of the three days that it lasts, liberty to do anything, and no one dares say a word to them. If they find kettles over the fire, they upset them; they break the earthen pots, knock down the dogs, throw fire and ashes everywhere, so thoroughly that often the cabins and entire villages burn down.
>
> (ibid. 17:177–9)

The next day, everyone again went through the longhouses where Angoutenc had passed, this time for the purposes of having their own desires guessed, by giving riddles:

> For example, some one will say, 'What I desire and what I am seeking is that which bears a lake within itself;' and by this is intended a pumpkin or calabash ... Another will intimate that

he desires an Andacwandet feast, – that is to say, many fornications and adulteries. His Riddle being guessed, there is no lack of persons to satisfy his desire ... As soon, then, as the Riddle is proposed, they immediately strive to guess it; and saying, 'It is that,' they at the same time throw the object to the person who demands and announces his desires. If this is really his thought, he exclaims that it has been found, and there upon there is rejoicing by all those in the cabin, who manifest their delight by striking against the pieces of bark that form the walls of their cabins; at the same time the patient feels relieved.

(ibid. 17:179–81)

On the third day of this particular feast, Angoutenc was again walked through all the longhouses, this time proposing her 'last and principal desire' in the form of a riddle. She related her troubles 'in a plaintive and languishing voice' and everyone fell over themselves to find out what it was that she desired. When her riddle had been solved, the entire village rejoiced. Although Angoutenc found herself much better after the feast, she did not feel herself to be entirely cured, attributing this to some failure to follow exact detail, or to some 'imperfection in the ceremony' (ibid. 17:187).

Games and Gambling

Other forms of ritualized and collectively sanctioned ways of expressing competition and aggression open to men and women were games and gambling. Although only men played lacrosse, both sexes gambled, playing the 'dish game' and *aescara*. Often teams of different villages played against each other and games went on for days. Betting was for high stakes. Losers were expected to take defeat graciously – but individuals who gambled away their household's property sometimes committed suicide out of shame. Games, like other activities associated with competition and with the expression of feelings, were sometimes undertaken to avert disaster, famine, disease or were played during ceremonies. Preparations for these games were elaborate. 'It is beyond my power', wrote Le Jeune, 'to picture the diligence and activity of our Barbarians in preparing themselves and in seeking all the means and omens for good luck and success in their games' (ibid. 17:203).

They assemble at night, and spend the time partly in shaking the dish and ascertaining who has the best hand, – partly in

185

displaying their charms, and exhorting them. Towards the end they lie down to sleep in the same cabin, having previously fasted, and for some time abstained from their wives, – and all this to have some favourable dream; in the morning they have to relate what happened during the night.

Finally, they collect all the things which they have dreamed can bring good luck, and fill pouches with them, in order to carry them. They search everywhere, besides, for those who have charms suitable to the game, or Ascwandics or familiar demons, that these may assist the one who holds the dish, and be nearest to him when he shakes it. If there be some old men whose presence is regarded as efficacious in augmenting the strength and virtue of their charms, they are not satisfied to take the charms to them, but sometimes even load these men themselves upon the shoulders of the young men, to be carried to the place of the assembly. And inasmuch as we pass in the country for master sorcerers, they do not fail to admonish us to bring our prayer, and to perform many ceremonies, in order to make them win.

(ibid. 17:203)

Once a game began the principal players took their place in the middle of the longhouse, surrounded by assistants whose role it was to attract good luck to their player, and to counter the spells of the other side. Betting was heavy, and people would wager everything they owned down to the clothing they wore.

Rituals of Warfare

But it was with warfare and all the rituals of torture and cannibalism that accompanied it that the Huron allowed themselves the widest latitude for aggressive expression. The decision to go to war often came out of the expressed wishes for revenge by those who were in some stage of a mourning ritual for a relative who had been killed by enemy warriors. Mourning rituals emphasized self-neglect and neglect of social duties to such an extent that other villagers might become concerned for their own safety, as the mourner could lose all control and become destructive in their grief. The formation of a war party, which allowed the anger and desire for destruction unleashed by the death of a relative to be safely discharged, followed proscribed patterns, including threats of being labelled cowards by the matrons (Ritcher 1983:532).

Ritcher, in an insightful article on Iroquoian warfare practices, maintains that this venting of grief over loss of relatives and the general sense of superiority that came from participating in the humiliation of the enemy were the underlying motivations for Iroquoian warfare. According to Ritcher:

> Mourners were not the only ones to benefit from the ceremonial torture and execution of captives. While grieving relatives vented their emotions, all of the villagers, by partaking in the humiliation of every prisoner and the torture of some, were able to participate directly in the defeat of their foes. Warfare thus dramatically promoted group cohesion and demonstrated to the Iroquois their superiority over their enemies.
>
> (ibid.: 535)

Feasts given to announce an intention to go to war also followed a set pattern and presaged a future feast of human flesh. Finally, the torture, death and ritual cannibalism, or the adoption of the prisoner into a household, were strictly controlled and undertaken within clear guidelines for such behaviours. To ignore the rituals was to invite defeat. In a letter addressed to the Father Provincial of the Province of France and dated 1642, Isaac Jogues described a ceremony conducted by his Iroquois captors, which was intended to appease the spirits for the Iroquois' failure to follow prescribed rituals.

> During the winter, at a solemn feast which they had made of two Bears, which they had offered to their demon, they had used this form of words: 'Aireskoi,[2] thou dost right to punish us, and to give us no more captives' (they were speaking of the Algonquins, of whom that year they had not taken one; these are, moreover, their chief enemies...) 'because we have sinned by not eating the bodies of those whom thou last gavest us; but we promise thee to eat the first ones whom thou shalt send us, as we now do with these two Bears'.
>
> (Thwaites 1896–1901, 39:221)

Warfare for the Huron, and for other Iroquoian people who shared in the same cultural traditions, while carried out on the pretext of easing the grief of those who had recently lost relatives to similar activities of the enemy, fulfilled a much wider function. It allowed the participants to express rage, anger and grief openly and safely, emotions which would otherwise have to go unexpressed in societies which scrupulously and ruthlessly prohibited any such feelings to be expressed towards kin and others with whom they had daily contact. According to Le Jeune, the Huron made a 'pretence of never getting angry, not because of the beauty of this virtue, for which they have not even a name, but for their own contentment and happiness, I mean, to avoid the bitterness caused by anger' (ibid. 8:231).

The Huron were expected to restrain themselves, by force if necessary, and not to express any anger towards other Huron. Le Jeune claimed to have heard only one man say out loud that he was angry and when this was overheard by others 'they kept their eyes on him, for when these Barbarians are angry, they are dangerous and unrestrained' (ibid. 8:231). According to Le Jeune the Huron were 'very much attached to each other and agree admirably'. Disputes, quarrels, and accusations were rarely heard; anger was reserved to be vented towards enemies, not towards fellow Huron.

Bressani echoes Le Jeune's observations, writing about a 'captain' who had been wounded by some young man. When this wounded clan leader saw that his clan members were angry enough to try to revenge themselves on the perpetrator of the crime he is reputed to have stopped them by saying: 'Enough; did you not feel the earth shake with horror at that audacity?' According to Bressani '[t]his causes them stoically to dissimulate their passions, especially that of resentment; and it is a great reproach to say to one who begins to grow angry, 'So you are getting angry?' (ibid. 39:267).

Women, although they did not go to war, clearly played an important role in decisions, preparation and the final culmination of a war party's efforts – the torture and eating of prisoners. It is important, too, to note the Huron's treatment of warriors who died during a battle. They were not accorded honours, but were treated with caution and interred in separate graves away from those who had died peacefully, lest their anger disturbed the others. The Huron believed that the souls of these dead warriors were destined to constantly wander, seeking revenge. The revenge that the Huron sought against their living enemies could in no way make up for the wrongs that were done to their slain relatives. Anyone who died a violent death was condemned to an eternity of unfulfilled, unrequited rage. Under these circumstances it is interesting that young men would take the risk to seek out enemies. And when they did take the risk, it is clear from the descriptions left to us by first-hand observers that they took every pain to minimize the possibility of their own death. Sagard described their methods as follows:

> Their warfare is, properly speaking, nothing but surprises and treachery. Every year in the spring, and during the whole summer, five or six hundred young Huron men, or more, go and scatter themselves over some Iroquois territory, five or six in one place, five or six in another... and they lie flat on their belly in the fields and woods and alongside the main roads and paths, and when it is night they prowl about everywhere and enter even the towns and villages to try to catch some one, whether man, woman, or child, and if they take them alive, they carry them off to their own country to put them to death over a slow fire.
>
> (Wrong (ed.) 1939:152)

Sagard also noted that the Huron did not torture women, girls or children, but usually gave them as presents to others who had recently lost someone in war (ibid. 1939:153).

The Europeans often branded the Huron as cowardly because of their use of surprise attacks, unwillingness to fight when outnumbered, and their contentment with taking a few captives in a battle. Champlain, in particular, could not understand why his allies would retreat if they sustained any casualties, even though in Champlain's eyes they were winning the battle.

The introduction of the fur trade added another dimension to this complex. In addition to the 'traditional' motives for undertaking raiding parties, was now added a further incentive, at least for the Iroquois who had been the enemies of the Huron. Lacking furs of their own, the Iroquois began a period of raiding the Huron who were bringing the furs down the St Lawrence to the French, but, more particularly, they also raided the Huron on their return when they had European goods. Raiding Huron trading parties became a way for the Iroquois to acquire European trade goods. However, this new feature in no way replaced earlier motives. Rather, the more they sought and fought for furs, the more deaths there were; the more they were compelled to seek revenge for slain comrades, the more they were compelled to renew their efforts at raiding (Ritcher 1983:540).

WOMEN, FEAR AND AGGRESSION

In all of the dream guessing rituals, gaming, warfare and prisoner torture and cannibalism of the Huron, displacement of aggression played a central role. A man is burned by his friends and relatives instead of by his enemies (a curious twist, because burning one's enemies allows the aggressors to displace the unacceptable feelings they might have towards close relatives and friends on to others who, as enemies, can be made to take the real intended victim's place). A dog is killed and eaten instead of the man who fears this fate. A woman walks through fire, and along with others becomes adept at handling that dangerous element without being burned. Presents are given in order to appease desires that would not be fulfilled if they had been expressed directly. Seemingly insane behaviour is encouraged in those who, under 'normal' conditions, would not be allowed such avenues of self-expression. Games are played with teams of assistants who direct negative spells towards the opponent and who avert the same negative spells coming towards their player from the supporters of the opponent.

It is clear that women were not excluded from any of this expression of aggression. Nor did they play a negligible part in the preparation for warfare, or in the carrying out of the ceremonies that crowned every successful warfare undertaking – the torture and eating of prisoners. First, women played a central role in providing the impetus for undertaking warring parties. It was often at their request that the male members of their clan began to organize themselves to go on a raid. Second, women provided the warriors with the food that they needed to sustain themselves on the way. They also spun the hemp that men needed to make their weapons and armour. One Jesuit observer reported, for example, that one of the chiefs of a large Huron village went around to all the longhouses

> exhorting the women to take courage and that when the young men should bring them some hemp to spin they should willingly render them the service so that they could make weapons to go to war against the Hiroquois in the spring.
>
> (Thwaites 1896–1901, 17:265)

Women's participation, it would seem, could make or break men's plans for warring. Moreover, women participated in the culminating ceremonies of warfare, and while they did not get glory for bringing in a prisoner, they did get the satisfaction of being able to vent as much rage and grief as they wished.

Likewise, women were not set apart from men as legitimized objects of aggression. Although, as the creation myths involving Aataentsic demonstrate, women's potential for destructiveness, and men's potential for creating and protecting were recognized, women were not segregated from men in the social world as more dangerous or morally weaker beings. All this was soon to change. When the Jesuits finally were able to set the moral direction, the appropriate objects of fear and aggression became redefined. New definitions of what was moral, new codes of behaviour, ways of interpreting emotions and of acting on them were put into place. Women, especially, were made into dangerous beings, the legitimate objects of men's aggression.

9

'CHAIN HER BY ONE FOOT'

Until the series of events which devastated their society in the mid-seventeenth century, Huron women and men maintained egalitarian positions in relation to one another. Although men and women were separated from each other by a social division of labour which structured their lives in very different ways, neither sex dominated the other on any of the dimensions that we have so far examined. As the bearers of the next generation Huron women were not subjected to control by men in the interests of either ensuring the reproduction of society as a whole or of providing an adequate supply of labourers for each kin corporate group. Until the arrival of the Europeans, at least, the Huron seem to have been relatively demographically stable, and capable, in spite of low birth rates combined with low life expectancies, to reproduce sufficient labour power without resorting to men controlling women's reproductive capacities.

Second, women and men held relatively egalitarian statuses in terms of their capacities to access the means of production necessary for subsistence production. Men and women were also equally able to gain access to the labour power of others in co-operative groupings when it was required to successfully complete a production task. Men and women, by virtue of birth and thus membership in a kin corporate group, as well as through marriage, had the right of access to the products of the labour of others; men and women of the appropriate, socially defined reciprocal kin categories had the right of use of the products of each other's labour. As long as any individual Huron had kin in the appropriately defined relational categories, or as long as others were willing to adopt an 'orphan' or 'stranger' into their descent group, no Huron went without access to the means of production, the co-operative labour of others necessary to undertake subsistence activities or the product of the labour of others defined as kin.

Third, Huron men and women were equal in terms of their abilities to share in the consumption of trade goods as well as in the decisions affecting community life, including warfare and the treatment of enemies taken as prisoners. No Huron women participated directly in trade, in political councils or in warfare. However, kin corporate structures were organized in such a way that men were bound by decision-making processes and redistributive networks that included women. Whatever men brought back into their wives' or their mothers' households – whether hunted meat, trade goods, prisoners of war, or decisions made in council on a course of action to be taken – passed through the hands of women as well as men. Women were not excluded from the enjoyment of trade goods or the consumption of meat and other foodstuffs that were exclusively produced by men. Nor were they excluded from the torture and eating of war prisoners. They took an active part in the decision-making processes that affected the entire life of the society. Women encouraged or discouraged men from going to war; they decided whether nor not they would comply with decisions made in council by clan representatives; they appointed or helped to depose those leaders.

Finally, neither men nor women were identified as being especially dangerous for the well-being of society. Although in Huron myth, women were more capable of evil actions, and men of good, in day to day living neither sex was singled out as being particularly worthy of fear. Nor was either sex made the object of societal expressions of aggression. Neither women nor men were identified as being more powerful, closer to God or more moral and capable of rational thought. If anything, women were considered to be more valuable than men, because they 'peopled the country'. Institutionalized structures channelled aggressive, jealous and fearful behaviour away from individuals within the society and outward to a well-defined enemy. When these feelings were expressed internally they were done so in ritualized, institutionalized ways – through sorcery, dream guessing or ritualized insanity. But whatever the means of discharging aggression, women, as a category, were never singled out as fitting objects. In Huron society women acted as subjects, with no greater or lesser rights to express their feelings than men.

It was this complex of institutional and ideological structures, centring on matrilineal, matrilocal kin corporate groupings, through which rights and obligations circulated in ways that assured the relatively egalitarian status of *all* members of the society, that had to be replaced if women were to be brought under the control of men. While the Jesuits were committed missionaries with a clear vision both of their task and of its importance to the salvation of the world, they were few in number compared to the Huron and they lacked the means of physical force necessary to conquer the natives of New France and to make them submit to Christianization. The disorganization of traditional institutional structures, the demoralization of the Huron (and the Montagnais) and the final subjugation of women to men was accomplished in quite a different manner. It was accomplished through the virtual annihilation of the institutional structures, especially the kin corporate groups, that had previously supported women and men in egalitarian positions. That disorganization took place on many levels – demographic, economic, political, ideological and emotional. The end result was that women were deprived of their status as independent subjects, and became objects against whom feelings of fear, aggression and hatred could legitimately be expressed. Women, formerly proud and free, were made submissive as 'lambs'; in short women became sacrificial victims for feelings which could no longer be discharged otherwise.

Yet, even as late as 1645 the struggle waged by the Jesuits against lawlessness, free divorce and diabolic practices was not going well. The missions to New France had not been blessed with frequent miracles; there had been few if any miraculous cures, no one received the gift of tongues or prophecy. The Jesuits had not been favoured with any significant sign or event that would 'make even the most impious acknowledge the power and majesty of Him whose greatness they proclaim' (Thwaites 1896–1901, 28:55). Nor had they received nearly enough money in aid and gifts which could have been employed to promote more conversions. Finally, they did not have

> force at hand, and the support of that sharp sword which serves the Church in so holy a manner to give authority to her Decrees, to maintain Justice, and to curb the insolence of those who trample under foot the holiness of her mysteries.
>
> (ibid. 28:55)

As Le Jeune wrote:

> what can be expected from these barbarous nations when it has not pleased God to bless us with frequent miracles, and to make the Faith more agreeable to them by the pleasant things that it would cause Heaven to shower, even in this life, on those who

should submit to his Laws; and when we have not here even such temporal aids as the succour, the benefits, and the gifts which have been employed with Savages in other countries of the World to procure their conversion?

(ibid. 28:55)

Lacking money, military force and divine intervention, the Jesuits' project in New France advanced only on the heels of the almost complete annihilation of the very people they sought to convert.

DISEASE, EPIDEMICS AND WARFARE

In 1634 the Jesuits made the first record of the appearance and spread of an epidemic disease in New France. Huron who went to Trois Rivières to trade in that year came into contact with Montagnais and Algonkian who were already there and dying in large numbers (ibid. 7:221). Huron traders, in turn, brought the disease back home with them and so many Huron fell ill and were incapacitated that autumn that crops could not be harvested and were left to rot in the fields (ibid. 8:87–9). Brébeuf, who observed the effects of the epidemic among the Huron, described the course of the disease as beginning with a high fever, followed by a rash, then impaired vision or blindness and terminating with diarrhoea. He described the rash as 'a sort of measles or smallpox, but different from that common in France' (ibid. 8:89), while Le Jeune described it as 'a sort of measles, and an oppression of the stomach' (ibid. 7:221).

Although some French fell ill, they did not suffer the same intensity of symptoms, and recovered within a few days. Few Huron died in this first round of epidemic disease, but those who fell ill recovered very slowly, and many remained in a weakened state during the winter months. Whatever the specific diseases, the first appearance of epidemics in New France coincided with the return of the Jesuits to that country. The epidemic of 1634 and the ones that followed were to reduce the Huron population by at least 50 per cent over a period of six years (Trigger 1976 II:499). While thousands of native people died during these epidemics, very few French even fell ill.

A series of far more deadly epidemics began in 1636. During the autumn of that year an influenza-type disease struck many Huron villages, lasting over the winter and into the spring. About ten per cent of the Nipissings who spent the winter among the Huron died as a result of this epidemic. A lower percentage of Huron than

Nipissings may have died, because the Huron had better housing and diet. Another, more virulent disease struck in 1637, this time affecting the entire confederacy, killing, within two days, many who fell ill (Thwaites 1896–1901, 15:69). Because no European became sick at the same time, modern scholars have argued that the epidemic of 1637 was a European childhood ailment, possibly scarlet fever (Dobyns 1983:22; Trigger 1986:231). In 1639 a smallpox epidemic killed several thousand Huron, and reduced the population to about 9,000, or about half of its pre-1634 size (Thwaites 1896–1901, 19:77–9, 123).

At the same time as the Huron were being decimated by epidemics, the Iroquois mounted a series of concentrated raids into Huron country. They also stepped up their attacks against those Huron traders going to their annual meetings with the French at Tadoussac and Trois Rivières. Meanwhile, counter-measures taken by the Huron met with serious defeat. In 1635 over 500 Huron warriors planned a surprise raid on a Seneca village.[1] Warned of this plan, the Seneca were able to take defensive measures and, in a surprise attack on the Huron, killed 200 and took another 100 prisoner. By 1640 the Iroquois were making frequent raids into Huron territory, attacking women and children as they worked in the fields, and carrying off prisoners, or entering villages at night by stealth, murdering several individuals and then making good an escape (ibid. 22:305). In the years that followed, the Iroquois began attacking and destroying entire villages. No longer content with surprise raids, or with challenging the men of the village to come out and fight, the Iroquois pursued a policy of surprise attacks with total pillage and destruction (ibid. 26:175).

'Disease, war, and famine', wrote Barthelemy Vimont in the *Relation* of 1643/4, 'are the three scourges with which God has been pleased to smite our neophytes since they have commenced to adore him' (ibid. 25:105). The effects on the Huron population were devastating. Whereas even eight years previously there had been eighty or 100 longhouses in a village, only five or six remained. A war leader who might have commanded 800 warriors, now had only thirty or forty. Fleets of 300 or 400 canoes used to arrive every summer to trade at Quebec; now only twenty or thirty came down. But, according to Vimont, 'the most pitiful part', was that 'the remnants of Nations consist almost entirely of women, widows or girls, who cannot all find lawful husbands, and who consequently are in danger of much suffering, or of committing great sins' (ibid. 25:109).

In 1643 the Iroquois mounted a devastating attack into Huron territory and hundreds of Huron were either killed or taken prisoner (ibid. 27:65). As a result, crops were again left unharvested and many Huron suffered from famine that autumn and winter. The French court was sufficiently concerned about the situation that in 1644 the queen made 100,000 francs available to send French soldiers to protect the Huron. These soldiers only stayed for one year, arriving back at Montreal in sixty Huron canoes in September of the following year.[2]

In 1647 the Seneca, Cayuga and Onondaga amassed a war party of over 1,000 men but called off their planned attack until the following year. In the summer of 1648, Iroquois warriors destroyed the village of Teanaostaiaé and another neighbouring town. Seven hundred people were either killed or taken prisoner, the rest fled the village, seeking refuge with other Huron (ibid. 34:99). The Huron most likely lost about one-tenth of their remaining population in this raid (Trigger 1976 II:753). The dislocation of so many survivors in mid-July meant that it was impossible for them to clear lands and plant new crops. As a consequence the Huron suffered, once again, from famine over the winter. The Jesuits reported that many wandered ten to twenty days in the woods without food other than a piece of bark or skin. Some ate the cords of their snowshoes (Thwaites 1896–1901, 27:109).

In the autumn of 1648 the Iroquois reassembled their large war party of 1,000 men for a final assault on the Huron. They spent the winter north of Lake Ontario in order to be in a good position to surprise the Huron in the early spring (ibid. 34:123–5). In March of 1649 they raided and destroyed the villages of Taenhatentaron and St Louis (ibid. 34:125–31; 39:247–51). Among the residents were the Jesuits Jean de Brébeuf and Gabriel Lalemant who were tortured and eaten. The Iroquois were finally turned back when they mounted an attack on the Jesuit mission at Sainte-Marie.

In panic, the surviving Huron decided to burn all their villages and to flee. Some took refuge among the Tionnontaté or the Neutral tribes. Others made their way to the French at Quebec, while still others took refuge on Christian Island, accompanied by the Jesuit Chaumonot. Chaumonot described conditions during the winter of 1649–50 as:

> The famine here has been very severe.... The greater number
> of these poor people ... had passed the whole Summer, a part
> also the Autumn, living in the woods on roots and wild fruits;

or taking, here and there, in the Lakes or Rivers, a few small fish, which aided rather in postponing for a little time their death, than in satisfying the needs of life. Winter having set in, ... [t]hen it was that we were compelled to behold dying skeletons eking out a miserable life, feeding even on the excrements and refuse of nature.... Even carrion dug up, the remains of Foxes and Dogs, excited no horror; and they even devoured one another, but this in secret; for although the Hurons, ere the faith had given them more light than they possessed in infidelity, would not have considered that they committed any sin in eating their enemies, any more than in killing them, yet I can truly say that they regarded with no less horror the eating of their fellow-countrymen than would be felt in France at eating human flesh. But necessity had no longer law; and famished teeth ceased to discern the nature of what they ate. Mothers fed upon their children; brothers on their brothers; while children recognized no longer, in a corpse, him whom, while he lived, they had called their Father.

(ibid. 35:87–9)

Many who did not starve to death died as the result of contagious diseases. Paul Ragueneau, however, saw a positive side to all of this:

it was in the midst of these desolations that God was pleased to bring forth, from their deepest misfortunes, the well-being of this people. Their hearts had become so tractable to the faith that we effected in them, by a single word, more than we had ever been able to accomplish in entire years. These poor people, dying of hunger, came of their own accord to see us, and besought of us Baptism, – which they beheld as near to them as was the death itself which they carried in their bosoms.

(ibid. 35:91)

CHALLENGES TO KIN CORPORATE ORGANIZATION

Demographic Disruption

The kin corporate structure of Huron society could tolerate a certain amount of demographic disruption; there were several different ways of socially reconstructing a kin relationship when death or some other disruption occurred, removing an important kinsman or kinswoman from those who depended on them. When this happened a Huron family could adopt someone to take the place of a recently deceased relative. In his *Relation* of 1639 Paul Le Jeune referred to

> a custom the Savages have of resuscitating or bringing back to life again their departed friends, especially if they were men of influence among them. They transfer the name of the dead to some other man, and lo, the dead is raised to life, and the grief of the relatives is all past.
>
> (ibid. 16:201)

This ceremony took place during a feast, and the person who was to assume a new identity was given a present which, if accepted, bound that person to 'take charge of the family of the deceased, so that his wards call him father' (ibid. 16:203). If the present was made to a warrior, he was committed to go to war to 'kill some of the enemy in place of the deceased who lives again in his person' (ibid. 16:203).

Sometimes it was a prisoner who was thus adopted. Huron prisoner-taking rituals dictated that every prisoner who was brought back to the country was adopted into some family. The adopting families were decided on by clan leaders who had organized the raiding parties, and prisoners were almost always awarded to a prominent family who had recently lost some member to the enemy, in order, as the Huron said, 'to dry up the tears' of the dead man's survivors. If the prisoner pleased the family they might decide not to have him tortured and eaten, but to allow him to live. If such was the decision the adopted prisoner was given the name, title and social position of the person he replaced. This was experienced first hand, as we have seen, by the Jesuit Isaac Jogues. It was also experienced by another Jesuit, François-Joseph Bressani, who was captured by the Mohawk in 1644. Taken from village to village, and tortured at each new location, Bressani was finally adopted by a Mohawk woman whose grandfather had been killed by the Huron. Bressani escaped the Mohawk only when his adoptive granddaughter later decided to sell him to the Dutch for about 200 livres' worth of trade goods.

Strangers who came to live among the Huron, particularly those who were considered important, and trading partners who came from other nations could also be adopted into families. Many Huron who traded with members of other tribes had 'relatives' in those tribes as trading partners. One of the Jesuits' first Huron male converts, Joseph Chihwatenha, for example, accompanied the Jesuits to visit the Tionnontaté, another Iroquoian group living to the west of the Huron, in order to help them establish a mission there. Although the Tionnontaté sent word that if the Jesuits set foot in their village they would most likely be put to death as sorcerers, the strength of the ties of obligation between 'relatives' is underlined by the fact that Chihwatenha was able to persuade his trading partner 'relatives' to provide lodging for himself and his Jesuit companions.[3]

Several families sometimes competed to adopt a newcomer depending on how important he or she was considered to be. When the Recollect first arrived among the Huron, for example, several different families tried to induce them to live with them and to be adopted. Le Caron, the head of the Recollect mission, decided against such a course of action, and requested a cabin be built for him outside the village where he was staying. The Jesuit Father de Quen, Superior at Sillery, found himself in an unsatisfactory position after having been adopted into the family of 'an old woman and her kindred'. After having accepted some beaver pelts from this adoptive family, de Quen was expected to take the place of a deceased relative and 'to do all for them that the deceased was accustomed to do, they had to be fed, lodged, etc., during the winter' (ibid. 27:97–9). Marginal notes to this entry in the Jesuit Journals read, 'gifts accepted are an injury', indicating the extent to which the Jesuits felt put upon by the demands of adoption.

The upshot was that the Jesuits decided to follow the same policy as had the Recollect on the grounds that it was spiritually dangerous for them to live with the Huron. Nakedness as well as the daily living practices of the Huron offended Jesuit sensibilities. 'Religious eyes', Charles Lalemant wrote to his brother Jérôme in 1626, 'could not support the sight of so much lewdness carried on openly' (ibid. 4:197). Such a decision, however, excluded the Jesuits from the redistributive networks that they would have belonged to had they allowed themselves to be adopted and to live with their 'kin'.

Sometimes an important Huron who had recently died was re-placed by another Huron, often a close relative who did not have the same social standing. Like the prisoners of war, this relative would be transformed into the person he or she was replacing, taking on not only their name, but also their social status and their duties. For example, when Joseph Chihwatenha was murdered (most likely by other Huron who opposed his conversion and his friendship with the Jesuits), his elder brother, Teondechoren, 'revived' Joseph's name. Teondechoren converted to Christianity, even though he had firmly resisted his brother's attempts to have him convert while he was still alive. As 'Joseph', Teondechoren remained a convert and, at least outwardly, continued in his brother's work (ibid. 21:149–51). But extensive demographic disruption, such as that experienced after 1634, seriously impaired the Huron's capacity to replenish their social relationships through adoption. When that disruption was combined with the factionalism caused by some of the Huron converting to Christianity, the consequences for individuals who found themselves without relatives was devastating. This point is forcefully illustrated by a poignant account given by Le Jeune about a Christian convert named 'Anne'.

Anne had two grown daughters and a niece, whom Le Jeune described as the 'sole supports of her old age, and all of this poor woman's riches'. These women, whose spouses had either been killed in the wars with the Iroquois or who had died in some epidemic, would have formed a longhouse and would have worked together to meet their food requirements. Misfortune struck, and Anne lost her two daughters and niece within a period of three weeks to epidemic diseases. Left with three small children to look after, she herself was so ill that she could barely manage to get around. She lacked food, fuel and clothing. Her sight and strength were failing, but because she persisted in her Christianity, no one else in the village would come to her aid.

> Throughout her village, they have speech enough and malice enough to bewail her misery, and accuse God as being powerless or unjust in his providence: but there was scarcely any one, even of her nearest relatives, who assumed the obligation of giving her any assistance. Her affliction has terrified many, and has made them lose courage, – fearing, they said, a like misfortune if they persisted in the Faith.
>
> (ibid. 19:235)

Having kin did not necessarily mean having access to their help. Contravention of rules or of moral values could result in isolation or even ostracism – a fate which meant great hardship, even death. Marriage patterns, rules of residence, rules of exchange and gender complementary as entitlement only worked when the individuals were united together into a specific social structure by a set of commonly accepted rules. Compliance with what others thought to be moral behaviour was the only real guarantee that each individual had of being able to take a share of the product of the labour of others.

Factionalism

Until just before the dispersal of the Huron by the Iroquois, Jesuit missionaries had little success in converting many Huron to Christianity. Those who converted did so for a number of reasons that had little to do with belief. The majority of the adult Huron who were baptized in the early years of the Jesuit mission, received the sacrament because they believed it would help them recover from sickness, or because they believed it would allow them to join relatives in Heaven who had been baptized and who had died. Others who were baptized were traders who saw baptism as a way of becoming relatives of the French with whom they sought trade relations. Jérôme Lalemant observed in the *Relation* of 1638/9 that the principal aim of those Huron who sought baptism was to secure long life and prosperity for themselves and for their children (ibid. 17:133; 18:19).

By the charter of the Company of New France, Christian natives were to be accorded the benefits of French citizenship, and to be given the same trading privileges as the French. Christian natives were given additional presents when they came to trade, as a sign of the 'affection' that the French had for all those who shared their religion (ibid. 12:257; 16:33). Moreover, from 1641 onward, when the French finally decided to sell arms to the Huron, only those who were professed Christians had the right to trade for them. By the early 1640s the Jesuits could write that whereas previously there was hardly a single Huron warrior who was a Christian, they could now count up to twenty-two believers in one band, 'all men of courage, and mostly Captains or people of importance'. They attributed this success to the fact that the use of guns was denied to the 'infidels' by the governor, while permitted to the Christian neophytes. 'It seems', one wrote, 'that our Lord intends to use this means in order to render Christianity acceptable in these regions' (ibid. 25:27).

By 1643 Huron going to Trois Rivières to trade with the French went in separate parties of Christians and non-Christians, with the Christians playing an ever-increasingly important role. While in 1648 less than 15 per cent of all Huron professed to be Christians, over 50 per cent of the 250 traders who arrived at Trois Rivières to trade had either been baptized or were receiving instruction (ibid. 32:179).

Becoming a Christian imposed many hardships on both the convert and his or her family. As Le Jeune saw the matter:

202

If a poor Barbarian becomes a Christian, he is immediately assailed by all those of his acquaintance, who lament and deplore him as if he were already lost, and it were all over with him. Some assure him, if it be winter time, that in the Spring (if he is still living) all his hair will fall off; others, that he need no longer count upon going hunting, trading, or to war, except with the certainty that thenceforth he will be unlucky in everything; they inspire in the women the fear that they will bear no more children. In short, they are all threatened, or rather assured, that what they fear the most in world will surely happen to them.

It is represented, besides, that thenceforth they will be defrauded of feasts, and consequently of the sole delight or bliss of the country; that, as a necessary result, they must renounce all the rights and intercourse of friendship with their kinsmen and compatriots. And if they be Captains who have charge of making the announcements and managing ceremonials, they are told that they may count upon seeing themselves despoiled of their influence and authority.

(ibid. 17:129)

The Jesuits expected that the converts would agree to marriages that would be binding for life, to give up their belief in dreams, to stop eating human flesh, attending feasts, curing ceremonies and other public gatherings where the Jesuits feared the Devil's influence might be present (ibid. 13:169–75). These prohibitions, in effect, socially isolated the Christians and cut them out of most aspects of public life. Forbidden to participate in most forms of public entertainment, not allowed to attend clan feasts where hunted meat was distributed, Christians found themselves outside traditional Huron society.

Converts were also forced to give up the charms, rituals and other means whereby they had previously secured good health and luck in gambling, hunting and war (ibid. 17:121, 129–31). Conversion was especially difficult when it involved clan leaders. According to the Jesuits, the duties of these leaders consisted in 'obeying the Devil, presiding over hellish ceremonies, and exhorting young people to dances, feasts and most infamous lewdness' (ibid. 23:185). Clan leaders who converted were usually forced to give up their ceremonial roles.

By the early 1640s the Huron were beginning to differentiate themselves into traditionalist and Christian factions in matters other than trade. The effects of this division were sometimes disastrous. In 1642, for example, some Huron, desperate for help against their enemies, consulted a famous shaman, asking him to consult his familiar spirit, in order to lead them in war. By way of invoking his familiar spirit, the shaman had a small cabin, 2 or 3 feet wide, built and filled it with heated stones. After 'throwing himself into the middle of this furnace', the door was closed and he began to sing inside, while everyone else danced around the outside. Finally he emerged with the news that the enemy army was approaching from the south and that if the Huron went out to engage them, they could put the enemy to flight and take many prisoners.

The Christian warriors, who refused to participate with traditionalists in their war party because of the involvement of the shaman, decided on principle not to accompany the traditionalists going towards the south. The Christians feared that if they were victorious, only the Demon would derive glory from the victory, while God's name would be blasphemed (ibid. 27:177). In order to avoid that sin, they decided to go towards the west. Meanwhile, the traditionalists did encounter the enemy but, lacking sufficient warriors, were soundly defeated.

Christians took the decision not to be buried with non-Christians in village cemeteries, or in the Feast of the Dead (ibid. 23:31). When travelling they endeavoured to stay only with other Christians, and not with fellow clan members, as was the traditional practice. They further determined only to reveal their problems and difficulties to fellow Christians, instead of to family members. Even friendships between Christians and non-Christians were discouraged. A non-Christian woman of high social standing decided, after having a dream in which a spirit instructed her, to form a friendship with a Christian woman. In order to seal this friendship she sent her intended friend a dog, a blanket and a load of firewood. She also gave a feast in honour of the alliance. When the Christian woman and her husband learned that the impulse for this gesture came from a dream, they rejected her offer and sent the presents back. Such an action encouraged Jérôme Lalemant to write: 'There is no bond of friendship that Faith will not sever rather than see a Christian separated from God' (ibid. 23:125).

The traditionalists, for their part, countered with accusations of witchcraft, and threats of death or in some cases with the murder of the converts. The Jesuits, for example, recorded the misfortune of one Christian whose relatives expelled him from their longhouse after the death of a baptized niece. Blaming the Christian for his niece's death, his relatives refused to allow him to live with them unless he renounced his conversion. Because this man had no other living relatives with whom he could live, he was forced to beg for food and 'to do his own cooking'. This made him the object both of ridicule and of threats against his life. He was branded a sorcerer and told to be prepared to die at any moment.

One woman who became a Christian, named Luce Andotraaon, gave up being a member of a dance society, described by a Jesuit as 'the most celebrated in the country, because it is believed the most powerful over the Demons to procure, by their means, the healing of certain diseases'. The society was quite exclusive and people were admitted only 'with ceremony, with great gifts, and after a declaration which they make to the grand masters of this Brotherhood, to keep secret the mysteries that are intrusted to them, as holy and sacred' (ibid. 30:23).

An important person in this society accosted Luce and told her of a secret plot against her by the leaders of that society to 'surprise her the next Summer in her field, to split her head, and remove her scalp, – by that means concealing the murder that would be committed, the suspicion of it being likely to fall on the Iroquois enemies' (ibid. 30:23). The only way for Luce to avert certain death was to renounce Christianity and return to the dance. These 'grand masters of the dance', as Lalemant called them, worked diligently to force others like Luce to give up their faith. Although some complied, others, Lalemant claimed, were animated in the 'expectation of a ruder war, and of a combat which may proceed even to blood, and which may make for us Martyrs' (ibid. 30:25).

THE FAILURE OF TRADITIONAL RELIGION

One of the most effective challenges to the traditionalists came directly from the Jesuits themselves. They were relentless in pointing out the ineffectiveness of the Huron shamans in stemming the deaths and destruction that the Huron faced, especially after 1634. The Jesuits recognized that a major source of opposition to their mission came from the shamans and from the Huron's reliance on their activities to control natural and supernatural forces, disease and even good fortune.

The Jesuits themselves by no means escaped accusations of witchcraft. As early as 1628 they were suspected of using magic to harm the country. In that year a drought affected the country and one of the more important shamans of the region where the Jesuits were staying accused them of frightening the thunderbird who caused rain with the red-painted cross that Brébeuf had erected outside of his cabin. Brébeuf refused to remove the cross. He did however agree to paint it white, under the condition that, if it didn't rain afterwards the shaman would be exposed as an imposter. When in fact it didn't rain, Brébeuf found himself in the position of being able to impose ritual conditions of his own on the village residents. He ordered them all to come to his cabin and to a bring dish of corn with them for 'poor families'. Once assembled he had them kiss the cross. According to Brébeuf, 'they did so well that the same day God gave them rain and in the end a plentiful harvest' (ibid. 10:47–9).

During the epidemics that followed in the 1630s the Jesuits were repeatedly accused of causing the illness, of protecting the French but not the Huron, and of wanting to see the Huron destroyed. Invariably the Jesuits would be asked by the Huron of the villages in which they were resident to participate in curing ceremonies or to help put an end to the epidemic. Just as invariably they would refuse. In 1636, for example, when invited by the clan leaders of the village of Wenrio to cure the epidemic that was raging in the village, Brébeuf announced that the end of the epidemic would only come when the Huron agreed to give up their old practices and to become Christians. While the residents of Wenrio agreed to these drastic measures, it soon became obvious to them that this did not bring an end to the epidemic (ibid. 13:169–75).

The Jesuits did many other things to mark themselves as sorcerers in the eyes of the Huron. They kept their cabin doors closed, and only accepted visitors at certain times of the day. They condemned curing rituals and refused to give presents to those people whose souls desired them. They were accused of giving infected charms to victims, of bringing a corpse with them from France that was kept in their chapel and that was spreading the disease, of having other objects such as a cloak or cloth that spread infection (ibid. 12:237–9; 13:147; 15:33). The Jesuits were viewed as powerful sorcerers who could send messages on paper, control the weather and avoid or easily recover from illness. Brébeuf, for example, increased his reputation by predicting the lunar eclipses of 1637 and 1638 (ibid. 15:139).

In spite of frequent accusations against them, and near-miss attempts against their lives, the Jesuits persisted in their proselytizing, and as Huron society began to disintegrate under the pressures of disease, famine and warfare, the Jesuits gained more and more of a following. Convinced that the Devil was rampant among the Huron, or that the Huron simply lived in superstition and ignorance, the Jesuits were determined to struggle to their own deaths to see them converted.

Many Huron could not reconcile what the Jesuits told them about God's love and forgiveness, and the actual events taking place in their daily lives. The traditionalists among them pointed to the death and destruction all around them, claiming that such calamities only began to occur when the Jesuits came to speak about Jesus Christ. Although God was supposed to be full of forgiveness, they argued, as soon as they embraced Christianity they were attacked and slaughtered by their enemies. The Iroquois, who did not believe in God, prospered, while the Huron, who had 'forsaken the ways of the ancestors, were being massacred even exterminated' (ibid. 25:35–7).

The newly and fervently converted countered with the argument that it was not such a great misfortune 'to leave the earth in order to be blessed in Heaven'. Some of them seemed to have drawn on the Jesuits' idea that God was punishing them for their own good, like a father punishes a child. The Iroquois were simply the instrument that God had chosen to use to punish them. Indeed, God had chosen to punish the Huron with the Iroquois, and not the Iroquois with the Huron because he loved them much, much more. The proof was that, while the baptized Huron went to Heaven, the Iroquois, unbaptized, all were cast into the fires of Hell (ibid. 25:37).

THE SUCCESS OF THE JESUITS' PROGRAMME

The views of the Jesuits, as recorded in the *Jesuit Relations*, became an essential part of the construction of lines of power between men and women in Huron and Montagnais societies only after the kin corporate structures of these societies received multiple blows which rendered them incapable of dealing with day to day existence. The eventual success of the Jesuits in imposing seventeenth-century Christian images of women and men on Huron and Montagnais societies is indicative of the extent to which they were finally able to obtain a strategic position within both societies from which they could define and enforce meanings. The more the Huron and Montagnais were undermined by famine, wars and European diseases, the more those disasters wrecked havoc with existing social structures and called traditional coping mechanisms into question, the more successful the Jesuits became in redefining the basis of social organization and its rationalization.

With the capacity of kin corporate structures to regenerate themselves undermined, with the rights of access to the means of production and the product of the labour of others taken away, with the basis for their participation in political decision-making processes destroyed and, finally, with traditions, myths and supporting ideologies discredited, Huron women found themselves with little institutional support from which they could exercise power. In place of kin structures which supported them, property relations which allowed them equal access, ideologies which accorded them equal status with men and channels of self-expression which allowed them to vent their anger and aggression, Huron women came under social rules, institutional structures and supporting ideologies which greatly reduced their capacity to participate on an equal footing with men in social life. In place of kin corporate structures were small family groupings, organized as producing and consuming units, under the control of a titular male head of household. Women were reduced to being the wards of their male relatives. But it was only with the adoption of Christian ideology that they were made into justifiable objects of fear and aggression.

Because the integrity and social cohesion of Huron and Montagnais societies was challenged under pressures of war, European disease and the fur trade, the Jesuits, as representatives of a new and apparently cohesive social order, were finally able to gain a strategic position in both societies. That position allowed them to define new images of men and women; images which reduced women's stature, redefined their powers, capabilities and characteristics and which identified them as the inferiors of men and dependants of their husbands and fathers. Moreover, as the French gained economic and military strength in New France, the Jesuits' position as the arbitrators of these newly-defined power relations was greatly strengthened.

As part of their programme to reform native society the Jesuits sought to substantially alter the sexual and emotional relations between men and women. It was not that all sexuality and emotional expressions were to be suppressed, rather they were to be given new modes of expression, meaning and moral sanction. But the new Christian modes of expression and the resulting sanctions were oppressive in that they denied spontaneity and relied instead on channelling emotional reactions along clearly defined and controlled lines. Those channels of expression denigrated women's power at every step, setting husbands, the church and a male God in a watchful hierarchy over them.

The images of native women presented in the pages of the *Jesuit Relations* reflect power relations between men and women that had been established within French society by the seventeenth-century. Those images came to replace traditional native representations through the operation of lines of power which transformed formerly independent women into suitable subjects of the French state. Less than two decades after the Jesuits began their missions in New France they were able to begin reporting major changes in the distribution of power between men and women.

Once the traditional economic bases of their societies had been smashed, first the Montagnais's, then the Huron's very existence came to depend on the charity handed out by the Jesuits and on the military protection given by French soldiers. Instead of traditional lines of power, in which individuals within kinship groups could decide to accept or reject decisions made by clan or tribal leaders, all Huron and Montagnais had to submit themselves to the authority of the Catholic Church and the French state. Any opposition to French rule brought sanctions against individuals, sanctions, moreover, which could not be easily evaded and which were clearly punitive. Women who refused to live with their husbands, for example, were put in prison, women who spoke to suitors against their parents' wishes were beaten, disobedient children were also chastised and beaten.

Commenting on this turn of events, the Jesuit Paul Le Jeune wrote:

Such acts of justice cause no surprise in France, because it is usual there to proceed in that manner. But, among these people – where everyone considers himself, from birth, as free as the wild animals that roam in their great forests – it is a marvel, or rather a miracle, to see a peremptory command obeyed, or any act of severity or justice performed. Some Savages, having

209

learned that, in France, malefactors are put to death, have often reproached us, saying that we were cruel, – that we killed our own countrymen; and that we had no sense. They asked whether the relatives of those who were condemned to death did not seek vengeance. The Infidels still have the same ideas but the Christians are learning, more and more, the importance of exercising Justice.

(ibid. 22:83–5)

What had changed, above all, was the way in which aggressive impulses were organized, legitimized and expressed. The Jesuits had succeeded in transforming Huron and Montagnais society because the Huron and Montagnais began to adopt the Jesuits' views and practices concerning subjugation and domination. Aggression, once displaced and directed towards traditional enemies who were tortured and eaten or acted out through ritual ceremonies, now was turned towards the self and towards women. With traditional social relations and ways of controlling and interpreting daily events undermined and with men established as arbitrators of right and wrong, seventeenth-century Christian doctrine, as interpreted by the Jesuits, became the accepted authority in establishing definitions of men, women, their natures and their interrelations. Huron and Montagnais women, formerly proud and free, had to become, in one Jesuit's own words, as 'gentle as little lambs'.

There are many examples of the ways in which aggression, fear and anger were redirected either towards the self or towards women once the Huron and Montagnais became Christianized. A young, recently married man, for example, who wanted to leave a wife whom he had come to hate, for a woman he loved, experienced torment which he only resolved through self-flagellation. The man, who was terribly afraid of committing a sin, went to his spiritual director and asked to be sent to prison or to be publicly flogged. Denied this punishment, 'he slips into a room near the Chapel, and, with a rope that he finds, he beats himself so hard all over the body that the noise reaches the ears of the Father, who runs in and forbids so severe a penance' (ibid. 22:67). In Vimont's view, however, the penance was not such a bad thing. 'The Devil', he wrote, 'who loves not the spirit of mortification, soon left him, and his temptation vanished' (ibid. 22:67).

At Tadoussac, Christianized native people began to perform extensive acts self-punishment, deciding that the ones assigned to them by their Jesuit confessors were not severe enough. 'They all resolved, by common consent, to perform a harder one and to scourge themselves in imitation of the holy Penitents of whom they had heard. They at once made a great discipline of heavy cords, full of large knots, which they tied to the end of a stick, to serve as a handle' (ibid. 27:191–3). Then, called to mass, one of their leaders stood up and addressed them, saying that he was afraid that the people of Tadoussac would not be saved, that they were too wicked, that they had committed too many offences and showed few signs of improvement. Claiming that he wished to atone for his sins he withdrew the 'great discipline, that was hidden beneath his robe', and showed it to the congregation, saying:

> 'This is not that Hell-fire that I have deserved. It is by a little straw, in comparison with what is suffered down below in the abode of the Demons. Even if my whole body were covered with blood from this whip, and my flesh were torn by blows, I would not even then consider that I had paid my debts and satisfied God's justice. But I know that he is infinitely good, and has mercy on those who ask pardon of him with all their hearts'.
>
> (ibid. 27:195)

Turning to another leader, he offered the discipline to him and begged him to 'strike and spare me not'. Other Christians followed his lead. 'They all came up, one after another, to perform their penance; each one decided what he wished to give and what he wished to receive' (ibid. 27:197). The Jesuit, who was about to say mass, was surprised at this behaviour 'which he did not expect from a people who know not yet what it is to suffer for God'. Not surprised enough, however, to stop them in case he might be 'opposing the workings of the holy Ghost'. Instead, 'he merely took care that it did not go beyond the bounds of prudence, and that there were no excesses' (ibid. 27:197). Even children were whipped:

> their fathers and mothers made them approach the Altar, took off their little garments, and begged him who held the whip to chastise them at his discretion, in proportion to their age and strength, – alleging that this chastisement was already due to their disobedience. These poor victims went there cheerfully; they knelt before the Altar, clasped their hands, and, without shrinking or shedding one little tear, they received the blows from the whip, which were gently delivered on their innocent

flesh. Some of the mothers even struck with their Rosaries, in the manner of the discipline, their little children still at the breast.

(ibid. 27:197)

One man asked that he be whipped as he walked around the church, so that he could endure the 'shame and be an object of opprobrium to all' (ibid. 27:199). This demand parallels the treatment that prisoners were given, within the longhouses, in the early stages of the ritual of torture. Men and women, who used to vent their aggression and anger against enemies, now directed it against themselves. In the early 1640s, some of the warriors from the Christianized village of Saint Joseph brought several Iroquois prisoners back from a war expedition. One old woman 'to whom the sight of these new guests was exceedingly unwelcome' asked for permission from the Jesuits to torture the prisoners. 'My Father,' she is reputed to have said, 'allow me to caress the prisoners a little . . . . They have killed, burned, and eaten my father, my husband, and my children. Permit me, my Father to caress them' (ibid. 27:237). Denied permission by the Jesuit, and told that whatever she gave to the Iroquois prisoners God would give back to her, she replied 'Then I will do them no harm' (ibid. 27:239).

Another woman, described as 'exceedingly vindictive, and . . . insanely furious against the Iroquois' was asked if she loved Our Lord:

'I love God more than I hate the Iroquois; that love alone which I bear to him prevents me from making them feel the injuries that they have done to me. I am the only one remaining of a large family; I am poor and forsaken. They have placed me in that condition for they roasted and ate all my relatives and all my friends. In fact, my heart would hate those people . . . but it has more love for God than hatred and aversion for them. That is why I wish them no evil.'

(ibid. 27:239)

Men now accepted that the women who aroused their sexual feelings could easily be a source of temptation sent to them by the Devil. One Christian Huron, who thought himself dying, summoned a Jesuit to hear his confession.

This poor man draws forth a little bundle of wood, like a bunch of matches, and showing it to the Father, said to him: 'There are all my sins, I have written them upon these pieces of wood, after our fashion, for fear of forgetting them'.

(ibid. 29:103)

His most regretted sin was that he loved a woman who was pursuing him.

'I did ... preserve for a long time the whiteness of my Baptism; I carried a long time the torch which they made me hold, well lighted, without extinguishing it. When that woman who has ruined me was endeavoring to gain me, I fled from her, at first; but little by little I took pleasure in her friendship. I thought of no harm in that, until I realized that my heart desired to be wicked; I drove her away from me, but she went not far, – very soon, she appeared before my eyes. Finally I began to love her; my heart trembled, reproaching me that I would forsake prayer. I was going to confess at once; but this demon, pursuing me, ruined me. I came to love her in good sooth; and, seeing well that I would have no peace near you, I left you and went away to the Island, and thence to the Hurons; love was blinding me. I sinned sometimes without remorse; more often; fear seized my soul'.

(ibid. 29:105)

This man became so frightened of his sin that he fell ill, and asked to be brought to the Jesuits at Trois Rivières in order to be confessed. His penitence served, he was allowed to re-enter the church, and he recovered his health.

Many Huron began to take on a sense of worthlessness, or a sense of lacking control over most aspects of their lives. Lalemant recorded this conversation with one of his converts in 1640, who to Lalemant's delight likened the relation of the Huron to God to that of dogs to their human masters:

we [are] at the disposal of God, just as the dogs which men feed are in their power: ... just as they, when they have a young dog that is turning out bad, kill him in order to obviate the harm that he might do, becoming larger – likewise God, foreseeing that a child will be bad if he became a man, anticipates him with death, by an effect of his goodness which men do not see. Just the same, although we give our dogs what suffices them for their food, they nevertheless eat what they find, and take it where they can. Thus, although God gives us sufficient for life, we are

213

never satisfied; we beat our dogs on these occasions, although we love them: likewise when we abuse God's favours, he chastises us, and yet he does not fail to love us; but those who serve him faithfully, God loves with more tenderness than a father loves his children.

(ibid. 19:145)

In accepting Christianity the Huron learned to be utterly submissive to what they learned to identify as the will of God. In so doing they had to accept a sense of themselves, their powers and their worth as being nothing. Another Huron was 'overheard' by Lalemant in prayer, exclaiming:

Alas! I am but dust in your presence, and the sweepings of a cabin that is cleaned. All men are nothing before you, – what can I then offer you, great God? All that I have, my God. You are the master of our lives; to-day I offer them to you, not only the life of my children, but mine, and that of all those in my family. If I am the last to die, I will say to you: 'Take my life, my God, all that you wish is reasonable.' To-day, my God, you can try me by taking me at my word. Yes, I will say nothing else than that your will is holy in everything which it ordains ... Have pity on me: it is enough for me that the present which I have just made is acceptable to you.

(ibid. 19:239)

But giving up their freedom, their adult status, their sense of being able to have an effect on the world they lived in caused many Huron immense anguish. Learning to redirect their anger, fears and aggressive impulses towards themselves, their children and towards women was met with a certain amount of resistance, often acted out in a version of the *Ononharoia*. During Easter of 1642, for example, a clan leader by the name of Astiskoua, who was living in the village of Saint Joseph, was called to Sainte-Marie, where the Jesuits had built their mission, to be baptized. The Jesuits wrote that Astiskoua had a 'good mind ... and as the Faith seemed to have entered into his heart, there was nothing savage about his sentiments; his discourse was full of zeal and fervour; his resolutions were in every way worthy of a Christian' (ibid. 23:143).

In spite of his outward appearances, when Astiskoua tried to enter the church to be baptized 'he felt an occult force that repelled him violently; he tried a second and a third time, still he could not see what stopped him, but he always felt repulsed' (ibid. 23:143). Although urged on by his wife and by the other Christians Astiskoua could not overcome the invisible force that was preventing him from entering the church. He was forced to leave, and after walking three leagues he entered the villages of Saint Jean and Saint Ignace, 'burst into the Cabins, smashed the doors and broke the Canoes, while no one dared to approach him'.

> He cried out that a Devil had entered into his body, and that this Demon had told him to take him for his father, to follow his guidance, and to rest assured that he had an affection for him; but that he must boldly kill all the French, as they alone were ruining the whole Country. It was impossible to restrain his violence. He ran about in the woods, forcing his way everywhere. The briars and thorns tore his whole body but could not stop him. After long wanderings, he arrived at his own Village; he beat, he struck, he wished to kill all whom he met. At last he was seized, bound, and questioned. It was ever the Demon, that enemy of Peace, that spoke.
>
> (ibid. 27:145)

By the time the Christians from Saint Joseph returned from Sainte-Marie, the rest of the villagers who were still traditionalists had also decided that the French should all be killed. 'The Demoniac', as the Jesuits dubbed Astiskoua, sought to vent his anger against the Christians, smashing everything in their longhouses and trying to destroy the chapel in his village. He poured water over the head of a woman, in mock baptizm, and threatened to burn a Christian man. When the Jesuits arrived in Saint Joseph, to see what could be done to calm him, they found that he had not eaten or slept for five or six days. After a few more days of treating the Jesuits to abusive behaviour, Astiskoua's possession suddenly ceased.

> The poor man was quite ashamed, when he was told what he had done. He came to see us at our House, and told us, as well as he could remember, how his disease had commenced, and how the Demon had worked upon him. He showed that he had lost neither Faith nor the desire to be Baptized, and asked pardon of us for what he had done, – if indeed he could be charged with any crime, in acts which his will had no share, and from which he had suffered more than any other. We are determined to do nothing rash in this Baptism; time will bring us more

knowledge. We hope that, with God's assistance, everything will result in the confusion of the Demons, and in the welfare of this little Church.

(ibid. 23:143–9)

The anguish that Astiskoua showed in giving up his independence and submitting to a capricious and difficult God is evident in his response. He was able to rely on the *Ononharoia*, the traditional form of dealing with overwhelming anxiety, that was still available to him in Huron society. However, it is revealing to note that both he and the Jesuits seem to agree that his madness was the result of a demonic possession. Caught between two worlds, Astiskoua chose to accept a Christian interpretation of the causes of his anxiety and his attempts to deal with it brought him back to the Jesuits.

AGGRESSION AND THE SUBJUGATION OF WOMEN

What shocked the Jesuits so much about the Huron and the Montagnais was that they expressed their aggressiveness so differently from what the Jesuits found acceptable. It made them seem to the Jesuits to indeed be savages, uncivilized, uncontrolled. The Huron and Montagnais seemed to recognize no social hierarchy; no authority. They did not know, love, worship and above all fear God. They had the temerity to consult the Devil in all they did, constantly inviting the wrath of God in punishment. Although they made the distinction between male and female, they assigned neither a dominant position, contrary to the rules of both nature and God. Finally, although they refused to inflict corporal punishment on each other – they would neither punish their children, nor adult wrongdoers – they did not hesitate to torture, kill and eat their enemies.

The struggle between the Jesuits and the Huron and the Montagnais was nothing less than a struggle over the recognition and acceptance of hierarchy and authority. The Jesuits tried to force the native people to the realization that their forms of domination and submission were the only forms that should be allowed to exist. All other types of authority were the work of the Devil. The Jesuits strove, therefore, to make the Huron and Montagnais comply with the understanding that men were women's superiors, and that women should express their true natures by being meek, mild and submissive.

The problem with freedom, in the Jesuits' view – although they were willing to concede that it might be the greatest pleasure of human life – was that it might 'degenerate into licence, or rather the liberty of wild asses'. It must therefore be regulated and subjected to 'rules emanating from eternal laws'. But the most irksome problem, and the source of the greatest opposition to the 'spirit of the Faith', was the fact that aspects of Huron and Montagnais life, from remedies for diseases to ceremonies for fishing, hunting and growing crops, councils of war and civil councils as well as what was done for pure amusement, 'almost all abounded in diabolical ceremonies'. The Jesuits were convinced that these ceremonies were so pervasive that to embrace Christianity for a Huron or a Montagnais was to have to 'die to the world at the very moment that one wishes to assume the life of a Christian'.

Even if the Devil really did not give the Huron and Montagnais the help they asked for, it was enough that they believed he did.

> They believe that he speaks to them in dreams, they invoke his aid; they make presents and sacrifices to him, – sometimes to appease him and sometimes to render him favourable to them; they attribute to him their health, their cures, and all the happiness of their lives.
>
> (ibid. 27:53)

This made them, in Jesuit opinion, 'slaves of the Devil, without gaining anything in his service'. 'Slaves of the Devil', maybe, but certainly not of anyone else. It was European culture, through the auspices of the Jesuits, that outlined for the Huron and the Montagnais who was to be whose inferior, who was to listen to whose advice, do whose bidding. Always it was women who were to follow, under the control of men. Christianity, in particular, provided a framework though which desire, fear and the need to act on those emotions could be formed, converted, made into a system of intra-psychic beliefs and combined with social practices and institutions to create a workable system of repressive authority, and subordinated objects. Christianity provided a very powerful means of tying women and men into a hierarchical ordering of their relations, into a system of domination and submission which ultimately dealt with eroticism in such a way as to stress women's inferiority, and men's dominance over them. Above all else Christianity provided a framework through which eroticism could be filtered, the aggressiveness associated with it rationalized on the basis of the dangerous closeness of women to the source of all evil temptation, the Devil.

In the Jesuits' version of Christianity, love, fear and domination were synonymous. The events that occurred which compelled the Huron and Montagnais to embrace Christianity were, finally, the catalyst that allowed this combination of emotions to be firmly fixed in their personalities. In the place of their old cultural freedoms and truths now seen to cause them terrible 'deprivation and suffering', the native converts had 'miracle, mystery and authority' (Benjamin 1988:5). In short, the freedom of women, which had formerly rested on containment and on the release of aggressive impulses through ritualized displacement towards enemies, or through dream guessing and ritual insanity, was now discredited along with the entire culture.

With conversion to Christianity and settlement in Christianized villages women no longer married except to Christian men approved by the Jesuits. They no longer divorced whenever they felt they had good reason, nor did they have sexual relations with whomever they pleased. They ceased to oppose their husbands' will, or ever stand up to men, when they thought they had reason, without the fear of facing humiliating and often physically painful consequences.

If the Jesuits are to believed, in being Christianized women developed very different attitudes, and saw the Jesuits not as their destroyers, but as the source of their salvation. A member of one group of elderly Huron women, the youngest of whom was more than 60 years old, remarked to Le Jeune who had just baptized her: 'My son, thou hast made us live again; our hearts are full of joy, – they tell us that thy words are true, and that we shall go to heaven' (ibid. 18:145). The eldest of the five had even begun to 'remember' the myths and beliefs of her people in an entirely new way, in keeping with her new found Christianity. She is reputed to have remarked:

> 'It seems to me that our Ancestors believed something of what the Fathers teach; for I remember that when I was quite young, my father, who was very old, related to us that he who has made all, and who provides our food, was displeased when any one did wrong, and that he hated the wicked and punished them after their death'.
>
> (ibid. 18:145–7)

Now not only did women submit to public humiliation, as did Marie Meiaskawat during her wedding ceremony, but they began to police their own behaviour. Zealous women took to locking up young girls inside their French-style houses or in grain storage areas at night to prevent them from meeting clandestinely with young men. Young women themselves applied to the Jesuits for protection against young men during the night (ibid. 25:185). Girls wept when accused of some unvirtuous behaviour. Certain women ask not to be stripped of their beaver wrappings after death for modesty's sake. Others claimed to hate men who tried to speak freely to them. Le Jeune was able to remark that 'such scruples are pardonable in girls, and show in what esteem purity is held here, where formerly its name was hardly known' (ibid. 25:185–7).

Once they were able to establish a few Christian villages the Jesuits organized the election of village leaders by secret ballot. In Sillery, the first Christian village to be established, one of the first acts of these duly elected chiefs was to summon the women to a council in order to admonish them to be baptized. Once there the women, who had up to this point refused baptism, were blamed for being 'the cause of all misfortune', and were warned that they must obey their husbands from now on. The Jesuit de Quen, who served at the village named Saint Joseph, reported the following conversation with the women who had been summoned to the council, and who had subsequently come to 'beg' him for baptism. According to de Quen, the women came to tell him that:

'Yesterday the men summoned us to a Council, the first time that women have ever entered one; but they treated us so rudely that we were greatly astonished. "It is you women," they said to us, "who are the cause of all our misfortunes, – it is you who keep the demons among us. You do not urge to be baptized; you must not be satisfied to ask this favour only once from the Fathers, you must importune them. You are lazy about going to prayers; when you pass before the cross, you never salute it; you wish to be independent. Now know that you will obey your husbands; and you young people, you will obey your parents and our Captains; and, if any fail to do so, we have concluded to give them nothing to eat".'

(ibid. 18:105–7)

Paul Le Jeune, in whose *Relation* of 1640 this report appeared, added his own comment that:

[T]hese new Preachers... are so much the more wonderful as they are new and very far removed from the Savage methods of action. I believe, indeed, that they will not all at once enter into this great submissiveness that they promise themselves; but it will be in this point as in others, they will embrace it little by little.

(ibid. 18:107)

The new Christian captains had ruled that women who left their husbands, if captured, were now to be beaten and thrown in jail. Their resolve to carry this out was put to the test shortly after the elections when:

> A young woman having fled ... into the woods, not wishing to obey her husband, the Captains had her searched for, and came to ask us (the Jesuits), if, having found her, it would not be well to chain her by one foot; and if it would be enough to make her pass four days and four nights without eating, as penance for her fault.

(ibid. 18:107)

A second young woman, who had been baptized, and who was living in the village of Saint Joseph, also decided to leave her husband. When she refused to return to him the 'Assembly of Captains' met and decided to take 'harsh measures' against her, resolving to send her to prison in Quebec, under the guard of two of their number. The young woman fled, was caught, tied up and put into a canoe. When she saw that her choice was to go back to her husband, or to go into a dungeon, 'she humbly begged to be taken back to Saint Joseph, promising that hence forward she would be more obedient' (ibid. 22:81–3).

Even the Jesuits were surprised by this behaviour, pointing out in the *Relations* that formerly such acts of 'violence' were looked upon with 'horror' and were 'more remote from their customs than Heaven is from earth'. In fact, some young men, who were not yet converted to Christianity, on seeing this young woman tied up and forced into a canoe, threatened to kill anyone who laid a hand on her. The Christian 'captains', who seemed now to be in control responded that 'there was nothing that they would not do or endure in order to secure obedience to God' (ibid. 22:83).

A year later, another young woman living at Sillery tried to leave her husband, 'without just cause'. The most 'zealous Savages' decided to have a prison built for her at Sillery and had her seized and locked up in it. It was reported that she entered the prison 'peaceably, suffering herself to be led like a lamb'. She spent the day and the night of 2 January, 'the severest season of the winter', without fire, food or covering. The next day Father de Quen gave her a bit of bread and some straw to rest on. That evening she was released, when they decided that they had done enough to 'inspire terror in her and in several others' (ibid. 24:39).

Now women who were chastised by their husbands for disobedience felt themselves guilty of a sin, and were compelled to confess as much to the Jesuits. A baptized women, for example, attended some public feast or game against the expressed wishes of her husband. When she returned home he chastised her saying:

> If I were not a Christian, I would tell you that, if you did not care for me, you should seek another husband to whom you would render more obedience; but, having promised God not to leave until death, I cannot speak to you thus although you have offended me.
>
> (ibid. 18:135)

This woman felt compelled to ask for her husband's forgiveness, and appeared in the Jesuit's cabin the next morning to confess saying, 'My Father, I have offended God, I have not obeyed my husband; my heart is very sad; I greatly desire to make my confession of this' (ibid. 18:135).

Somehow, in a period of less than thirty years, the Huron and the Montagnais had gone from being as free as 'wild animals' to administering French-style justice to compel dissenters to obey an impersonal and universally applicable set of rules and regulations. What is even more astonishing is that those rules and regulations, along with the kind of individual-centred corporal punishment that was meted out to offenders, had been, only a few years previously, abhorrent to the Huron and the Montagnais.

CHANGING THE VICTIM/REDIRECTING AGGRESSION

The subjugation of Huron and Montagnais women to men rested, ultimately, on a major refocusing of aggressive impulses within both societies. That refocusing had a number of elements, and included, most importantly, the denigration of women and their exclusion from full membership as being, unequivocally *of* the society. Huron and Montagnais women were given the ambiguous role of being both essential to society, but potentially the cause of all its problems.

Until the complete disorganization of Huron and Montagnais societies fear, anger and aggressive impulses were dissipated outside of the group, towards traditional enemies who were taken as prisoners and later tortured and eaten. Fear, anger and aggressive impulses were also dissipated within the society through a number of institutionalized rituals, including a formalized type of 'insanity', gambling, dream guessing and curing ceremonies involving witchcraft, and counter-witchcraft.

The Huron, in particular, were able to direct the more malevolent feelings and actions towards victims brought into the community from outside. In a series of highly ritualized activities, they turned their intended victims into a member of their community, going so far as to adopt the prisoner of war into a family whose members were mourning the loss of a relative killed in warfare. The intended victim was thus simultaneously marked by his difference, and by his similarity.[4] He was made part of the community, even to the extent of being given the place of someone who had been recently killed. But he was also marked – damaged by being brutalized – the moment he arrived in his captor's village.

This ambiguity, and the almost transparent nature of the transference made by the members of a Huron community towards their intended victim, is quite remarkable. The Huron tortured their victims as 'brother', 'cousin', 'uncle'. As they undertook the torture, often of the most sadistic and sexually explicit nature, they made claims to be helping the victim, to be endeavouring to make the victim more comfortable. They explicitly claimed to be giving the victim the loving care he had a right to claim as their relative.

The violence that at any moment threatened to disrupt the collective life of the Huron was thus transferred on to a sort of reconciliatory victim who literally stood in for *male* relatives. The Huron rarely tortured women. Instead they adopted them into their families, and often such women were married, and their children were raised as members of the society. Men, within Huron society were legitimate objects of aggression, but only specific men, prisoners who were made both of and not of the community.

Once the violence towards the victim began in earnest, once the torture rituals were underway, everyone in the community – men, women and children – participated. As the transference took place the victim went from his status as quasi member of the community to a radically different other – something which could be destroyed with impunity, which had to be cut out and annihilated. In this way, the victim was at one and the same time exterior to the community and central to it. When the violence towards the victim was over, peace was temporarily restored to the community. The eating of the torture victim was the last act in the denial of the true nature of the violent impulses. The torture victim, no longer of the community, no longer 'uncle', 'brother' or 'cousin' became like hunted meat; something to be consumed in a ritualized feast. A living being whose spirit needed to be appeased, for certain, but a being whose remains could be disposed in garbage middens, along with the remains of any other hunted animal used as meat.

The Christianization of the Huron and the Montagnais changed, fundamentally, the way in which aggression, fear, anger and violence were rationalized and exteriorized. It changed, too, the way in which victims were identified. Women became legitimate objects of aggression; they became victims, scapegoats.[5] Women were identified and held responsible for internal tensions and societal disasters. In place of traditional practices for dissipating societal aggression, the Christianization of the Huron and Montagnais allowed new forms of transference to take place. All women became potential victims. Facing a situation that seemed intolerable, the Huron and the Montagnais embraced Christianity along with the legitimate categories of victims it offered them. The Huron and Montagnais exchanged one set of delusions for another, one set of unconscious and inadequate reasons for persecuting victims for another set, these ones derived from Christian theology. Women figured prominently among the chosen victims of Christian theology, as it was put into practice during the sixteenth and seventeenth centuries.

10

CONCLUSIONS

Although the Jesuits were eventually successful in converting the Huron and the Montagnais to Christianity they faced a considerable amount of resistance, especially from women. Moreover, women's resistance was offered from a position of relative strength from within both societies. The institutionalized arrangements through which power was brought into play and the ideological, symbolic and emotional representations of women assured them of subject status in both societies.

Being male or female was the most significant division between people in both Huron and Montagnais societies. Men and women were simultaneously different from each other and clearly set apart by those differences. They were also brought together by those differences. Neither the Huron nor the Montagnais could exist, as societies, without the bringing together of the two sexes. Although the two sexes were perceived as different and enjoyed different life experiences, tasks and even emotional characteristics, their differences made a necessity out of the almost daily co-operation between the two groups. Men could not exist without women, nor women without men. The two sexes complemented each other – and the survival of any given individual and of the society as a whole was predicated on the working of that complementarity, whether it was for emotional life, for the making of children, to have goods available or to have access to shelter and to protection from enemies. In short, both male and female were necessary if each individual was to be able to deal with day to day living.

The sexual division of labour, of social and emotional tasks, of ways of being in the world and relating to it through others all focused on what were seen as fundamental differences between women and men, and on their pressing need to constantly interact.

The nature of this interdependence in Huron society is under-scored in the *Relations* in the conversations of some of the first Christianized men, who were very concerned about the effects of their newly adopted religion on their chances of finding a wife given that the majority of Huron women did not yet follow the same laws. These young Hurons were concerned that if they were not allowed to remarry when their wives left them, they would find themselves in a wretched state, because it was the women who cultivated the land.

I have argued in agreement with Coontz and Henderson (1986a), that in matrilineal, matrifocal societies such as the Huron, men needed women even more than women needed men. A man could easily find himself 'without a home, always wandering' if no woman would take him in. The radical sexual division of labour which existed in both Huron and Montagnais societies created a situation in which complementarity acted as a powerful attraction, guaranteeing simultaneously difference and interdependence. Men and women may have worked in different spheres, and at different tasks, produc-ing different resources. But in order to exist they had to pool those resources. Huron men knew they could not live well without a wife, that women contributed to their emotional and physical well-being, and they felt vulnerable. On an almost daily basis the labour necess-ary to assure life, and, after that, emotional security, depended on the two sexes working together; more specifically working together as partners concerned not only with daily existence but also with cre-ating and raising the next generation.

It is little wonder that the Jesuits, in promoting a reorganization of society in which domination and subordination played a major role, were concerned with fixing men's domination over women. In the new society promoted by the Jesuits, fear and aggression were not primarily dealt with by identifying and scapegoating a few outside surogate victims, but by a daily submission of one's conscience to detailed scrutiny for possible sins. In this world-view women were always more susceptible to the influence of the Devil, being by nature weaker and less virtuous than men. Thus it was incumbent upon a man not only to examine his own conscience and to keep it in order, but also to make sure that his women were also kept in good moral standing.

In order to successfully introduce Christianity, especially as it related to a reorganization of marriage, familial life and relations between men and women, traditional institutional structures, as well as people's emotional lives, had to be substantially altered. The seventeenth-century Jesuits understood that a major part of their mission among the native peoples of New France was to restructure the lines of power. Their task was to introduce hierarchy, and thus domination and subjugation, where equality had previously existed. They were concerned with relations between men and women because those relations did not conform to the pattern of domination and submission called for by seventeenth-century Christian doctrine. They sought to undermine the relative freedom and equality of women and men because they found in that freedom a dangerous obstacle to the new morality they sought to instil. Christianity depended, in the final analysis, on fear and submission, on the recognition of hierarchies and on the subjugation of inferiors to their betters. It depended on one half of society being made submissive to the other half.

Twentieth-century theorists have a quite different agenda when considering questions about men, women and their interrelations – questions that were once the preserve of theologians and moralists. No longer sure of the exact nature or significance of bodily differences between men and women, no longer convinced of the origins of those differences in some divine plan, and certainly no longer concerned with the struggle between the forces of good and evil, of God and Satan, contemporary theorists have devoted a great deal of scholarly attention to reformulating western thinking about relations between men and women. Generally speaking, late-twentieth-century theories fall into one of two large categories. Certain theorists argue (usually on the basis of biological differences between the sexes) that women have universally been subjugated to men, that men have always and everywhere dominated women. Others point to specific historical or contemporary examples to demonstrate that the domination of women by men has not been universal.

No amount of analysis of the Huron and Montagnais will ever settle the problem of the universal origins of women's subjugation. I did not find a solution to Engels' riddle of the 'world historic defeat of women', nor could I determine the global conditions under which patriarchy is instituted. Yet the information available on the Huron and Montagnais contains a clear record of massive change. It covers a time period when women's independence – the basis of their subjectivity – was successfully challenged. During the seventeenth century Huron and Montagnais women and men *came* to recognize themselves as something different from what they formerly were. Women *took on* the status of dependants, of the subjugated, of objects; while men embraced the role of women's rulers. What was previously unthought or, rather, which did not appear in the consciousness of the Huron or Montagnais – that women were weak, dependent and at the same time dangerous, the cause of all the misfortune in society – was accepted as a truth. And the means of controlling the obvious danger provoked by women was produced in the same moment: women had to be subjugated to men.

In order for women and men to come to see themselves differently, and to act accordingly, there had to have been an extensive reorganization of society. That reorganization was clearly the outcome of the intervention of the French, as colonists, fur merchants, administrators and especially as missionaries. In order for the relations between Huron and Montagnais women and men to be so profoundly altered, in order for women to be subjugated to men, the people of these two societies had to first be exposed to another society, whose members were devoted to bringing their version of reality to the rest of the world. The Jesuit missionaries who proselytized the Huron and Montagnais were driven by a truth through which they were convinced that the salvation of the world was dependent on their efforts in the New World and elsewhere. Those efforts, most importantly, included the ever necessary struggle against the forces of evil, in order to secure a future for the forces of good.

That Huron and Montagnais women *came* to be subjugated to men is a persistent piece of evidence that the denial of subject status to women is *not* a natural part of the human condition. The power to act, to be represented as a subject, was, originally, not the exclusive domain of men in either Huron or Montagnais societies. What emerges from a study of these two seventeenth-century societies, even one carried out on the basis of information gathered by the very men who were dedicated to introducing subjugation and domination into those societies, is a picture of a complex and delicately balanced series of power relations in which authority, submission and domination were always in play but usually stalemated.

Yet it is also the case that much of what the Jesuits sought to instil in Huron and Montagnais society – domination and subjugation – was already there, although culturally and institutionally handled in ways that the Jesuits attributed to the influence of the Devil. Fear, aggressiveness, hatred and the displacement of these emotions already played a key role in the management of Huron daily living. It took a series of massive crises, and the determination of a few Jesuit missionaries, to redirect them elsewhere.

The unprecedented pressures from famine, disease and warfare together provoked a total collapse of the institutional structures designed to deal with crises on such a large scale. In the midst of this collapse the knowledge that people had available to them about how to mitigate the effects of the crises, how to intervene in the flow of events and to turn them once again into conditions favourable for human existence, all failed. In the face of such a massive failure of their ability to order human relations, and relations between humans and other forces, the world-view, knowledge, beliefs and institutional structures the Jesuits offered must have appeared to them as the only credible solution. Identification with, and submission to the power of the Jesuits' God must have fulfilled some of the Huron's hopeful fantasies that some omnipotent being controlled their lives. It was an easy next step to identify women with the old, and now proven dangerous, practices of the very culture that seemed to have led them to this terrible impasse. Men, at least, could then be free to be identified with the new God, and with all that was to be done for salvation. Huron and Montagnais women came to accept their role as the 'other', as both dangerous and inferior to men. The traditions which formerly supported them were totally discredited. Women, along with the men who survived, turned to Catholicism and to the Jesuits' support as their only hope for life. But with Jesuit aid, came a persuasive demand for, and justification of, women's subordinated status, and the domination of women by men. A vicious cycle began. The more women were subjugated, the less they were experienced by men (and also by themselves) as truly human. The less human they became, the more easy it was to justify their subjugation.[1]

Yet we cannot blame Christianity or even western culture for the existence of women's subjugation. While the potential for men to dominate women exists everywhere, as does the potential for women to submit to this domination, the potential for resistance also exists. The submission of women to men occurred among the Huron and the Montagnais only under exceptionally disruptive circumstances. Institutional structures and powerful technologies of the self had formerly existed within Huron and Montagnais societies, and had effectively allowed women to maintain a subject status, even in the face of powerful pressures to the contrary. It was only when the cultural fabric of both societies was all but destroyed by genocidal wars, famine and epidemic disease that both women and men finally embraced their new status as the dominated and the dominant; as objects and subjects.

NOTES

1 'PROUD, DISOBEDIENT AND ILL-TEMPERED'

1 The *Relations* were originally published by the Parisian publisher, Sebastian Cramoisy, who numbered among the original members of Cardinal Richelieu's Company of New France. The Company was established to hold the trade monopoly with the colonies in New France (Thwaites 1896–1901, 4:257).
2 Megera was one of the three furies in Greek mythology.
3 One of the best such studies to date is Maurice Godelier (1982).
4 See Elisabeth Badinter (1989) for a discussion of the issue of complementarity.
5 Claude Dulong (1984) has captured the daily lives of French women of the seventeenth-century in such a way to show the extent of this inequality.
6 According to Foucault, history should be analysed according to the intelligibility of 'struggles, of strategies and tactics'. In this way only will 'the intrinsic intelligibility of confrontations' be accounted for (1978:33).

2 'THE BLOOD OF MARTYRS IS THE SEED OF CHRISTIANS'

1 The idea of an Antichrist had its origins in pre-Christian traditions. According to old Babylonian, Canaanite and Hebrew New Year traditions, while order had been imposed on chaos the menace of chaos still existed (Cavendish 1975:17).
2 See Jean Delumeau (1978) on whose work this section draws extensively.
3 On this issue see Dulong (1984), especially chapter 1.
4 A chevalet was an instrument of torture, 'a sort of a wooden horse, with a sharp back, on which soldiers who had committed disorders were placed, with cannon balls attached to their feet'.
5 For an excellent discussion of the role of 'poisonous pedagogy' in establishing adult personality structures see Alice Miller (1983), especially chapter 1.

6 This was common practice among religious during the seventeenth century.

3 'THAT THEY MAY ALSO ACQUIRE A FRENCH HEART AND SPIRIT'

1 See, for example, Dessert (1984), chapter 6.
2 See Dessert (1984), especially part one, for an analysis of the relation between power and money in seventeenth-century France.
3 Cartier was introduced to François I by Jean Le Veneur, Bishop and count of Lisieux, Abbé of Mont St Michel and grand almoner of France in 1532, when François I made a pilgrimage to Mont St Michel. Cartier was a pilot, and relative of the bursar of the abbey who had previously undertaken other voyages to Brazil and the 'new land'. Le Veneur apparently persuaded the king that it would be a good idea to entrust a mission of discovery in the New World to Cartier, promising to contribute to the costs of such a voyage. Papal bulls reserving territories in the New World to Spain and Portugal stood in François I's way. An agreement between him and the pope, however, clarified the situation: 'the papal bull dividing up the new continents between the crowns of Spain and Portugal concerned only already-known continents and not lands subsequently discovered by the other crowns' (Trudel 1973:11).
4 Cartier took back to France

> ten captive Iroquois: the old chief Donnacona, his sons Domagaya and Taignoagny, the girl of twelve and two little boys who had been given to him by Donnacona in September 1535, a girl of eight or nine whom he had received in the same period from the chief of Achelacy, and three Indians (two of them personages of importance) who are not further identified.
>
> (Trudel 1973:32)

5 Marc Lescarbot (1907–14:17) and cited in Dickason (1977:101).
6 See Aveling (1981), especially chapter 5.
7 Following the assassination attempt agents for Henri IV had found libellous material coming from the Catholic League in the room of a Jesuit, Father Guignard. It was enough to get the entire order expelled from the country.
8 Shortly after he sold his interest to his nephew, Montmorency became involved in a plot to overthrow the king. He was subsequently executed for his efforts.
9 Fouqueray describes Ventadour as a great noble, disgusted with the world, who had retired from court and who only wished to contribute to the glory of Jesus Christ. Ventadour chose a Jesuit, Philibert Noyrot, as his confessor. Noyrot, like Ventadour, was completely devoted to the project of evangelizing the Indians (1925:293).
10 In addition, the marquise de Guercheville was also persuaded to sell her rights to trade to Richelieu. Most likely Noyrot's influence was behind both sales.

11 Members included the Marquis Deffiat, superintendent of finance, Champlain, Claude de Rouemont, Sabastian Cramoisy (the printer), Jean de Lauson, intendant of Canada, the Commander de Razilly, Louis Houel, secretary of the king and controller of the salt works at Brouage, and other merchants from Paris, Rouen, Dieppe and Bordeaux (Thwaites 1896–1901, 4:257).

12 According to Thwaites, it is most likely Le Jeune was congratulating Richelieu for clamping more restrictions on to the Huguenots (1896–1901, 8:311).

4 'THE MALE IS MORE FITTED TO RULE THAN THE FEMALE'

1 Members of both of these two orders arrived at Quebec, 1 August 1639 (Thwaites 1896–1901, 8:311).

2 For an excellent discussion of the attitude of Christian theology towards marriage, sexuality, virginity and pleasure see Marie-Odile Métral (1977).

3 See Prudence Allen (1985) especially pp. 1–3. Throughout this section I have greatly relied on Allen's work. Allen argues that there are three basic theories of sex identity: sex unity, sex polarity and sex complementarity. Sex unity claims that women and men are equal, that there are no significant differences between them. Sex polarity claims that men and women are significantly different *and* that one sex (usually male) is superior to the other (usually female). Finally sex complementarity holds that while men and women are significantly different they are also equal. See also Lloyd (1984).

4 Michel Foucault has suggested that a fundamental trait of western thought has been to identify sex and pleasure, to make sex the law of all pleasure. This identity justifies the need to restrain sexuality and provides the possibility of its control. The ideas of sex/pleasure identity and the renunciation of sex except as an act of procreation were originally Stoic and not Christian themes. They were adopted by the early Christians, Foucault says, when Christianity was integrated into the state structures of the Roman Empire 'for which Stoicism was the quasi-universal philosophy' (1979:73).

5 Cited in R. W. Southern (1986).

6 Muchembled (1987:13). See also Claude Dulong (1984) especially chapter 6. Dulong points out that three-quarters of those who were executed as witches were women.

7 According to Lawson–Tancred, Plato never compromised or qualified his central psychological message, that the soul is a non-physical, spiritual substance. As such it was inherently free from the causal *nexus*, and restricted only by its penitentiary entrammelment in a mortal body (1986:43).

8 See Prudence Allen on this question. She argues that Plato devalues the material aspect of existence and views the body as an unimportant and negative aspect of human existence (1985:81). In keeping within the Christian tradition of identifying the body as a significant part of human

existence, Allen wishes to develop her own justification for differences between men and women. While she wishes to retain the idea that women and men are equal on the level of capacities, she also wishes to retain the Christian emphasis on the significance of the differences in their bodies.

9   The material on Pythagoras was written down by others and attributed to him.
10 Translation cited in Jean-Louis Flandrin (1979:126).
11 J. J. Surin (1730:236) (first published in 1657).
12 J. J. Surin (1730:230–3).

5 'THIS LITTLE FURY OF HELL'

1   On this issue see Trigger (1986) especially chapter 2.
2   The Jesuits established their first seminary for native boys at Quebec in 1635. At first they had hoped to train these boys to become co-adjutors who could then be sent back to work among their own people. Not only did the Jesuits get very few Huron and Montagnais boys for their seminary, but they soon discovered that young people were not taken very seriously by their elders. The Jesuits were then forced to alter their plans, and set out to attract older men to their seminary.

6 'WOMEN SUSTAIN THE FAMILIES'

1   This area is about 60 miles north of present day Toronto.
2   This meaning is suggested by Heidenreich (1971:21–2) and by Trigger (1976:27).
3   Thwaites (1896–1901, 16:227). The spellings follow those set by Trigger (1976).
4   Trigger (1976:30). For a discussion of alternate spellings, sources and possible meanings of these names see Heidenreich (1971:301–2).
5   For a detailed discussion of contemporary population estimates as well as current methods of estimating Huron population size see Heidenreich (1971:91–103). For another opinion see Dickinson (1980:173–9).
6   The Jesuit Paul Ragueneau, in his *Relation* of 1648/9, speaks of 'eight Captains, from eight nations that constitute the Huron country' (Thwaites 1896–1901, 33:243, 257). Bressani's *Relation* of 1652/3 makes the same reference.
7   According to Steckley the Huron names for the eight clans were 'Ancnion, en – bear, Oskennonton – deer, Andia8ich – turtle, Ets8tai – beaver, Annaarisk8a – wolf, H8enh8en – loon, or sturgeon, Andesonk – hawk, Andatsatea – fox (1982:32).
8   For a discussion of nineteenth-century theories of kinship, sexual relations and social evolution see Rosalind Coward (1983).
9   See, for example, Alfred Kroeber (1952); Mischa Titiev (1953:511–30); Meyer Fortes (1953:17–41) and Edmund Leach (1961). Cited in Eric R. Wolf (1982:89).
10 See Kathleen Gough (1961:631–54). Another view may be found in Cara Richards (1967). Richards's position is supported by Brian

Hayden (1977:3–9). Both Richards and Hayden question the 'matrilocal nature' of household units. Hayden goes so far as to argue that 'trade was responsible for the development of longhouse residential units, that these units were corporate groups held together by the benefits of trade, and that the archaeological records demonstrate a degree of economic orchestration and specialization within the longhouses previously unsuspected' (1977:3). This interpretation has been rejected by other Huron scholars.

11 But see Cara Richards (1967) for a different argument.

12 Le Jeune called these men 'Jugglers'.

7 'AMONG THESE TRIBES ARE FOUND POWERFUL WOMEN OF EXTRAORDINARY STATURE'

1 Heidenreich (1971) estimates that fish constituted about 7 per cent of the total caloric intake of the Huron during the period after European contact.

2 See for example Thwaites (1896–1901, 17:39).

3 Warfare was inspired by a desire for revenge against those who killed a relative.

4 Trigger suggests that Huron traders brought back trade goods that were either difficult for men to manufacture or that performed much better than the ones already being used by men. The implication here is that men made the choices about what to trade for and did so solely on the basis of their own convenience. Because it was easier for them to trade for women's tools rather than to manufacture the tools themselves, they chose that option. A more likely reason, I suggest, that so many iron axes were imported into Huronia is because women found them to be much more efficient tools than the stone ones made by men, and that women requested that men trade for them (Trigger 1986:201).

5 See for example, Burton (1985); Coontz and Henderson (1986a); Coward (1983); and Lerner (1986).

6 Compare this with Lerner's list (1986:23).

7 Draper's explanation for this has an ultimately biological referent. Changes in the !Kung political, economic and social situation, in Draper's opinion, only act to allow for the development of already existing tendencies inherent from birth. 'The sexes begin life with different repertories of response potential and ... in reaction to some categories of stimuli, at least, the sexes will respond differentially' (Draper 1975:602–15).

8 Nor, as Maurice Godelier has shown, is the lack of commodity exchange, or of private property, sufficient, in itself, to guarantee women an undominated position in society. 'The oppression of women by men', he argues, 'is a social reality not born with the emergence of classes, but pre-exists them and is of an entirely different nature' (1982:10).

9 The Jesuits referred to village leaders as 'captains'.

10 See also Thwaites (1896–1901, 13:123) for references to the relationship between women and their children.

8 'DEATH OVER A SLOW FIRE'

1 The name of another Huron clan, who lived in a different village (Thwaites 1896–1901, 13:270).

2 Jogues believed this to be the deity who presided over wars.

9 'CHAIN HER BY ONE FOOT'

1 The Seneca are one of the Five Nation Iroquois.

2 These soldiers apparently brought back 30,000 or 40,000 francs worth of beaver pelts, causing a dispute with the habitants of Quebec over the proceeds of the trade (Thwaites 1896–1901, 24:89).

3 But even here, Chihwatenha stretched his welcome to the limit, and the Jesuits were expelled from the longhouse of Chihwatenha's relatives when it was discovered that they were baptizing the sick. They were later allowed to return, on the basis that hospitality between kin had been violated by their expulsion (Thwaites 1896–1901, 20:51–3).

4 René Girard makes this argument about sacrificial animals. 'In order to polarize effectively the malevolent aspects of community life', Girard writes, 'the victim must differ from members of the community but also resemble them... the victim must live among the members of the community and adopt their customs and characteristic habits' (1987b:69). Although Girard is making his argument to explain the domestication of animals, his insight into the role of victim, and the relation between victim and collectivity is clearly applicable to situations in which the victim is human.

5 On the issue of scapegoating see especially Girard (1987a). Girard argues that in order to be genuine, scapegoating must remain unconscious; persecutors do not realize they have chosen the victim for inadequate reasons (p. 78).

10 CONCLUSIONS

1 Benjamin's (1988) work is particularly relevant here.

BIBLIOGRAPHY

Allen, Prudence (1985) *The Concept of Woman: The Aristotelian Revolution 750 BC–AD 1250*, Montreal: Eden Press.

Anderson, Karen (1985) 'Commodity exchange and subordination: Montagnais–Naskapi and Huron women, 1600–1650', *Signs*, 11, 1:48–62.

Anderson, Perry (1974) *Lineages of the Absolutist State*, London: New Left Books.

— (1978) *Passages From Antiquity to Feudalism*, London: New Left Books.

Aquinas, St Thomas (1923–9) *The 'Summa Contra Gentiles' of Saint Thomas Aquinas*, 4 vols, literally translated by the English Dominican Fathers, New York: Benzinger Bros.

— (1940) *In Octo Libros Policorum Aristotelis Expositio Sev. de Rebus Civilibus*, Peculiaris editio Alumnis Universitatis Lavallensis, Quebec: Tremblay and Dion.

— (1948) *Summa Theologiae*, vols 1–3, translated by the English Dominican Fathers, New York: Benzinger Bros.

— (1952a) *On the Power of God (Quaestiones Disputatae de Potentia Dei)*, literally translated by the English Dominican Fathers, Westminister; Maryland: Newman Press.

— (1952b) *Truth*, 3 vols, translated from the definitive Leonine text by R. W. Mulligan, J. V. McGlynn, and R. W. Schmidt, Chicago: Henry Regnery Co.

Aristotle (1924) *Metaphysics*, 2 vols: a revised text with introduction and commentary by W. D. Ross, Oxford: Clarendon Press.

— (1937) *Parts of Animals*: With an English translation by A. L. Peck, London and Cambridge, Mass.: William Heinemann and Harvard University Press.

— (1943) *Generation of Animals*: with an English translation by A. L. Peck, London, Cambridge, Mass.: William Heinemann and Harvard University Press.

— (1947) *De Anima, in the Version of William of Moerbeke; and the Commentary of Saint Thomas Aquinas*, translated by Knelm Foster and Silvester Humphries, with an introduction by Ivor Thomas, New Haven: Yale University Press.

— (1974) *The Politics of Aristotle*: with English notes by Richard Congreve, 2nd edn, London: Longmans, Green and Company.

Aveling, J. C. H. (1981) *The Jesuits*, London: Blond & Briggs.

Bachofen, J. J. (1968) *Myth, Religion and Mother-Right*: selections of Bachofen's writings including *Das Mutter-Recht* (1861), London: Routledge & Kegan Paul.

Badinter, Elisabeth (1989) *Man/Woman: The One is the Other*, London: Collins Harvill.

Bender, Barbara (1975) *Farming in Prehistory*, London: John Baker.

Benedicti, Jean (1600) *La Somme des Pechez et remède d'iceux*, Paris: Chez Iamet et Pierre Mettayer. Imprimeurs et Libraries Ordinaires du Roy.

Benjamin, Jessica (1988) *The Bonds of Love: Psychoanalysis, Feminism and the Problem of Domination*, New York: Pantheon Books.

Biggar, H. P. (ed.) (1922–36) *The Works of Samuel de Champlain*, 6 vols, Toronto: The Champlain Society.

— (1930) *A Collection of Documents Relating to Jacques Cartier and the Sieur de Roberval*, Ottawa: Publications of the Public Archives of Canada, no. 14.

Bishop, Morris (1964) *Champlain: The Life of Fortitude*, New York: Alfred A. Knopf.

Broderick, J. (1934) *The Economic Morals of the Jesuits*, London: Oxford University Press.

Brown, S. E. and Buenadventura–Posso, E. (1980) 'Forced transition from egalitarianism to male domination: the Bari of Colombia', in Mona Etienne and Eleanor Leacock (eds) *Women and Colonization*, New York: Praeger.

Brown, Peter (1988) *The Body and Society: Men, Women and Sexual Renunciation in Early Christianity*, London: Faber & Faber.

Burton, Clare (1985) *Subordination: feminism and social theory*, Sydney: George Allen & Unwin.

Capul, Maurice (1984) *Internant et Internement Sous L'Ancien Régime*, 4 vols, Paris: CTNERHI.

Cavendish, R. (1975) *The Powers of Evil: Western religion, magic and folk belief*, London: Routledge & Kegan Paul.

Charmot, François (1951) La pédagogie des Jésuites, ses principes – son actualité, Paris: Spes.

Coontz, Stephanie and Henderson, Peta (1986a), 'Property forms, political power and female labour in the origins of class and state societies', in S. Coontz and P. Henderson (eds) *Women's Work, Men's Property: the origins of gender and class*, London: Verso.

— (eds) (1986b) *Women's Work, Men's Property, the origins of gender and class*, London: Verso.

Coward, Rosalind (1983) *Patriarchal Precedents: sexuality and social relations*, London: Routledge & Kegan Paul.

Delumeau, Jean (1978) *La Peur en Occident, XIVème–XVIIIème siècles*, Paris: Fayard.

Dessert, Daniel (1984) *Argent, pouvoir et société au Grand Siècle*, Paris: Fayard.

Dickason, Olive Patricia (1977) 'Renaissance Europe's view of Amerindian sovereignty and territoriality', *Plural Societies* 8, 3–4:97–107.

Dickinson, John A. (1980) 'The pre-contact Huron population. A reappraisal', *Ontario History* 72,3:173–9.

Dobyns, H. F. (1983), *Their Number Became Thinned: Native American Population Dynamics in Eastern North America*, Knoxville: University of Tennessee Press.

Donohue, John W. (1963) *Jesuit Education: An Essay on the Foundation of its Ideas*, New York: Fordham University Press.

Draper, Patricia (1975) 'Cultural pressure on sex differences', *American Ethnologist* 2, 4:602–15.

Dubois, Jean, (ed.) (1977) *Larousse de la langue française: Lexis*, Paris: Larousse.

Du Creux, François (Crexius) (1951–2) *The History of Canada*, 2 vols, Toronto: The Champlain Society.

Dulong, Claude (1984) *La Vie Quotidienne des Femmes au Grand Siècle*, Paris: Hachette.

Engels, Frederick (1972) *The Origins of the Family, Private Property and the State*: introduction and notes by Eleanor Burke Leacock, New York: International Publishers.

Etienne, Mona (1980) 'Women and men, cloth and colonization: the transformation of production–distribution relations among the Baule (Ivory Coast)', in Mona Etienne and Eleanor Leacock (eds) *Women and Colonization*, New York: Praeger.

Etienne, Mona and Leacock, Eleanor (eds) (1980) *Women and Colonization*, New York: Praeger.

Flandrin, Jean-Louis (1979) *Families in Former Times: Kinship, Household and Sexuality*, London: Cambridge University Press.

Foucault, Michel (1979) 'Truth, and power', in Meaghan Morris and Paul Patton (eds) *Michel Foucault: Power, Truth, Strategy*, Sydney: Feral Publications.

— (1980) *The History of Sexuality, vol. I: An Introduction*, New York: Pantheon.

Fouqueray, Henri (1925) *Histoire de la Compagnie de Jésus en France, des origines à la suppression (1528–1762). Tome IV, Sous le ministère de Richelieu, première partie (1624–34)*, Paris: A. Picard et Fils.

Gailey (1980) 'Putting down sisters and wives: Tongan women and colonization', in Mona Etienne and Eleanor Leacock (eds) *Women and Colonization*, New York: Praeger.

Garrard, Charles (1969) 'Iron trade knives on historic Petun sites', *Ontario Archaeology* 13:3–15.

Girard, R. (1987a) 'Generative Scapegoating', in Robert Hemerton-Kelley (ed.) *Violent Origins: Walter Burkert, René Girard, and Jonathan Z. Smith on Ritual Killing and Cultural Formation*, Stanford: Stanford University Press.

— (1987b) *Things Hidden since the Foundation of the World*, Stanford: Stanford University Press.

Godelier, Maurice (1981) 'The origins of male dominance', *New Left Review* 127:3–14.

— (1982) *La Production des Grands Hommes*, Paris: Fayard.

Goubert, Pierre and Roche, Daniel (1984) *Les Français et l'Ancien Régime*, 2 vols, Paris: Armand Colin.

Gough, Kathleen (1961) 'The modern disintegration of matrilineal descent groups', in David M. Schneider and Kathleen Gough (eds) *Matrilineal Kinship*, Berkeley: University of California Press.

Grant, J. W. (1984) *Moon of Wintertime: Missionaries and the Indians of Canada in Encounter Since 1534*, Toronto: University of Toronto Press.

Guibert, Joseph de (1964) *The Jesuits: Their Spiritual Doctrine and Practice; a historical study*, Chicago: Institute of Jesuit Sources.

Hayden, Brian (1977) 'Corporate groups and the late Ontario Iroquoian longhouse', *Ontario Archaeology* 28:3–16.

Heidenreich, Conrad (1971) *Huronia: A History and Geography of the Huron Indians, 1600–1650*, Toronto: McClelland and Stewart.

Hindess, Barry and Hirst, Paul Q. (1975) *Pre-Capitalist Modes of Production*, London: New Left Books.

Kidd, K. E. (1953) 'The excavation and historical identification of a Huron ossuary', *American Anthropologist*, 18:359–79.

Kroeber, Alfred (1952) *The Nature of Culture*, Chicago: University of Chicago Press.

Lafitau, Joseph-François (1839) *Moeurs, coutumes et religions des sauvages américains*. Tome I, Paris: Librairies Classique de Périsse Frères.

Latta, Martha (1971) 'Archaeology of the Penetang Peninsula', *Palaeoecology and Ontario Prehistory*, II, DAUTRR, 2:116–36.

—— (1976) 'The Iroquoian cultures of Huronia: a study of acculturation through archaeology', unpublished PhD thesis, Toronto: University of Toronto.

Lawson-Tancred, Hugh (1986) 'Introduction' to Aristotle *De Anima (On the Soul)*, New York: Penguin.

Leach, Edmund (1961) *Rethinking Anthropology*, London: Athlone Press.

Leacock, Eleanor (1978) 'Women's status in egalitarian society: implications for social evolution', *Current Anthropology*, 19:241–55.

—— (1980) 'Montagnais women and the Jesuit programme for colonization', in Mona Etienne and Eleanor Leacock (eds) *Women and Colonization*, New York: Praeger.

Lerner, Gerda (1986) *The Creation of Patriarchy*, New York: Oxford University Press.

Lescarbot, Marc (1907–14) *The History of New France*, 3 vols, translated by W. L. Grant, Toronto: The Champlain Society.

Lévi-Strauss, C. (1969) *Elementary Structures of Kinship* (1949), Boston: Beacon Press.

Lloyd, Genevieve (1984) *The Man of Reason: 'Male' and 'Female' in Western Philosophy*, Minneapolis: University of Minneapolis Press.

Maclean, Ian (1980) *The Renaissance Notion of Woman: A Study in the Fortunes of Scholasticism and Medical Science in European Intellectual Life*, Cambridge: Cambridge University Press.

Marie de L'Incarnation, mère (1876) *Lettres de la révérende mère Marie de l'Incarnation (née Marie Guyart), première supérieure du monastère des Ursulines de Québec*, 2 vols, Tournai, France: V. H. Casterman.

Meillassoux, Claude (1981) *Maidens, Meal and Money: Capitalism and the Domestic Community*, Cambridge: Cambridge University Press.

Métral, Marie-Odile (1977) *Le Mariage: les hésitations de l'Occident*, Paris: Aubier.

Miller, Alice (1983) *For Your Own Good: Hidden Cruelty in Child-Rearing and the Roots of Violence*, New York: Farrar Straus Giroüx.

Moore, Henrietta L. (1988) *Feminism and Anthropology*, Minneapolis: University of Minneapolis Press.

Morgan, L. H. (1871) *Systems of Consanguinity and Affinity of the Human Family*, Washington: Smithsonian Contributions to Knowledge, vol. 17.

— (1975) *League of the Iroquois* (1851), introduction by Wm N. Fenton, New York: Citadel Press.

Muchembled, Robert (1987) *Sorcières, Justice et Société aux 16ème et 17ème Siècles*, Paris: Imago.

Oury, Dom Guy (1971) *Marie de l'Incarnation, Ursuline (1599–1672): Correspondance*, Solesmes: Abbaye Saint-Pierre.

Otis, Leah L. (1987) *Prostitution in Medieval Society: The History of an Urban Institution in Languedoc*, Chicago: University of Chicago Press.

Plato (1959) *Timaeus*, translated by Francis M. Cornford, edited by Oskar Priest, Indianapolis: Bobbs-Merrill Company.

— (1987) *The Republic*, New York: Penguin.

Ramsden, P. G. (1978) 'An hypothesis concerning the effects of early European trade among some Ontario Iroquois', *Canadian Journal of Archaeology*, 2:101–5.

Reiter, Rayna R. (ed.) (1975) *Toward an Anthropology of Women*. New York: Monthly Review Press.

Richards, Cara (1967) 'Huron and Iroquois residence patterns 1600–1650', in Elizabeth Tooker (ed.) *Iroquois Culture, History and Prehistory*, Albany: University of the State of New York.

Ritcher, D. K. (1983) 'War and culture: the Iroquois experience', *William and Mary Quarterly*, 40:528–59.

Rogers, Susan C. (1975) 'Female forms of power and the myth of male dominance: a model of male/female interaction in peasant society', *American Ethnologist*, 2:727–56.

— (1978) 'Woman's place: a critical review of anthropological theory', *Comparative Studies in Society and History*, 20:123–62.

— (1980) 'The use and abuse of anthropology: reflections on feminism and cross-cultural understanding', *Signs*, 5, no. 31.

Rosaldo, Michell and Lamphere, Louise (eds) (1974) *Women, Culture and Society*, Stanford: Stanford University Press.

Sacks, Karen (1975) 'Engels revisited: women, the organization of production and private property' in Rayna R. Reiter (ed.) *Toward an Anthropology of Women*, New York: Monthly Review Press.

— (1976) 'State bias and women's status', *American Anthropologist*, 78:565–9.

Sanday, Peggy Reeves (1973) 'Towards a theory of the status of women', *American Anthropologist*, 75:1682–1700.

— (1974) 'Female status in the public domain', in Michell Rosaldo and Louise Lamphere (eds) *Women, Culture and Society*, Stanford: Stanford University Press.

— (1981) *Female Power and Male Dominance: on the origins of sexual inequality*, Cambridge: Cambridge University Press.

Schneider, David M. and Gough, Kathleen (eds) (1961) *Matrilineal Kinship*, Berkeley: University of California Press.

Schwickerath, Robert (1904) *Jesuit Education: its history and principles viewed in light of modern educational problems*, St Louis: Herder.

Sinclair, T. A. (1986) 'Translator's introduction' to Aristotle, *The Politics*, New York: Penguin.

Southern, R. W. (1986) *Western Society and the Church in the Middle Ages*, Harmondsworth: Penguin.

Steckley, John (1982) 'The clans and phratries of the Huron', *Ontario Archaeology*, 37:29–34.

Summers, Montagu (ed.) (1971) *The Malleus Maleficarum of Heinrich Kramer and James Sprenger*, New York: Dover Publications Inc.

Surin, J. J. (1730) *Catéchisme spirituel de la perfection chrétienne* (1657), vol. 2. Paris:

Thwaites, Rubin Gold (1896–1901) *Jesuit Relations and Allied Documents*, 73 vols, Cleveland: Burrows Brothers.

Titiev, Mischa (1953) 'The influences of common residence on the unilateral classification of kindred', *American Anthropologist*, 55:17–41.

Tooker, Elizabeth (ed.) (1967) *Iroquois Culture, History and Prehistory*, Albany: University of the State of New York.

Townsend, William (1969) 'Stone and steel tools in a New Guinean society', *Ethnology*, 8, 2:169–205.

Tredennick, Hugh (1984) 'Aristotle in the Middle Ages', in Aristotle *Ethics*, New York: Penguin.

Trigger, Bruce (1976) *The Children of Aataentsic*, 2 vols, Montreal: McGill-Queen's University Press.

— (1986) *Natives and Newcomers: Canada's 'Heroic Age' Reconsidered*, Montreal: McGill-Queen's University Press.

Trudel, Marcel (1973) *The Beginnings of New France, 1524–1663*, Toronto: McClelland and Stewart.

Tüchle, Hermann, Bouman, C. A. and Le Brun, Jacques (1968) *Réforme et Contre-Réforme*, Paris: Editions du Seuil.

Vogel, Cornelia J. de (1966) *Pythagoras and Early Pythagoreanism: An Interpretation of Neglected Evidence of the Philosopher Pythagoras*, Assen: Van Gorcum.

Weedon, Chris (1987) *Feminist Practice and Poststructuralist Theory*, London: Basil Blackwell.

Wolf, Eric R. (1982) *Europe and the People Without History*, Berkeley: University of California Press.

Woodrow, Alain (1984) *Les Jésuites: histoire de pouvoirs*, Paris: Jean-Claude Lattés.

Wright, J. V. (1966) *The Ontario Iroquois Tradition*, Ottawa: National Museum of Canada Bulletin 210.

— (1967) *The Laurel Tradition and the Middle Woodland Period*, Ottawa: National Museum of Canada Bulletin 217.

Wrong, G. M. (ed.) (1939) *The Long Journey to the Country of the Hurons*, Toronto: The Champlain Society.

INDEX